# A Brief History of International Criminal Law and International Criminal Court

Cenap Çakmak

# A Brief History of International Criminal Law and International Criminal Court

palgrave
macmillan

Cenap Çakmak
International Relations
Eskisehir Osmangazi University
Eskisehir, Turkey

ISBN 978-1-137-56735-2 ISBN 978-1-137-56736-9 (eBook)
DOI 10.1057/978-1-137-56736-9

Library of Congress Control Number: 2017936781



Cover illustration: evdokiageorgieva

Printed on acid-free paper

This Palgrave Macmillan imprint is published by Springer Nature
The registered company is Nature America Inc.
The registered company address is: 1 New York Plaza, New York, NY 10004, U.S.A.

*Dedicated to the memory of my mother*

# Preface

International criminal law is a nascent part of international law that attracts growing attention because of mass atrocities and heinous international crimes committed in different parts of the world. This body of international law is designed to prosecute the individuals responsible for the commission of these crimes and provide redress. Most destructive and egregious crimes have always attracted attention. However, historically, the solutions developed to address such acts have remained inadequate and failed to restore justice. The strong emphasis upon sovereign prerogatives of the nation states and their heads has been the main factor for the lack of strong mechanism in global stage to deal with these crimes.

International criminal law has emerged to fill this void. This book seeks to present a historical depiction of how international criminal law has evolved from a national setting to a truly international outlook. To this end, it first evaluates how international criminal law has evolved from a historical perspective. Particular attention is paid to how the first permanent international criminal court was made. In this section, the role of NGOs and other relevant actors is also taken into account to show that the making of international law and politics has become an intricate business. In the final section, the general features of the ICC and how it stands in world politics and affects the interstate affairs is analyzed.

The book is intended to serve as an introductory text for advanced courses on international criminal law or humanitarian law in both legal studies and political science-related fields including international relations. However, it may also be used as a supplemental reading for public international law courses as well. In addition, general readership may find it useful as the area of international criminal law is particularly popular because of its relation to the ongoing atrocities in different parts of the world.

The errors in the book remain solely mine while those who have extensively made contributions deserve credit.

Istanbul, 2016 Dr. Cenap Çakmak

# Contents

# Historical Background: Evolution of International Criminal Law, Individual Criminal Accountability, and the Idea of a Permanent International Court

It is generally agreed that international law is based on the consent of states. In other words, states, and the intergovernmental organizations they create, are the main units of international law, which thus governs the interactions between the states as legitimate actors. However, in rare instances, a natural person may become a subject of international law; in other words, international law prescribes rules that apply to real persons as well. International criminal law is a body of law that generates rules that govern certain acts committed by real persons. With the exception of these rules, a real person's acts are generally governed by national laws. However, some acts by a real person are considered grave, and for this reason, states agree that these acts must be included in the scope and domain of international law. Although it does so in a complementary fashion, international criminal law argues that it operates in such cases of grave acts and it converts real persons into subjects of the international legal system.

International criminal law is a nascent part of international law, suggesting that it has not been an integral and indispensable part of the international legal system for long. However, it should also be noted that international criminal law has roots in terms of introducing ideas on



C. Çakmak, *A Brief History of International Criminal Law and International Criminal Court*,
DOI 10.1057/978-1-137-56736-9_1

how to prosecute grave crimes committed against large numbers of people in times of both war and peace. This volume seeks to analyze how these ideas emerged in a historical context and were then transformed into the legal mechanisms that led to the emergence and development of a separate body of international law.

It is possible to divide the evolution of international criminal law into three main parts. Before there was international criminal law, all criminal acts including the most heinous ones—popularly called international crimes—were prosecutable by national jurisdictions alone. The principle of sovereignty called for exclusive jurisdiction over these actions, suggesting that only the state where the relevant criminal activity took place would be authorized to address the crime. Known as territoriality, this principle still remains the primary choice in enforcing criminal codes.

However, given the gravity of international crimes, the doctrine of universal jurisdiction was developed to address the problem of impunity for the perpetrators of criminal activities that had devastating impact. The doctrine suggests that a state should be able to claim jurisdiction over certain crimes even if those crimes were not committed in its territories. The principle was initially invoked for privacy, but its scope was later expanded to include other international crimes as well, including hijacking, genocide and crimes against humanity. However, out of fear of political retaliation, only a few states relied on this doctrine to prosecute perpetrators of international crimes that had not been committed in their territories. With few exceptions (famous examples include the Pinochet trial and Israel's prosecution of former Nazi military officer Adolf Eichmann), individual states remained indifferent to cases of international crime simply because they did not have strong political motivation to get involved.

The establishing of ad hoc tribunals and hybrid courts can be considered a response to individual states' reluctance to prosecute perpetrators of international crimes in cases in which they had no strong interest or will. Because ad hoc tribunals were not run by a single state, judges, prosecutors and the other powerful players in these initiatives would have no fear of political retaliation, and because the tribunals would be formed by the UN Security Council, they would not suffer from a lack of legitimacy or effectiveness. Ad hoc tribunals made tremendous contributions to the evolution of international criminal law. However, they were not without problems. The Nuremberg and Tokyo tribunals that were called after the end of World War II were strongly criticized because they allegedly delivered the justice of victorious powers and served their interests. Despite their contributions, particularly those of the Nuremberg trials, the controversy over their impartiality still remains. Another problem with ad hoc tribunals is whether or not they effectively deter future perpetrators. In addition, assembling these tribunals takes a great deal of time, requires strong willingness and is costly, all of which led to what was popularly called tribunal fatigue.

In an effort to address this problem, the international community created a permanent international criminal court that held automatic jurisdiction over certain crimes without requiring prior authorization by states or the relevant international institutions. The emergence of a permanent international criminal court was hailed as a major breakthrough in ending impunity and holding the perpetrators of international crimes accountable under international law. However, the court was to be viewed as a product of collective efforts and action involving progressive states paying attention to protecting human rights, relevant international institutions including the UN and representatives of global civil society.

By nature and definition, states are expected to preserve their domination and supremacy on the international political stage; for this reason, they would normally be expected to claim jurisdiction over their nationals even if the acts of these nationals could be considered harmful to the entire international system. The principle of sovereignty, the basis of the state's supremacy in international politics, is the main source of this claim. For this reason, even though they consented to its creation, the states could be persuaded by nonstate actors to develop international criminal laws that clearly restricted the states' prerogatives as political actors. In particular, civil society actors and even individuals who served and acted as norm entrepreneurs made extensive contributions to the emergence of the international criminal law that was also created by the states.

In assessing the role of global civil society in creating the first permanent global institutions to address the gravest crimes, it is essential to first trace the idea behind creating such a body. Along this journey, it is also necessary and relevant to examine how the individual human being became a subject of international law and how international criminal law gradually evolved over the course of the nineteenth and twentieth centuries. Of course, it is not possible to explore the details,[1] and thus, this section focuses on the aforesaid subject only to the extent that this attempt to explore the historical background reveals how the developments in international criminal law and the evolution of individual criminal responsibility have limited the state's domain and sphere of influence in global politics.[2]

[1] There is a vast literature on various aspects of international criminal law. Among others, see the following: Ilias Bantekas and Susan Nash, *International Criminal Law* (London: Cavendish, 2001); M. Cherif Bassiouni, (ed.), *Introduction to International Criminal Law* (Ardsley NY: Transnational Publishers, 2003); *International Criminal Law* (Ardsley, NY: Transnational Publishers, 1998); (ed.), *International Criminal Law,* 3 vols. (Ardsley-on-Hudson: Transnational Publishers, 1986); *International Criminal Law: A Draft International Criminal Code* (Alphen aan den Rijn, The Netherlands; Germantown, MD: Sijthoff & Noordhoff, 1980); Bassiouni and Ved P. Nanda (compiled and edited), *A Treatise on International Criminal Law* (Springfield, IL: Thomas, 1973); Antonio Cassesse, *International Criminal Law* (Oxford: Oxford University Press, 2003); Rodney Dixon, Karim Kahn and Richard May (eds.), *Archbold: International Criminal Courts: Practice, Procedure and Evidence* (London: Sweet & Maxwell, 2002); Sterling Johnson, *Peace Without Justice? Hegemonic Instability or International Criminal Law* (Aldershot, Hants, UK; Burlington, VT: Ashgate, 2003); Kriangsak Kittichaisaree, *International Criminal Law* (Oxford; New York: Oxford University Press, 2001); Helen Malcolm and Rodney Dixon (eds.), *International Criminal Law Reports* (London: Cameron May, 2000); Donald W. van Ness, *International Standards and Norms Relating to Criminal Justice: Conventions, Guidelines, Rules and Recommendations Promulgated by the United Nations, Council of Europe, Organization of American States, Organization of African Unity and Commonwealth of Nations* (Bethesda, MD: Pike & Fischer, 1997); Jordan J. Paust, Leila Sadat and M. Cherif Bassiouni (eds.), *International Criminal Law: Cases and Materials* (Durham, NC: Carolina Academic Press, 2000), Geert-Jan A. Knoops, *The Prosecution and Defense of Peacekeepers Under International Criminal Law* (Ardsley, NY: Transnational Publishers, 2003); Bruce Broomhall, *International Justice and the International Criminal Court: Between Sovereignty and the Rule of Law* (Oxford and New York: Oxford University Press, 2003); Christoph Safferling, *Towards an International Criminal Procedure* (Oxford: Oxford University Press, 2001); Iain Cameron, *The Protective Principle of International Criminal Jurisdiction* (Aldershot, UK; Brookfield, VT: Dartmouth Pub. Co., 1994).

[2] For a detailed account of the relationship between state sovereignty and international criminal law, see, among others, Jackson Nyamuya Maogoto, *State Sovereignty and International Criminal Law: Versailles to Rome* (Ardsley, NY: Transnational Publishers, 2003).

In the meantime, this section will also demonstrate that because of the lack of external pressure on the states, they have easily managed to resist the realization of a permanent international court, basing their resistance on the premise that such a court would damage the prominence and dominance of the nation-state and the principle of sovereignty that has kept the state in the role of the determinant actor in global politics. Although the idea that an international criminal court should be established to prevent future atrocities has often been voiced, because there has been no coordinated, single-minded global civil action, the state-centric world has not seen this long-desired international body come to fruition.

When presenting the historical developments concerning the issues under review here, scholars of international criminal law often choose between focusing on the evolution and current application of the idea of universal jurisdiction as a whole—that is, the crimes that fall under the scope of universal jurisdiction, the relevant international legal arrangements, etc.—and simply listing the most outstanding historical developments pertinent to the core subject of international criminal responsibility. However, to make the subject clearer by clarifying the relevant concepts, both the historical developments and the whole subject of universal jurisdiction are examined here.

## A Brief Historical Survey of International Criminal Law and Individual Criminal Responsibility

For practical reasons, it is possible to divide the history of international criminal law into three parts. Although there may be some serious overlaps between the periods, such a division seems to be helpful in understanding the development and evolution of individual criminal responsibility in a clearer, more precise fashion. Given that the state-centric world system was dominant over the course of the nineteenth and twentieth centuries and that the evolution of international criminal law is closely related to this system, it would be wise to choose important historical turning points in order to explain this evolution. Undoubtedly, these historical points are the two world wars, which, as one may easily expect, brought the idea that those responsible for large-scale death should be tried and convicted. Therefore, in general terms, the evolution of international criminal law is examined in four phases: pre-World War I; the interwar period, that is, the period between World War I and World War II; the period between the end of World War II and the collapse of the Soviet Union; and the period since the end of the Cold War. Although the last period does not involve a *real* war, given that it relates to another type of war, it is not unusual to regard it as a historical turning point.

# Part I

## The Evolution of International Criminal Law: A Historical Overview

# Prior to World War I

Over the past 500 years, the global community has sought numerous ways to address the most serious crimes that concerned and equally horrified the whole world.[1] Bassiouni even argues that there is evidence of a tribunal that held individuals responsible for war crimes in Greece in 405 BC.[2] Schabas joins this view, saying, "War criminals have been prosecuted at least since the time of ancient Greece, and probably well before that."[3] Others also refer to similar examples from ancient China, India, and Japan.[4] Therefore,

[1] Sandra L. Jamison, "A Permanent International Criminal Court: A Proposal That Overcomes Past Objections," *Denver Journal of International Law & Policy*, Vol. 23, Issue 2, 1995, p. 419.

[2] M. Cherif Bassiouni, *Crimes Against Humanity in International Criminal Law*, 2nd rev. ed. (Cambridge, MA: Kluwer Law International, 1999), p. 517.

[3] William A. Schabas, *An Introduction to the International Criminal Court* (Cambridge, UK and New York, NY: Cambridge University Press, 2001), p. 1.

[4] Adriaan Bos, "The International Criminal Court: A Perspective," in Roy p. Lee (ed.), *The International Criminal Court: The Making of the Rome Statute: Issues, Negotiations, Results* (The Hague: Kluwer Law International, 1999), p. 465 and Yves Beigbeder, *Judging War Criminals: The Politics of International Justice* (New York: St. Martin's, 1999), pp. 4–5, cited in Paul Bowers, *The International Criminal Court Bill (HL), Bill 70 of 2000–2001,* Research Paper 01/39, 28 March 2002, through House of Commons Library, United Kingdom, 28 March 2002, accessed via: http://www.parliament.uk/commons/lib/research/rp2001/rp01-039.pdf, p. 13, *footnote 8.*



C. Çakmak, *A Brief History of International Criminal Law and International Criminal Court*,
DOI 10.1057/978-1-137-56736-9_2

it could be argued that the world has always shown an interest in and a desire for a superior judicial body with the power to address the most heinous crimes, given that such crimes have always been committed. However, both historians and international lawyers often agree that such a body did not come into existence until the end of the fifteenth century. Although it is asserted that "the concept of a permanent ICC has intrigued the international community since the thirteenth century,"[5] in fact, "the concept of an international tribunal with its own super-national criminal justice power" can be traced to the fifteenth century.[6] In this vein, it is generally accepted that the first known international criminal trial was conducted in 1474. It is contended that international criminal rules were first enforced and invoked when an ad hoc tribunal was established to try Peter von Hagenbach, who was accused and convicted of such crimes as "murder, rape, perjury, and other crimes in violation of 'the laws of God and man.'"[7] It is essential to note that those crimes were committed against a civilian community during his military occupation of Austria.[8] Given that the referenced crimes were war crimes and that von Hagenbach was

---

[5] Brook Sari Moshan, "Women, War, and Words: The Gender Component in the Permanent International Criminal Court's Definition of Crimes Against Humanity," *Fordham International Law Journal,* Vol. 22, Issue 1, 1998, p. 165.

[6] Scott W. Andreasen, "The International Criminal Court: Does the Constitution Preclude Its Ratification by the United States?," *Iowa Law Review,* Vol. 85, Issue 2, 2000, p. 703.

[7] Damir Arnaut, "When in Rome? The International Criminal Court and Avenues for U.S. Participation," *Virginia Journal of International Law,* Vol. 43, Issue 2, 2003, p. 532.

[8] Roseann M. Latore, "Escape Out the Back Door or Charge in the Front Door: U.S. Reactions to the International Criminal Court," *Boston College International & Comparative Law Review,* Vol. 25, Issue 1, 2002, p. 162. It should be noted that the trial of Peter von Hagenbach is often cited by many others as the first international criminal proceeding. For instance, see, among others, Jamison, "A Permanent International Criminal Court: A Proposal that Overcomes Past Objections," p. 421; M. Cherif Bassiouni, "From Versailles to Rwanda in Seventy-Five Years: The Need to Establish a Permanent International Criminal Court," *Harvard Human Rights Journal,* Vol. 10, Issue 10, 1997, p. 11; Jules Deschênes, "Toward International Criminal Justice," in Roger p. Clark and Madeleine Sann, (eds.), *The Prosecution of International Crimes* (New Brunswick, NJ: Transaction Publishers, 1996), pp. 30–32; James D. Meernik and Kimi L. King, "The Effectiveness of International Law and the ICTY—Preliminary Results of an Empirical Study," *International Criminal Law Review,* Vol. 1, Issue 3–4, 2001, p. 344; Aryeh Neier, *War Crimes: Brutality, Genocide, Terror, and the Struggle for Justice* (New York: Times Books, 1998) and Walter Gary Sharp, Sr., "International Obligations to Search for and Arrest War Criminals: Government Failure in the Former Yugoslavia," *Duke Journal of Comparative & International Law,* Vol. 7, Issue 2, 1997, p. 417.

tried by a criminal tribunal of 28 judges from different locations and political entities, including Alsace, Rhineland, Switzerland, and Austria,[9] it is understandable that many refer to this famous occasion as the first attempt to hold a foreign individual responsible for perpetrating crimes that are today believed to fall under the definition of international crimes.

However, it should be noted that the view that the Peter von Hagenbach case can be viewed as the earliest precedent for holding an individual criminal responsible at the international level is challenged and questioned, because it is not obvious that the law that was applied and even the tribunal itself were truly international or that the crimes committed during the invasion were in fact war crimes.[10] This view is also objectionable in that it does not seem possible to talk about an international order based on the interactions between nations. It is also interesting to note that no other "international" criminal court that tried individuals responsible for international crimes can be cited for the period before the world war, a fact that raises doubts about the credibility of the view stated above concerning the first international criminal trial. Although there have been attempts to address serious international crimes, particularly war crimes, they were not international in nature and did not foresee the establishment of an international criminal court. Among these attempts, the most notable one is likely the so-called Lieber Code,[11] a set of rules that regulated the conduct of war. Drafted by Francis Lieber from Columbia University and applied by Abraham Lincoln during the American Civil War, these rules could be cited as the earliest modern codification of the laws of war.[12] They were significant because they explicitly proscribed inhumane conduct of war and

[9] Marlies Glasius, "Expertise in the Cause of Justice: Global Civil Society Influence on the Statute for an International Court," in Marlies Glasius, Mary Kaldor and Helmut Anheier (eds.), *Global Civil Society 2002* (Oxford: Oxford University Press, 2002), p. 138.

[10] See, for instance, Timothy L. H. McCormack, "Selective Reaction to Atrocity: War Crimes and the Development of International Criminal Law," *Albany Law Review*, Vol. 60, Issue 1, 1997, pp. 690–692.

[11] For a brief discussion of the process through which the Lieber Code was prepared as well as biographical snapshots of the code's author, Dr. Lieber, see George B. Davis, "Doctor Francis Lieber's Instructions for the Government Armies in the Field," *American Journal of International Law*, Vol. 1, Issue 1, 1907, pp. 13–25.

[12] Schabas, *An Introduction to the International Criminal Court*, p. 1.

enforced notable punishments for inhumane acts committed during war, including the death penalty.[13] The importance of these rules notwithstanding, they were national regulations that applied to US nationals only, and similar endeavors in other parts of the world were no different. Therefore, prosecution for war crimes "was only effected by national courts, and these were and remain ineffective when those responsible for the crimes are still in power and their victims remain subjugated."[14]

Nevertheless, it would not be fair to say that the above rules have remained entirely national regulations. Although these rules have not been incorporated in any international texts that regulate the conduct of war,

---

[13] Instructions for the Government of Armies of the United States in the Field, prepared by Francis Lieber, LL.D., Originally Issued as General Orders No. 100, Adjutant General's Office, April 24, 1863, Washington 1898: Government Printing Office. Those could be reached at http://www.yale.edu/lawweb/avalon/lieber.htm. Some important provisions from the Orders are as follows:

Art. 33.

It is no longer considered lawful—on the contrary, it is held to be a serious breach of the law of war—to force the subjects of the enemy into the service of the victorious government, except the latter should proclaim, after a fair and complete conquest of the hostile country or district, that it is resolved to keep the country, district, or place permanently as its own and make it a portion of its own country.

Art. 37.

The United States acknowledge and protect, in hostile countries occupied by them, religion and morality; strictly private property; the persons of the inhabitants, especially those of women: and the sacredness of domestic relations. Offenses to the contrary shall be rigorously punished.

Art. 67.

The law of nations allows every sovereign government to make war upon another sovereign state, and, therefore, admits of no rules or laws different from those of regular warfare, regarding the treatment of prisoners of war, although they may belong to the army of a government which the captor may consider as a wanton and unjust assailant.

Art. 70.

The use of poison in any manner, be it to poison wells, or food, or arms, is wholly excluded from modern warfare. He that uses it puts himself out of the pale of the law and usages of war.

Art. 76.

Prisoners of war shall be fed upon plain and wholesome food, whenever practicable, and treated with humanity.

They may be required to work for the benefit of the captor's government, according to their rank and condition.

Art. 80.

Honorable men, when captured, will abstain from giving to the enemy information concerning their own army, and the modern law of war permits no longer the use of any violence against prisoners in order to extort the desired information or to punish them for having given false information.

[14] Schabas, *An Introduction to the International Criminal Court*, p. 1.

they have had a great deal of impact on works that are relevant to codifying legal rules on war crimes and similar atrocities. Professor Bluntschli, who was charged with "the preparation of a draft of the proposed compilation of the recognized rules and usages of war" for an international meeting held in Brussels in 1874, relied heavily on the instructions prepared by Dr. Lieber. The impact of the instructions on Bluntschli's works was so significant that the outcome of the Brussels meeting "bears in every article a distinct impression of the Instructions."[15] Considering the heavy influence and practical usage of the Brussels Code,[16] which was prepared with primary reliance on Lieber's code during the proceedings of the 1899 Hague Conference,[17] it could be said that the Lieber instructions in fact became—although indirectly—internationally recognized rules. Despite the fact that they had been promulgated during an internal war, they did not lose eminence with time and continued to partially impact the international codifications of the Lieber Code's subject matter.

However, whether or not the above case constitutes a precedent for international criminal proceedings, it is clear that it did not significantly affect or contribute to inquiries into international criminal justice because the first proposal to create a permanent international court was made in 1872, when Switzerland's Gustave Moynier, one of the founders of the International Committee of the Red Cross, suggested creating an international criminal court to address violations of the 1864 Geneva Convention[18] in the Franco-Prussian War of 1870–1871,[19] far later than the supposedly first international criminal tribunal was established in 1474.

[15] Davis, "Doctor Francis Lieber's Instructions for the Government Armies in the Field," p. 22.

[16] The text of the outcome of the Brussels Conference could be found at: Project of an International Declaration Concerning the Laws and Customs of War, Adopted by the Conference of Brussels, August 27, 1874, reprinted in *The American Journal of International Law,* Vol. 1, Issue 2, Supplement: Official Documents, 1907, pp. 96–103.

[17] Ibid., p. 23.

[18] *Laws of War: the Geneva Convention for Amelioration of the Condition of the Wounded on the Field of Battle* (also known as the Red Cross Convention); adopted at Geneva, August 22, 1864, entered into force June 22, 1865. The text of the Convention can be reached through the website of *the* Avalon *Project of Yale University* at: http://www.yale.edu/lawweb/avalon/lawofwar/geneva04.htm.

[19] Arnaut, "When in Rome? The International Criminal Court and Avenues for U.S. Participation," p. 532. Unlike the von Hagenbach case, there is agreement and thus certainty

The main reason for and impetus behind this proposal was the reluctance of states to comply with the provisions of the Geneva Convention cited earlier. Although that Convention was signed by a large number of states at the time, large-scale atrocities were committed in the Franco-Prussian War.[20] During the discussions after that war, whereas many who referred to the uselessness of the aforesaid Convention and other related arrangements were in favor of abolishing the rules of war given that the rules were not being observed during wartime, Moynier took the opposite position and argued that the rules should be backed by an international criminal court so that the Convention would have a deterrent effect on warring parties.[21] However, his proposal was met with skepticism and was eventually

---

that the proposal for establishing a permanent international criminal court was first made by Gustave Moynier in 1872. See, for example, Christopher Keith Hall, "The First Proposal for A Permanent International Criminal Court," *International Review of the Red Cross,* Issue 322, 1998, p. 57–74; Christopher W. Mullins, David Kauzlarich and Dawn Rothe, "The International Criminal Court and the Control of State Crime: Prospects and Problems," *Critical Criminology,* Vol. 12, Issue 3, 2004, p. 289; Marie Törnquist-Chesnier, "NGOs and International Law," *Journal of Human Rights,* Vol. 3, Issue 2, 2004, p. 256; Christopher K. Hall, "La Primera Propuesta de Crecion de un Tribunal Penal Permanente," 145 Revista Internacional de la Cruz Roja, 63–82 (1998), as cited in Héctor Olásolo, "The Prosecutor of the ICC Before the Initiation of Investigations: A Quasi-judicial or a Political Body?," *International Criminal Law Review,* Vol. 3, Issue 2, 2003, p. 87. On January 3, 1872, Moynier presented his draft for establishing a permanent international criminal court at a meeting of the International Committee for the Relief of the Wounded (later to become the Red Cross), which was set up under the *Geneva Convention for the Amelioration of the Condition of the Wounded in Armies in the Field, 1864.* This proposal was published in the *Bulletin International des Sociétés de secours aux militaries bleséss* on January 28, 1872. See, Morten Bergsmo, "Folkerettslig belysning av 'etisk rensing' i det tidligere Jugoslavia," pp. 75–133 in Bård-Anders Andreassen and Elin Skaar (eds.), *Forsoning eller rettferdighet? Om beskyttelse av menneskerethighetene gjennom sannhetskommisjoner og rettstribunaler* (Oslo: Cappelen Akademisk Forlag, 1998), p. 98, cited in Tom Syring, "Good Governance and the ICC: Strengthening Besieged Democratic Regimes by International Means, The Logic of Institutional Empowerment," Paper presented at Arbeidsgruppe Internasjonal Politikk (Working Group on International Politics), Oslo, December 19, 2002, p. 7, *footnote 3.*

[20] It is interesting to note that Moynier, the first to propose creating a permanent criminal court, was not originally in favor of such an institution. However, the atrocities committed in the Franco-Prussian War appeared to radically change his mind. See Hall, "The First Proposal for A Permanent International Criminal Court," p. 57

[21] For a detailed examination of Moynier's proposal, see Hall, "The First Proposal for A Permanent International Criminal Court," pp. 57–74. This article also includes the text of Moynier's proposal, "Draft Convention for the Establishment of an International Judicial Body Suitable for the Prevention and Punishment of Violations of the Geneva Convention."

largely ignored.[22] It should be noted that the proposal was too extreme and radical[23] given the political circumstances of the time and the dominance of power politics.

The proposal drafted by Moynier was very brief, with ten articles only, and modest in terms of scope and reference to an international body that was to have the authority to prosecute war crimes. Article 1 of the draft provided that "in order to ensure the implementation of the Geneva Convention of 22 August 1864, and of its additional articles, there will be established, in the event of a war between two or more Contracting Powers, a tribunal to which may be addressed complaints concerning breaches of the aforementioned Convention."[24] Therefore, the draft did not refer to a separate statute that would govern the proposed court but suggested that the 1864 Geneva Convention be observed. The court Moynier proposed lacked a permanent panel of judges. Article 2 stated that the adjudicators would be nominated by three powers to be chosen by the President of the Swiss Confederation as soon as a war was declared.[25] Furthermore, the draft did not determine the venue where the judges would sit once they were appointed; this choice was left to the judges.[26] The proposed tribunal was not to be authorized to act on its own, but it was recognized as having the power to address the complaints addressed to it by the interested governments.[27] The tribunal was to determine whether the accused was guilty or not. If guilt were to be established, then the tribunal would also have the authority to impose a penalty in accordance with the existing rules of international law.[28] However, the tribunal would not be able to enforce its decisions. Rather, the draft

[22] Marlies Glasius, "How Activists Shaped the Court," Crimes of War Project, The International Criminal Court: An End to Impunity? *The Magazine* Section, December 2003, accessed via: http://www.crimesofwar.org/print/icc/icc-glasius-print.html.

[23] Hall, "The First Proposal for A Permanent International Criminal Court," pp. 57–74.

[24] Article 1 of Draft Convention for the Establishment of an International Judicial Body Suitable for the Prevention and Punishment of Violations of the Geneva Convention, reprinted in ibid.

[25] Ibid., Article 2.

[26] Ibid., Article 3.

[27] Ibid., Article 4.

[28] Ibid., Article 5.

provided that "the tribunal will notify its judgments to interested governments. The latter shall impose on those found guilty the penalties which have been pronounced against them."[29]

The brief review of the draft above suggests that Moynier's proposal was in effect very modest by contemporary standards. There is no argument that it was daring and striking at the time, but it should have been acceptable to states given its modesty and noninterference with national sovereignty. Despite this fact, states did not show interest in the proposal, which demonstrated the dominance of power politics and the observation of national sovereignty and national interests. According to Hall, the lack of support for and interest by the international law experts of the time in Moynier's proposal was one of most important reasons for the failure to enact it.[30] In other words, if the draft had been supported by nonstate figures, there might have been at least some prospect of creating the institution it called for.

However, because arms technology was increasingly improving, and thus, wars were becoming more deadly, the people became more concerned about the implications of war. This necessitated adopting certain rules on the conduct of war. As a consequence, attempts to develop a law of war that would be helpful in minimizing the negative effects of warfare accelerated the codification of international legal arrangements regarding the conduct of war, beginning in particular at the end of the nineteenth century.[31] Two developments are worth mentioning in this regard: The Hague Conventions of 1899 and 1907, where the first attempts to create an international penal code were made. The initial proposal for the 1899 conference was made by Czar Nicholas II of the

---

[29] Ibid., Article 6.

[30] Hall comments on this matter as follows: "A century and a quarter after Gustave Moynier's daring proposal, the prospects are increasingly bright that the international community will adopt a treaty establishing a permanent international criminal court. In dramatic contrast to the response of leading international law experts in 1872, more than three hundred non-governmental organizations throughout the world have joined forces in an NGO Coalition for an International Criminal Court to mobilize public support for the prompt establishment of an effective court." Hall, "The First Proposal for a Permanent International Criminal Court," pp. 57–74.

[31] Seha L. Meray, *Devletler Hukukuna Giriş,* revised 3rd ed., 2nd vol. (Ankara: Ankara University Press, 1965), p. 428.

Russian Empire on August 24, 1898.[32] The proposal was accepted by 26 countries, and eventually the Peace Conference was held at The Hague. The Czar assumed the same role at the second Hague Conference held in 1907 by issuing the formal invitation. However, this time the proposal for the conference came from the United States, and 44 countries participated.[33]

Those conventions were "the first significant codification of the laws of war in an international treaty."[34] The Convention of 1899 created the Convention for the Pacific Settlement of Disputes and a Court of Arbitral Justice.[35] Also known as the Permanent Court of Arbitration

---

[32] It is interesting to witness that the proposal for a conference that could have limited state sovereignty was made by a head of state, who should have been eager to preserve the sovereignty of the state he represented. However, considering that the Czar made the proposal to "diminish the burden of taxation for military and naval expenditures which presses down with enormously increasing weight upon the shoulders of the people," it could be concluded that his sincerity in demanding world peace was questionable. William I. Hull, The Two Hague Conferences and their Contributions to International Law 3 (1908), cited in Leila Nadya Sadat, "The Establishment of the International Criminal Court: From The Hague to Rome and Back Again," *Michigan State University-DCL Journal of International Law*, Vol. 8, Issue 1, 1999, p. 97, note 1. In fact, it was not a concern for Russia only. The following quotation eloquently explains one of the most outstanding motives behind states' willingness to hold a multilateral conference in which discussions and deliberations on reducing armaments took place: "It was a world with an Arms Race going on, and with military-industrial complexes to feed it. The costs were enormous, and came not just from the numbers of men involved. These were years when . . . there was much application of scientific invention to military purposes. New weapons and new means of delivering them were being developed every year. As soon as one military establishment had acquired a new military marvel, every state with which it might come into conflict felt the lack of an equivalent. It was repeatedly claimed, and not by socialists and liberals alone, that the costs were becoming too heavy to bear" Geoffrey Best, "Peace Conferences and the Century of Total War: The 1899 Hague Conference and What Came After," *International Affairs,* Vol. 75, Issue 3, 1999, pp. 619–620.

[33] Sadat, "The Establishment of the International Criminal Court: From the Hague to Rome and Back Again," pp. 97–98.

[34] Schabas, *An Introduction to the International Criminal Court,* p. 2. "They include an important series of provisions dealing with the protection of civilian populations . . . Other provisions of the Regulations protect cultural objects and private property of civilians." Ibid.

[35] Jamison, "A Permanent International Criminal Court: A Proposal that Overcomes Past Objections," p. 421. Four Hague Conventions were adopted at the Hague Convention of 1899: CONVENTION (I) FOR THE PACIFIC SETTLEMENT OF INTERNATIONAL DISPUTES (HAGUE I) (July 29, 1899), entered into force September 4, 1900, accessed via: http://www.yale.edu/lawweb/avalon/lawofwar/hague01.htm, CONVENTION WITH RESPECT TO THE LAWS AND CUSTOMS OF WAR ON LAND (HAGUE, II) (July 29, 1899), entered into force

(PCA),[36] this court is especially significant because it is viewed by some scholars as one of the earliest predecessors of the permanent International Criminal Court. Two reasons are referred to for this assertion. First, it is commented that the establishment of the PCA foresaw that interstate disputes could sometimes be resolved through legal endeavors and would not necessarily be matters of political rivalries. Second, its establishment triggered a general tendency toward international adjudication.[37]

However, it is worth noting that the Court whose creation was proposed at the 1899 Hague Conference had important defects. The most important one is explained as follows:

> The Hague Tribunal is not in the true sense a permanent court, it is permanent only in name. Its membership of judges is not confined to a few selected men who sit as a permanent court ready at all times to do its business and receiving a fixed salary during an appointment for life.[38]

Instead of a permanent court, what was proposed at The Hague was "a list of referees" from whom judges might be selected as "occasion offers. A clerk's office and a council to run it is all that is permanent or continuous in the organization." The judges were to be selected from a pool of 104. They were basically to be called from their vocations for a few months "to decide a certain dispute in their capacities as judges and

September 4, 1900, accessed via: http://www.yale.edu/lawweb/avalon/lawofwar/hague02.htm, CONVENTION FOR THE ADAPTATION TO MARITIME WARFARE OF THE PRINCIPLES OF THE GENEVA CONVENTION OF AUGUST 22, 1864, adopted July 29, 1899, entered into force, September 4, 1900, accessed via: http://www.yale.edu/lawweb/avalon/lawofwar/hague993.htm and Declaration on Prohibiting Launching of Projectiles and Explosives from Balloons (Hague, IV); July 29, 1899, entered into force, September 4, 1900.

[36] For brief information on the attempts made before The Hague Conference of 1899 with regard to international arbitration, see William L. Penfield, "International Arbitration," *American journal of International Law,* Vol. 1, Issue 2, 1907, pp. 330–341.

[37] Sadat, "The Establishment of the International Criminal Court: From The Hague to Rome and Back Again," p. 98, at note 2.

[38] R. Floyd Clark, "A Permanent Tribunal of International Arbitration: Its Necessity and Value," *American Journal of International Law,* Vol. 1, Issue 2, 1907, p. 343.

then lapse back again into the private life and environment from which they came."[39]

The Hague Convention of 1907 is significant in that while during the previous convention, it was decided that submission to the court would be optional, at the Convention of 1907, attempts were made to make the court's jurisdiction obligatory. However, although the preconditions for the court's entering into force were set at the Convention, because these conditions would not be met later, the court never went into effect.[40] The Convention also witnessed the first comprehensive codification of laws of war.[41] Thirteen conventions on various aspects of warfare were adopted at the conference in 1907, although one was never ratified and thus never enforced.[42] Overall, the primary objective of these conventions was to create rules and procedures that would eliminate unnecessary suffering by warring persons and ensure that noncombatants would not be targeted in the wars.[43]

However, despite the novel arrangements, The Hague conventions fell short in many respects.[44] First, although the Hague Convention of

---

[39] Ibid., p. 344.

[40] Sadat, "The Establishment of the International Criminal Court: From The Hague to Rome and Back Again," p. 422.

[41] Gerard E. O'Connor, "The Pursuit of Justice and Accountability: Why The United States Should Support the Establishment of an International Criminal Court," *Hofstra Law Review,* Vol. 27, Issue 4, 1999, p. 935.

[42] These are: Convention for the Pacific Settlement of International Disputes (1907), Convention Respecting the Limitation of the Employment of Force for the Recovery of Contract Debts (1907), Convention Relative to the Opening of Hostilities (1907), Convention Respecting The Laws and Customs of War on Land (1907), Convention Respecting the Rights and Duties of Neutral Powers and Persons in Case of War on Land (1907), Convention Relating to the Status of Enemy Merchant Ships at the Outbreak of Hostilities (1907), Convention Relating to the Conversion of Merchant Ships into War-Ships (1907), Convention Relative to the Laying of Automatic Submarine Contact Mines (1907), Convention Concerning Bombardment by Naval Forces in Time of War (1907), Convention for the Adaptation to Maritime War of the Principles of the Geneva Convention (1907), Convention Relative to Certain Restrictions with Regard to the Exercise of the Right of Capture In Naval War (1907), Convention Relative to the Creation of an International Prize Court (Never Ratified) and Convention Concerning the Rights and Duties of Neutral Powers in Naval War (1907). All are accessible at: http://www.lib.byu.edu/~rdh/wwi/hague.html.

[43] O'Connor, "The Pursuit of Justice and Accountability: Why The United States Should Support the Establishment of an International Criminal Court," p. 935.

[44] In fact, it is indicated in the preamble to the Conventions that they are incomplete. Schabas, *An Introduction to the International Criminal Court,* p. 2.

1907 managed to codify the laws of war, only states, not individuals, were obliged to comply with the rules adopted at the conference. In other words, the conventions "were meant to impose obligations and duties upon States, and were not intended to create criminal liability for individuals."[45] Furthermore, the enforcement of the laws was "primarily through reparations imposed upon a defeated state, or through reprisal or retaliation, which tended to escalate the spiral of savagery."[46]

More importantly, most conventions adopted at the Hague conventions to maintain the rules of laws of war lost a significant portion of their power because of the reservations they contained. As with the Conventions of 1864 and 1906, the Hague Convention of 1907 stated that any state that was party to the conventions was obliged to abide by the rules contained in them as long as all other state parties complied as well. This was called the "clause of solidarity" (Clause de solidaritè). According to this clause, if any state violated a convention or a nonparty entered the war, there was the strong possibility that other states would not consider themselves obliged to comply with the provisions of that convention.[47]

There is one simple and equally solid explanation for the weak provisions of the conventions discussed above: states were concerned with preserving their sovereign rights. There was an obvious link between the attempts to regulate warfare that were adopted at the two Hague conferences and the notion of sovereignty that was prevalent in world politics at the time. It was generally assumed that a head of state had authority over his state and that a state could not be bound by any law other than its domestic legal rules unless it explicitly consented to be so bound.[48]

However, it should be noted that notwithstanding the shortcomings of The Hague Conventions of 1899 and 1907 stated above, there was at

[45] Ibid.

[46] Bryan F. MacPherson, "Building an International Criminal Court for the 21st Century," *Connecticut Journal of International Law*, Vol. 13, Issue 1, 1998, pp. 4–5.

[47] Meray, *Devletler Hukukuna Giriş*, p. 434.

[48] Sadat, "The Establishment of the International Criminal Court: From The Hague to Rome and Back Again," p. 102.

least one attempt to invoke their provisions within a few years after their codification. The Carnegie Endowment for International Peace, a non-governmental organization, established a commission of inquiry to investigate atrocities committed especially against civilians and prisoners of war during two Balkan Wars of 1912 and 1913.[49] In its report, the commission referred to the Hague conventions as a basis for its description of war crimes.[50] However, it is worth remembering that the attempt was not led by states. Therefore, the Carnegie Endowment initiative could only be cited as a reference to the Hague conventions.

Another reference to the Hague conventions was made significantly later. The Statute of the International Criminal Tribunal for the Former Yugoslavia of 1993[51] relied heavily on the conventions as the main basis for codifying the customs and laws of war. Indeed, the Rome Statute of the International Criminal Court also borrows from those conventions in its Article 8(2)(b), (e) and (f).[52] This is a clear recognition of those long-ignored international legal arrangements on the laws of war as an authoritative base with respect to their coverage. Moreover, it is argued that the current permanent international criminal court is "the culmination of a process that goes back to the Red Cross and Hague Conventions on the conduct of warfare in the nineteenth and twentieth centuries,"[53] which is in effect a statement that gives full credit to the Hague conventions and acknowledges their prominence in international criminal law.

---

[49] M. Cherif Bassiouni, "Establishing an International Criminal Court: Historical Survey," *Military Law Review,* Issue 149, 1995, p. 53.

[50] *Report of the International Commission to Inquire into the Causes and Conduct of the Balkan Wars* (Washington, DC: Carnegie Endowment for International Peace, 1914), reprinted as George F. Kennan and Thomas M. Franck, *The Other Balkan Wars: A 1913 Carnegie Endowment Inquiry in Retrospect* (Washington, DC: Carnegie Endowment for International Peace, 1993).

[51] Statute of the International Tribunal for the Prosecution of Persons Responsible for Serious Violations of International Humanitarian Law Committed in the Territory of the Former Yugoslavia since 1991, U.N. Doc. S/25704, annex (1993) and S/25704/Add.1 (1993), adopted by Security Council on 25 May 1993, U.N. Doc. S/RES/827 (1993). The Statute's text can be reached at: http://www.un.org/icty/legaldoc-e/index.htm.

[52] Schabas, *An Introduction to the International Criminal Court,* p. 3.

[53] Giulio M. Gallarotti and Arik Y. Preis, "Toward Universal Human Rights and the Rule of Law: The Permanent International Criminal Court," *Australian Journal of International Affairs,* Vol. 53, Issue 1, 1999, p. 95.

There is in fact one more point, an important one given the subject matter of this study, that needs to be emphasized. Although the two above-mentioned multilateral conferences are in general viewed as attempts by the states that participated in the conferences, the input and encouragement of civil elements throughout the process cannot be overlooked. Although it may not be possible to refer to an organized civil society of that time, the "nonstate" parties' contributions to both the inauguration of the conference and the principles and rules adopted there suggest that the achievements made by those conferences at least partially belong to civil society.

The 1899 Hague Convention in particular witnessed the visible contribution of different elements of civil society. The peace societies of the time were interested in the conference. In particular, the Inter-Parliamentary Union's participation is worth noting because this organization had been involved in international peace congresses since the 1880s. An additional point worth mentioning is that women actively joined and assumed effective roles in these organizations. Aside from peace movements and early human rights organizations, professional groups, especially those of international lawyers, made contributions during the conference. There were also gatherings of masses before the conference, although these are not comparable with contemporary gatherings.[54]

Of course, the magnitude of these groups' presence at the conference, the scope of their contributions to the deliberations and their influence on the decisions to be made by the states' delegates were limited, modest and by no means comparable with the works of today's global civil society. However, even considering just the fact that the Convention was "the first ever occasion on which an intergovernmental... conference was accompanied by a great show of organized public opinion in its support"[55] reveals how important and crucial the participation of the "organized public" was. Although they were aware of their limits, the

[54] Best, "Peace Conferences and the Century of Total War: The 1899 Hague Conference and What Came After," pp. 620–621.

[55] Ibid., p. 623.

organizations formed by "the people" wanted to be taken seriously by the delegations during the Convention. Otherwise, they might have formed an alternative conference to the official one. They also attempted to influence the outcome through lobbying and informal meetings. However, as was already noted, their contribution was modest largely owing to their limited influence and resources. Best refers to another reason for this limited influence: not all participant states had civil elements present at the conference.[56] In any case, the important point is that the success of the conference, if any, cannot be attributed to the states alone but must include the civil elements that participated as well.

[56] Ibid., p. 624.

# The Interwar Period

It could be argued that the failures to create an international judicial body that would be empowered to prosecute war criminals over the course of the nineteenth century, which witnessed the outstanding impacts of the Industrial Revolution on arms technology, significantly contributed to the outbreak of World War I. Although it is not possible to prove that point with certainty, it is clear that power politics and the struggle between nations over sharing the world's economic and strategic assets were the major reasons for the war. The fact that the warring parties largely ignored the sanctity of human life led to a deadly war. Therefore, it should not be surprising that "the true impetus for the creation and acceptance of international jurisdiction over individuals committing war crimes was World War I, the first military conflict that truly took place on a world-wide scale."[1]

During the war, there were many instances in which civilians were murdered, tortured, deported, or subjected to other inhumane or

[1] Andreasen, "The International Criminal Court: Does the Constitution Preclude Its Ratification by the United States?," p. 703.



C. Çakmak, *A Brief History of International Criminal Law and International Criminal Court*,
DOI 10.1057/978-1-137-56736-9_3

degrading treatments. This marks one of the most obvious differences between World War I and the wars of the past: the previous wars were mainly fought between the armies of the warring parties, whereas World War I for the most part did not distinguish the civilian population from the warring personnel. For this reason, civilians were to a large extent directly affected by and involved in the deadly campaigns. In particular, the inhumane conduct of war by the Germans led to popular protest.

But perhaps the most notorious part of World War I was the mass killings of a huge number of Armenians in an aggressive campaign which many international legal scholars now call genocide.[2] A discussion of how international criminal law has evolved cannot be regarded properly done without inclusion of the campaign by the Ottoman Turks to destroy a sizeable Armenian people in the early twentieth century. Even though the question as to whether the killings of the Armenians in this period was truly genocide remains part of a political controversy particularly because of the lack of a judicial verdict by an international court, that episode was a catalytic event in the development of international criminal law and the establishment of political mechanisms to address these events. For example, it has been documented that diplomatic exchanges between the British Foreign Minister and his Russian counterpart about what to do about the Turkish massacre and dislocation of the Armenian people led to the first use of the term "Crimes Against Humanity" in international diplomacy and law.[3]

The scholarship of the international criminal law seems to be in a strong agreement that the campaign against Armenians and their dislocation in the hands of the Ottoman army was indeed genocide, even

[2] See Richard G. Hovanassian, *The Armenian Genocide in Perspective* (New Brunswick, NJ: Transaction Books, 1986); Vahakn D. Dadrian, *The History of the Armenian Genocide: Ethnic Conflict from the Balkans to Anatolia to Caucasus* (Providence: Berghahn, 1995); Jay Winter, *America and the Armenian Genocide of 1915* (Cambridge: Cambridge University Press, 2003); Yair Auron, *The Banality of Indifference: Zionism and the Armenian Genocide* (New Brunswick, NJ: Transaction Books, 2000); Vahakn Dadrian, *Warrant for Genocide: Key Elements of Turko-Armenian Conflict* (New Brunswick, NJ: Transaction Publishers, 2003); Richard G. Hovanassian, *The Armenian Genocide: History, Politics, Ethics* (New York: St. Martin's Press, 1992).

[3] Michelle Tusan, "Crimes Against Humanity: Human Rights, the British Empire, and the Origins of the Response to the Armenian Genocide," *American Historical Review,* Vol. 119, Issue 1, 2014, pp. 47–77.

the first genocide of the twentieth century.[4] Some accounts even argue that Hitler referred to the inaction and indifference of the major powers to what happened to Armenians during World War I when he decided to wipe out the Jews in Europe, stressing that the world would tacitly endorse his action this time again. Therefore, they attributed the gross nature of Holocaust to the failure of addressing what they call first genocide of the century.[5] Raphael Lemkin, a prominent Polish scholar who coined the term genocide and laid down the ground for the adoption of the UN Convention on the prevention of the crime of genocide, referred in his article to the mass murders of the Armenians as one of the cases that had gone unnoticed and that required to be labeled as international crime.[6] Ironically, however, despite the gravity of the campaign, the victorious powers in the war failed to ensure establishment of proper domestic and international mechanisms to prosecute the offenders and punish the culprits.

Mostly because of this failure, the Armenian genocide issue still remains a political dispute, particularly between the Turkish state, which denies to assume collective responsibility, and the Armenian Diaspora. In the absence of a judicial verdict (or even an attempt to create a judicial mechanism), the whole issue becomes even more political in nature, with the involvement of national parliaments in recognition of the killings as genocide. Turkey strongly objects to these initiatives, sometimes calling them as a plot or conspiracy, and asks reliance on historical archives in an attempt to reopen the debate. But the Turkish argument attracts little attention because international legal scholars have no (or little, at best) doubt on how to characterize the Ottoman campaign against the Armenian population.

[4] See Richard D. Kloian, *Armenian Genocide: First 20th Century Holocaust* (San Francisco, CA: Armenian Commemorative Committee, 1980).

[5] See, for instance, Vahakn Dadrian, "The Historical and Legal Interconnections Between the Armenian Genocide and Jewish Holocaust: From Impunity to Retributive Justice," *Yale Journal of International Law,* Vol. 23, Issue 2, 1998, pp. 503–559; Dadrian, "Convergent Aspects of the Armenian and Jewish Cases of Genocide," *Holocaust and Genocide Studies,* Vol. 3, Issue 2, 1988, pp. 151–169; particularly Kevork B. Bardakjian, *Hitler and the Armenian Genocide* (Cambridge, MA: Zoryan Institute, 1985).

[6] Raphael Lemkin, "Genocide," *American Scholar,* Vol. 15, Issue 2, April 1946, p. 229.

Apparently, the most plausible explanation for the fact that the issue has not been properly settled is that the mass murders stayed unattended by the international players of the time. Unlike atrocities committed by the Germans, little has been done to address the Armenian genocide (or crimes against humanity, as referred to in official documents). But this does not necessarily mean that the whole case has been forgotten or untouched. Historical records indicate that there have been some (but insufficient) attempts to at least report some of the offenses, without, however, amounting to criminal prosecution at a domestic or international level.

Scholars, particularly historians, present strong evidence by relying on primary sources to document the details of the Armenian genocide. Naim-Andonian Documents are considered one of the strong historical evidence of the Armenian genocide. The material, published in Armenian, French, and English languages, features the texts of the 52 very important official telegrams. Named after Naim Bey who explained the classified messages and added extensive notes to the original texts, and Aram Andonian who annexed complementary notes, the documents reveal that part of the Ottoman government devised plans on the extermination of the Armenian population.[7] Even though the authenticity of the papers is challenged,[8] leading historian Dadrian describe them as foundation of "the autonomy of a genocide."[9]

Additional historical evidence includes the writings of American envoy Hans Morgenthau,[10] documents presented to Viscount Bryce, British Secretary of State for Foreign Affairs,[11] and even memoirs of a

[7] The English version is in a condensed form: Na'im Bek, *The Memoirs of Naim Bey* (London: Hodder and Stoughton, 1920).

[8] Şinasi Orel and Süreyya Yuca, *The Talat Pasha Telegrams: Historical Fact or Armenian Fiction?* (Istanbul and London: K. Rustem and Brother, 1986).

[9] Vahakn N. Dadrian, "The Naim-Andonian Documents on the World War Destruction of Ottoman Armenians: The Anatomy of a Genocide," *International Journal of Middle East Studies*, Vol. 40, Issue 2, 2008, pp. 172–179.

[10] Hans Morgenthau, *Ambassador Morgenthau's Story* (Garden City, NY: Doubleday Page and Co., 1918) and Morgenthau, *Secrets of the Bosphorus* (London: Hutchinson, 1918).

[11] Arnold J. Toynbee, *The Treatment of Armenians in the Ottoman Empire: Documents Presented to Viscount Grey of Fallodon, Secretary of State for Foreign Affairs* (London: Hadder and Stoughton, 1916).

Venezuelan volunteer who fought on the side of the Ottomans.[12] Archival records also contribute a great deal to the scholarship. A number of official documents have been compiled or reprinted in secondary sources.[13] The same is also true for national archives. Dadrian, for instance, documents the Armenian genocide with reference to the German and Austrian sources.[14] He also studied the proceedings of a military tribunal established by Turkish authorities to prosecute the perpetrators of crimes against Armenians for documentation purposes.[15]

In other words, the problem with the Armenian genocide is not whether or not there is sufficient evidence and detail to depict what happened to more than 1.5 million Armenians who were residing in the Ottoman territories; the problem is that there was no significant attempt to hold the perpetrators responsible for committing international crimes, particularly crimes against humanity. As a result, historical studies do a great job by presenting clear evidence of what really happened, but fall short to identify what measures should be taken in the legal terrain. It is therefore possible to argue that the issue, in legal terms, has been left unconcluded.

As early as May 1915, the Allies, referring to the reports and documents proving commission of mass murders, formally accused the Ottoman state of crimes against humanity and further demanded for proper mechanisms by which masterminds of the massacres would be individually held liable. In 1919, shortly after the end of the war, the British even pressured the Ottoman authorities into setting up a special

---

[12] Rafael de Nogales, *Four Years Beneath the Crescent* (New York, NY: Scribner's, 1916).

[13] See Armen K. Hovanassian, "The United States Inquiry and the Armenian Question, 1917–1919: The Archival Papers," *Armenian Review*, Vol. 37, Issue 1, 1984, pp. 146–163.

[14] Vahakn N. Dadrian, "Documentation of the Armenian Genocide in German and Austrian Sources," in I. Charny (ed.), *The Widening Circle of Genocide* (New Brunswick, NJ: Transaction Publishers, 1994). Also see, Dadrian, "The Armenian Question and the Wartime Fate of the Armenians as Documented by the Officials of the Ottoman Empire's World War I Allies: Germany and Austria-Hungary," *International Journal of Middle East Studies*, Vol. 34, Issue 1, 2002, pp. 59–85.

[15] Vahakn N. Dadrian, "The Documentation of the World War I Armenian Massacres in the Proceedings of the Turkish Military Tribunal," *International Journal of Middle East Studies*, Vol. 23, Issue 4, 1991, pp. 549–576.

court-martial in Istanbul.[16] The Ottoman authorities did set up this tribunal and even indicted several top figures.[17] However, the prosecutions did not suffice to deliver full justice and turn into a true confrontation. Describing the Istanbul Tribunal as "the Nuremberg that failed," Bass comments that this case shows that "the enormous political difficulties of mounting prosecutions against foreign war criminals can be so great that a tribunal can *crumble*."[18]

The most serious attempt to prosecute the international crimes perpetrated against Armenians was to insert provisions in the Peace Treaty of Sevres in 1920 concluded between the victorious powers of World War I and the Ottoman Empire. However, the treaty did not enter into force and was further replaced by the Treaty of Lausanne in 1923 which, on the contrary, contained no provision on the prosecution of these crimes. The Treaty of Sevres contains two separate sets of provisions on the crimes committed during the war in a separate section dedicated to "penalties." The first set refers to the violations of laws and customs of war and envisages establishment of a tribunal for criminal prosecution:

> The Turkish Government recognises the right of the Allied Powers to bring before military tribunals persons accused of having committed acts in violation of the laws and customs of war. Such persons shall, if found guilty, be sentenced to punishments laid down by law. This provision will apply notwithstanding any proceedings or prosecution before a tribunal in Turkey or in the territory of her allies.
>
> The Turkish Government shall hand over to the Allied Powers or to such one of them as shall so request all persons accused of having committed an act in violation of the laws and customs of war, who are specified either by name or by the rank, office or employment which they held under the Turkish authorities. (Article 226)[19]

[16] Gary J. Bass, *Stay the Hand of Vengeance: The Politics of War Crimes Tribunals* (Princeton; Oxford: Princeton University Press, 2000), p. 107.

[17] See Vahakn N. Dadrian, "The Turkish Military Tribunal's Prosecution of the Authors of the Armenian Genocide: Four Major Court-Martial Series," *Holocaust and Genocide Studies*, Vol. 11, Issue 1, 1997, pp. 28–59.

[18] Bass, *Stay the Hand of Vengeance*, p. 106.

[19] The Peace Treaty of Sevres, August 10, 1920, Article 226.

Subsequent articles further require the surrender of the persons accused of having committed these offenses and provision of any information or documents that might be of help in the process of criminal prosecution to the Allied Powers by the Ottoman state. A review of these articles reveals that the section covering articles 226–229 is more focused on the violations against the combatants of the Allied Powers rather than offenses against large masses.

The second set of provisions, on the other hand, applies to the massacres committed during the war, without, however, making any explicit reference to the Armenian genocide:

> The Turkish Government undertakes to hand over to the Allied Powers the persons whose surrender may be required by the latter as being responsible for the massacres committed during the continuance of the state of war on territory which formed part of the Turkish Empire on August 1, 1914.

The Allied Powers reserve to themselves the right to designate the tribunal which shall try the persons so accused, and the Turkish Government undertakes to recognize such tribunal.

> In the event of the League of Nations having created in sufficient time a tribunal competent to deal with the said massacres, the Allied Powers reserve to themselves the right to bring the accused persons mentioned above before such tribunal, and the Turkish Government undertakes equally to recognise such tribunal. (Article 230)[20]

The Allied Powers did not raise the issue of prosecuting the perpetrators of crimes against humanity during World War I after the war mostly because of political considerations. It appears that the Armenian genocide has not been a big issue during the diplomatic deliberations at the backstage of Lausanne, following the pattern that has been observed in interstate relations before under which crimes against people went mostly unnoticed and untouched.

[20] Ibid., Article 230.

Of course, it is not possible to speculate as to whether or not similar tragedies would have taken place if the Armenian genocide had been properly addressed and the perpetrators had not enjoyed impunity, a problem that the large section of the activities towards creating an international criminal legal system now seeks to deal with. But the widespread culture of impunity and the indifference of the interstate system to mass murders reflects that the international political order in the early twentieth century was based on the supremacy of the nation states and the preservation of their sovereign privileges. As a result, the case of the Armenian genocide has become a victim of the implicitly acknowledged code that applied to the interstate relations back in the twentieth century.

Interestingly, German international crimes attracted greater attention during and after the war. One of the most notorious atrocities committed by German troops was the "Sack of Louvain," in which they executed over 200 civilians and burned portions of a Belgian city. Over 60,000 civilians were forced by Germans to move from the occupied parts of Belgium to labor camps.[21] German troops, after invading Belgium, also committed war crimes in France; there were numerous reports of German atrocities in France. In particular, the destruction of the Cathedral at Rheims and the large-scale pillage, rape and murder of civilians could be cited in this regard.[22] The aerial bombardment of London by Germans, which caused civilian casualties, was another significant and unforgettable incident that incited public protest and outcry. In 1915, the Germans went even further and wielded poisonous gas.[23] Furthermore, Germany targeted commercial and passenger vessels: In May 1915, a German U-boat sank the vessel Lusitania, killing 1,198 civilians.[24] Along with the Lusitania incident, the execution of Nurse Edith Cavell, who was the head of a training school for nurses in Brussels, and who was executed with Kaiser's

[21] James F. Willis, *Prologue to Nuremberg: The Politics and Diplomacy of Punishing War Criminals of the First World War* (Westport, CT: Greenwood Press, 1982), p. 9.

[22] Ibid., p. 13.

[23] Ibid., p. 19.

[24] Ibid., p. 20.

authorization for assisting and hiding Allied troops, has over time become the symbol for German atrocities during the war.[25] These two infamous incidents are frequently cited in order to emphasize the civilian losses and inhumanities of World War I.

With the end of World War I, the victorious powers in particular sought to address the war's atrocities. Of course, the attempts to address the crimes committed during the war focused only on the defeated states, not the victorious powers. In fact, even at the dawn of the war, there were numerous calls for justice and numerous expressions of concern over the large-scale commission of war crimes and other outlawed behaviors. For instance, in 1915, Elihu Root, former Secretary of War and State under Theodore Roosevelt, stated, "The civilized world will have to determine whether what we call international law is to be continued as a mere code of etiquette or is to be a real body of laws imposing obligations much more definite and inevitable than they have been heretofore."[26] Theodore S. Woolsey, a former law professor from Yale University, proposed establishing an international criminal court to prosecute the German atrocities.[27] A similar proposal was advanced by historian Hugh H. L. Bellot, who "urged that, in the event of an Allied victory, the Central Powers should be required to accept the convening of a criminal court to prosecute those war criminals who remained unpunished."[28]

The examples cited above and countless others resulted in a collective demand by people for the punishment of those responsible for wartime atrocities. Because of the lack of an independent and permanent international body that could address crimes similar to those committed during the world war, the major powers attempted to get involved in the process for the sake of maintaining justice. However, their attempts

[25] Matthew Lippman, "Towards an International Criminal Court," *San Diego Justice Journal,* Vol. 3, Issue 1, 1995, p. 3.

[26] Elihu Root, "The Outlook For International Law," *Proceedings of American Society of International Law,* Vol. 9, 1915, pp. 2–4, cited in Lippman, "Towards an International Criminal Court," *San Diego Justice Journal,* Vol. 3, Issue 1, 1995, p. 5, at note 22.

[27] Lippman, "Towards an International Criminal Court," p. 6.

[28] Ibid., pp. 8–9.

were ineffective, largely owing to considerations of national interests. Nevertheless, the period after World War I is significant in that during this period, there were a number of attempts to enforce the laws of war. Although most of these attempts failed, they left a legacy for future generations.

There appeared a possibility for establishing an international criminal tribunal to prosecute war crimes at the Paris Peace Conference of 1919, which was convened by the victorious powers of the war.[29] At the conference, a Commission on the Responsibility of the Authors of the War and on Enforcement and Punishment was appointed to seek a resolution for addressing the crimes committed during the war. The commission was charged with inquiring into and reporting on the following:

1. The responsibility of the authors of the war.
2. The facts concerning the German Empire's—and its allies'—breaches of the laws and customs of war.
3. The degree of responsibility for these offenses that was attributable to particular members of the enemy forces.
4. The constitution and procedure of a tribunal that would be appropriate for the trial of these offenses.
5. Any other matters directly related or ancillary to the above that could arise in the course of the inquiry and that the commission found to be useful and relevant for consideration.[30]

The commission appointed three subcommissions. Sub-Commission I on Criminal Acts was appointed to "discover and collect the evidence necessary to establish the facts relating to culpable conduct which (a) brought about the World War and accompanied its inception, and (b) took place in the course of hostilities." Sub-Commission II on the

[29] Andreasen, "The International Criminal Court: Does the Constitution Preclude Its Ratification by the United States?," p. 702.

[30] Report of the Commission on the Responsibility of the Authors of the War and on Enforcement of Penalties, presented to the Preliminary Peace Conference, March 29, 1919, Official English text, reprinted from Pamphlet No. 32, Division of International Law, Carnegie Endowment for International Peace, Washington, DC in *American Journal of International Law,* Vol. 14, Issue 1, 1920, pp. 95–154.

Responsibility for the War assumed the role of considering whether, based on the findings of the Sub-Commission on Criminal Acts relating to the war's initiation, "prosecutions could be instituted, and, if it [was] decided that prosecutions could be undertaken, to prepare a report" that indicated the individuals who had been found guilty and the court that would be competent to prosecute the offenses. The Sub-Commission III on the Responsibility for the Violation of the Laws and Customs of War was to consider whether, based on the findings of the Sub-Commission on Criminal Acts relating to the conduct of war, prosecutions could be instituted and in which court those prosecutions would proceed.[31]

The relevant subcommission determined that the responsibility for initiating a policy of aggression "rests first on Germany and Austria, secondly on Turkey and Bulgaria"[32] and consequently concluded that "the war was premeditated by the Central Powers together with their Allies, Turkey and Bulgaria, and was the result of acts deliberately committed in order to make it unavoidable" and that "Germany, in agreement with Austria-Hungary, deliberately worked to defeat all the many conciliatory proposals made by the Entente Powers and their repeated efforts to avoid war."[33] In relation to the outlawed acts committed during the war, the commission that was assigned to work on this matter also concluded that "the war was carried on by the Central Empires together with their allies, Turkey and Bulgaria, by barbarous or illegitimate methods in violation of the established laws and customs of war and the elementary laws of humanity."[34] The commission of outlawed acts was so widespread that the same commission also recommended creating a committee for the purpose of collecting and classifying information and preparing a complete list of facts concerning violations of the laws and customs of war that had been committed by the German Empire and its allies on land and sea and in the air during the course of the war.[35]

[31] Ibid., pp. 97–98.
[32] Ibid., p. 98.
[33] Ibid., p. 107.
[34] Ibid., p. 115.
[35] Ibid.

The commission further concluded that individuals who were thought to have been involved in inhumane conduct of war should be held responsible for violating the laws and customs of war and of the laws of humanity.[36] The commission dismissed the sovereign immunity defense and asserted that otherwise, "the greatest outrages against the laws and customs of war and the laws of humanity...could in no circumstances be punished. Such a conclusion would shock the conscience of civilized mankind."[37] It especially referred to the punishment of the Kaiser and stressed that the principles of the laws and customs of war and the laws of humanity would be meaningless if the Kaiser were not brought to trial while "other offenders less highly placed were punished."[38] However, although it referred to the Kaiser and other high-ranking officials as liable for numerous atrocities committed during the war, the commission concluded that it would be unprecedented to hold the Kaiser and other German officials "criminally" liable for waging a war of aggression against Belgium and Luxembourg.[39]

Although the commission also contended that those found guilty of the prescribed crimes could be tried in national courts, it recommended that an international criminal court be created for cases in which the accusations against the suspects were being levied by more than one state.[40] The commission asserted that each of the Allies had the authority to prosecute prisoners of war who were believed to have violated the laws and customs of war. However, it also proposed a single, consolidated high tribunal for cases involving individuals who allegedly committed war crimes and similar crimes against civilians and troops from multiple allied countries. This tribunal was to be authorized to apply "the principles of the law of nations as they result from the usages established among civilized peoples, from the laws of humanity and

[36] The relevant conclusion in the report reads as follows: "all persons belonging to enemy countries, however high their position may have been, without distinction of rank...are liable to criminal prosecution." Ibid., p. 117.

[37] Ibid., p. 116.

[38] Ibid., p. 117.

[39] Ibid., p. 118.

[40] MacPherson, "Building an International Criminal Court for the 21st Century," p. 5.

from the dictates of public conscience."[41] The tribunal was to be composed of four persons, and, if it found the accused guilty, it would have the power to sentence him to a punishment that might be "imposed for such an offence or offences by any court in any country represented on the tribunal."[42] Cases were to be selected by a prosecuting commission of five members who were to be appointed by the governments of the United States, the British Empire, France, Italy, and Japan.[43]

However, despite the shocking findings regarding wartime atrocities and the novel proposals for remedies that were contained in the commission's report, not all nations favored punishing those who were accused of having committed war crimes and other relevant crimes. In particular, the United States sought a stable peace rather than criminally prosecuting war criminals. For the United States, the greatest threat to the international order was Russian Communism.[44] For this reason especially, the US representatives submitted a number of reservations regarding the commission's report.[45] The American representatives on the commission objected to the references to the "laws and principles of humanity" contained in the report and further argued that they were too vague and general and thus could not be proper guides for enforcing international criminal law.[46] The United States also strongly objected to imposing criminal liability on heads of state. The American representatives argued that such individuals were only accountable to domestic authorities and thus that holding them responsible for committing acts that required criminal prosecution before a foreign or international tribunal would be a serious abrogation of state sovereignty.[47] According to the

---

[41] Report of the Commission on the Responsibility of the Authors of the War and on Enforcement of Penalties, p. 121.

[42] Ibid., p. 122.

[43] Ibid., pp. 122–123.

[44] Lippman, "Towards an International Criminal Court," p. 16.

[45] The text of the "Memorandum of Reservations Presented by The Representatives of The United States to the Report of the Commission on Responsibilities," is annexed to the Report of the Commission on the Responsibility of the Authors of the War and on Enforcement of Penalties, pp. 127ff.

[46] Ibid., p. 134.

[47] Ibid., pp. 135–36, 144, 148.

dissenting representatives, the existing national tribunals, rather than an international one, for prosecuting war crimes were more reliable because those tribunals already possessed well-established laws, procedures, and punishments. For criminal acts concerning more than one country, the American representatives proposed gathering the members of the relevant national courts.[48] The reason by the American representatives stated for their objection to the high tribunal proposed by the commission was that there was no precedent for such a tribunal and it was "unknown in the practice of nations."[49] They also referred to the fact that there was "no international statute or convention making a violation of the laws and customs of war—not to speak of the laws or principles of humanity—an international crime, affixing a punishment to it, and declaring the court which has jurisdiction over the offence."[50] Accordingly, the American representatives openly stated that the United States was not willing to cooperate in the establishment and proper functioning of the proposed high tribunal.[51]

In addition to the United States, Japan also objected to certain of the proposals contained in the commission's report. Although their objections were not as ardent as those of the United States, they referred to almost the same concerns. Japanese delegates questioned establishing an international tribunal after a war had ended and the existence of an international penal law that would apply to those who were found guilty of war crimes. In this vein, they also noted the possible consequences that "would be created in the history of international law by the prosecution for breaches of the laws and customs of war."[52]

At the conference that was held following the submission of the commission's report, the Allied powers also discussed Germany's

[48] Ibid., p. 142.

[49] Ibid., p. 145.

[50] Ibid., p. 146.

[51] "In view of their objections to the uncertain law to be applied... and in view also of their objections to the extent of the proposed jurisdiction of that tribunal, the American representatives were constrained to decline to be a party of its creation... They therefore refrained from taking part either in the discussion of the constitution or of the procedure of the tribunal" Ibid., pp. 148–149.

[52] "Reservations by the Japanese Delegation," Annex III to Report of the Commission on Responsibilities, pp. 151–152.

surrender and negotiated a treaty in which they dictated the terms. The deliberations at the conference also included issues concerning prosecuting high-level officials and war criminals from the defeated powers for "crimes against the laws of humanity." Ultimately, the victorious powers concluded the Treaty of Versailles with Germany on June 1919.[53] The treaty included a provision for establishing an ad hoc international criminal tribunal to prosecute Wilhelm II of Germany for initiating the war.[54] However, he fled to neutral Holland, which refused his extradition.[55] Although the Allied powers requested his extradition through diplomatic channels, because it became evident that Holland would never cooperate, they made no formal attempts to have Holland submit the Kaiser to the international tribunal that would try him.[56]

The failure to try the Kaiser should be viewed as a great disappointment and a step backward, given the salience of the accusations directed at him and that he was being held responsible for initiating the war and thus causing deaths in great numbers. Wilhelm II, the Kaiser of Germany, was especially held directly responsible for the slaughter of civilians in Belgium.[57] In the early days of the war, he wrote in a note to the Austrian Kaiser:

> My soul is torn, but everything must be put to fire and sword: men, women and children and old men must be slaughtered and not a tree or house be left standing. With these methods of terrorism, which are alone capable of affecting a people as degenerate as the French, the war will be over in two months, whereas if I admit considerations of humanity it will

[53] Treaty of Peace Between the Allied and Associated Powers and Germany, concluded at Versailles, June 28, 1919 (Treaty of Versailles). The treaty text can be reached at: http://history.acusd.edu/gen/text/versaillestreaty/all440.html.

[54] Treaty of Versailles, Article 227. This article states: "A special tribunal will be constituted to try the accused, thereby assuring him the guarantees essential to the right of defence. It will be composed of five judges, one appointed by each of the following Powers: namely, the United States of America, Great Britain, France, Italy and Japan."

[55] Schabas, *An Introduction to the International Criminal Court,* p. 3.

[56] O'Connor, "The Pursuit of Justice and Accountability: Why The United States Should Support the Establishment of an International Criminal Court," p. 936.

[57] Lippman, "Towards an International Criminal Court," p. 9.

> be prolonged for years. In spite of my repugnance I have therefore been obliged to choose the former system.[58]

Despite this "confession" and solid evidence proving Kaiser's involvement and clear connection with the wartime commission of crimes, concerns over sovereign rights and the view that heads of states were immune against prosecutions prevailed.

The Treaty of Versailles also provided for prosecuting German officials who were accused of violating the laws of war. However, in that case, there would be no international tribunal but national courts of the Allied powers.[59] The Treaty of Versailles, as noted earlier, created the Commission on the Responsibilities of the Authors of War and on Enforcement of Penalties. The crimes considered by the commission included rape, the use of poisonous gas, murders, massacres, and waging aggressive war, for which it proposed a tribunal consisting of 22 members.[60] The commission completed its work and submitted its report, which contained of a list of 895 alleged war criminals.[61]

In addition to the failure to prosecute the Kaiser in an international tribunal, the Allied powers could not proceed with prosecuting war criminals. Although the Treaty of Versailles provided for their prosecution by the victorious powers' national courts, "by 1921, the zest of the Allies to set up joint or even separate military tribunals had waned, and

---

[58] This note was reprinted in William Adams, "The American Peace Commission and the Punishment of Crimes Committed During War," *Law Quarterly Review,* Vol. 39, 1923, pp. 245–248, cited in Lippman, "Towards an International Criminal Court," pp. 9–10, at note 42.

[59] Treaty of Versailles, Articles 228 and 229. Article 229 states:

> Persons guilty of criminal acts against the nationals of one of the Allied and Associated Powers will be brought before the military tribunals of that Power.
>
> Persons guilty of criminal acts against the nationals of more than one of the Allied and Associated Powers will be brought before military tribunals composed of members of the military tribunals of the Powers concerned.

[60] Jamison, "A Permanent International Criminal Court: A Proposal that Overcomes Past Objections," p. 422.

[61] Bassiouni, "From Versailles to Rwanda in Seventy-Five Years: The Need to Establish a Permanent International Criminal Court," p. 16.

new developments in Europe required that Germany not be further humiliated."[62] The Allies were also greatly concerned about jeopardizing "the durability and stability of the already fragile Weimar Republic,"[63] founded after the defeat of Germany in World War I. Moreover, it should be noted that Germany had refused to surrender the accused for prosecution by the Allies.[64] The German stance and determination were very well received by the Allies, and thus, they must have decided that Germany would never cooperate with them on this matter. As a consequence, the Allies, instead of establishing a separate Allied tribunal, devolved this authority to Germany and asked for the prosecution of a limited number of the suspects before the Supreme Court of Germany.[65]

As a response to the request by the Allied forces, Germany passed the legislation that would make possible the trial of the alleged war criminals identified by the victorious powers. Although it had already introduced legal arrangements to implement the Treaty of Versailles' relevant provisions, with the new legislation, Germany proceeded with the trials. They took place in Leipzig, and for that reason, they are known as the Leipzig trials. Because the Supreme Court authorities were empowered to decide which cases would be brought to trial under German law, German authorities requested all relevant information from the Allies. The Allies submitted only 45 names from the original list of 895 who had previously been recommended by the commission to the German authorities for prosecution.[66]

However, it should be noted that the information and evidence concerning those 45 persons' involvement in war crimes was substantial

---

[62] Ibid., p. 19.

[63] O'Connor, "The Pursuit of Justice and Accountability: Why The United States Should Support the Establishment of an International Criminal Court," p. 936.

[64] MacPherson, "Building an International Criminal Court for the 21st Century," p. 6.

[65] Bassiouni, "From Versailles to Rwanda in Seventy-Five Years: The Need to Establish a Permanent International Criminal Court," p. 19.

[66] It is argued that the Allies originally sought to try 1,580 war criminals, a figure that contrasts with the commission's list of 895. However, the Allies reduced this number to 854. See MacPherson, "Building an International Criminal Court for the 21st Century," p. 6. However, despite this conflict, it is certain that the Allies submitted 45 names for possible prosecution.

because both the 1919 commission's extensive works and the Allies' supporting documentation were made available to the German Supreme Court. Despite the strong evidence, only 12 military officers were ultimately prosecuted before the *Reichsgericht,* the German Supreme Court.[67] However, the German Court's stance toward even those who were prosecuted was very mild. Not all prosecuted suspects were convicted, and even those who were convicted received sentences of imprisonment ranging from a few months to a few years. Most did not even serve their full sentences.[68] Nevertheless, two of the judgments of the Supreme Court at Leipzig are particularly important. They concerned the sinking of two hospital ships and the killing of the war survivors, and they are often cited "as precedents on the scope of the defense of superior orders."[69] However, there were no proceedings against any of the war crime suspects other than those of the Leipzig court. In sum, "No international trials of Germans accused of war crimes ever took place, and no international court arose out of World War I,"[70] and "the international community allowed many Germans who were believed to be guilty of war crimes to escape prosecution."[71]

Undoubtedly, the Allies were reluctant to seek justice and try the individuals responsible for war crimes during World War I, and they were extremely eager to preserve their national interests.[72] This can clearly be seen in their urgent action to sign an armistice with Germany on November 11, 1919, and their postponement of the trials, which began roughly two years after the armistice. This surely means that the Allies were ready to sacrifice justice "on the altars of [their]

---

[67] Bassiouni, "From Versailles to Rwanda in Seventy-Five Years: The Need to Establish a Permanent International Criminal Court," p. 20.

[68] MacPherson, "Building an International Criminal Court for the 21st Century," p. 6.

[69] Schabas, *An Introduction to the International Criminal Court,* p. 4.

[70] Andreasen, "The International Criminal Court: Does the Constitution Preclude Its Ratification by the United States?," p. 704.

[71] O'Connor, "The Pursuit of Justice and Accountability: Why The United States Should Support the Establishment of an International Criminal Court," p. 936.

[72] For a detailed account on this matter, see, Willis, *Prologue to Nuremberg: The Politics and Diplomacy of Punishing War Criminals of the First World War.*

international and domestic politics."[73] This also reflects the fact that during the interwar period, "the political will of the world's major powers [was] paramount over all else."[74]

Notwithstanding that the Allies did not work hard to achieve justice after World War I by prosecuting and convicting the individuals responsible for large-scale crimes, the interwar period was "important because the proponents of international law moved to establish a permanent system of international criminal justice and a standing court to try violators of international law."[75] There were numerous attempts to establish an international legal order that was more sensitive and responsive to the demands of justice.

The earlier attempt worth noting in this regard is the one made by the Executive Council of the League of Nations. During 1920 and 1921, it established an Advisory Committee of Jurists whose main task was to prepare a draft statute for a Permanent Court of International Justice. The draft statute submitted by this committee was signed and ratified by many states in 1922.[76] The committee also became involved with the issue of creating an international criminal tribunal following World War I. Baron Descamps of Belgium, a member of the advisory committee, proposed establishing a "high court of international justice" and suggested that the court's jurisdiction include offenses that were "recognized by the civilized nations but also by the demands of public conscience." Although the Third Committee of the Assembly of the League rejected this proposal, declaring that the idea of creating such a court was "premature,"[77] the proposal is significant because it refers to public demands. There were other attempts, especially by individuals and nongovernmental

[73] Bassiouni, "From Versailles to Rwanda in Seventy-Five Years: The Need to Establish a Permanent International Criminal Court," p. 20.

[74] Bassiouni, "Establishing an International Criminal Court: Historical Survey," p. 51.

[75] O'Connor, "The Pursuit of Justice and Accountability: Why The United States Should Support the Establishment of an International Criminal Court," p. 938.

[76] Jamison, "A Permanent International Criminal Court: A Proposal that Overcomes Past Objections," p. 423.

[77] Schabas, *An Introduction to the International Criminal Court,* pp. 4–5.

organizations, which seriously studied creating an international criminal court.[78] This is an important fact that reflects that civil society was much more concerned with achieving international justice.

A subsequent attempt and call for an International Court of Justice was made in 1922 at a meeting held by the International Law Association. Bearing in mind the failed attempt of the Advisory Committee of Jurists to create an international criminal court, the meeting participants stressed the need for such an institution. Hugh H. L. Bellot, in his paper presented at the meeting, referred to the "crying need" for the establishment of an International High Court of Justice.[79]

Subsequently, Bellot prepared a comprehensive draft statute for an international criminal court. This draft was presented at the conference held by the International Law Association in Stockholm in 1924 for discussion and possible revisions.[80] The draft met with serious and strong criticisms. Although the most intense criticisms focused on the proposed court's alleged infringement upon national sovereignty, additional criticisms are also worth noting. One of the most eagerly objected features of Bellot's proposal was its recognition of individual complaints before the court. The critics argued that international law regulated interstate relations and did not recognize individuals as subjects.[81]

In 1926, a report and final draft of a Statute of a High Court prepared by the Permanent International Criminal Court Committee of the International Law Association was submitted and then discussed at a meeting held in Vienna.[82] The committee contended that creating such a court was not only an urgent need but also would be a practical means

[78] MacPherson, "Building an International Criminal Court for the 21st Century," p. 7.

[79] Hugh H.L. Bellot, "A Permanent International Criminal Court," The International Law Association, Report of the Thirty-First Conference, Buenos Aires, 1922, p. 63, cited in Lippman, "Towards an International Criminal Court," p. 38, at footnote 138.

[80] Hugh H.L. Bellot, "Draft Statute for the Permanent International Criminal Court," in International Law Association, Report of the Thirty-Third Conference, 1924, cited in Lippman, "Towards an International Criminal Court," p. 31.

[81] Ibid., pp. 101–102.

[82] International Law Association, Report of The Permanent International Criminal Court Committee Report of the Thirty-Fourth Conference, Vienna, 1926 (London, 1927), cited in Lippman, "Towards an International Criminal Court," p. 33, at footnote 161.

of resolving international conflicts. In reaching this observation, the committee noted that the prosecution of individuals before a foreign tribunal as well as the trial and punishment of war criminals by domestic courts were equally problematic[83]; the first could be easily dismissed and criticized by the accused's home country, and the latter was in general viewed as biased.

A later attempt was made at the 1928 Havana Conference of Central American states. The participants drafted a Code of International Law in which such crimes as piracy and slave trading were referred to as violations of international law. However, the code applied only to states. Moreover, this document was criticized because it allowed nations to benefit from a "good will" provision, which hindered any possible advance in the principle of universal criminal accountability.[84] In addition to this regional attempt, the 1929 Geneva Convention also contributed to international criminal law by expanding the scope of the earlier Geneva arrangements on the wounded and prisoners of war. Moreover, the Hague regulations on the conduct of war were exceeded by the Kellogg-Briand Pact, which declared that initiating a war of aggression was illegal.[85]

Although the earlier attempt had failed, there were many other efforts to create an international criminal court. During the 1930s, these attempts focused more on creating an international body that would address the issue of terrorism and punish the perpetrators of terrorist acts. These efforts culminated in holding a Convention on Terrorism that would meet twice in Geneva, on April 30, 1935 and on January 26, 1936.

[83] Ibid., pp. 109–110.

[84] Jamison, "A Permanent International Criminal Court: A Proposal that Overcomes Past Objections," p. 423.

[85] "Development in the Law: International Criminal Law," *Harvard Law Review*, Vol. 114, Issue 7, 2001, pp. 1950–1951. Article 1 of the Kellog-Briand Pact of 1929 states, "The high contracting parties solemnly declare in the names of their respective peoples that they condemn recourse to war for the solution of international controversies, and renounce it as an instrument of national policy in their relations with one another." This pact is also important in that it was referred to as the basis for the war crimes trials that were conducted following the end of WWII. See John A. Maxwell and James J. Friedberg (eds.), *Human Rights in Western Civilization: 1600-Present*, 2nd ed. (Dubuque, IO: Kendall/Hunt Publishing, 1994), p. 128.

The trigger of and incentive for these efforts could be associated with the assassination of King Alexander of Yugoslavia and a French foreign minister by a Croatian nationalist in October 1934. The extradition of the assassin was declined by Italy, where he had fled, on the grounds that the assassinations were political crimes. France responded to this action by submitting a memorandum to the League of Nations that called for codifying a convention on terrorism as well as creating a criminal court that would be authorized to prosecute terrorists.[86] In December 1934, a Committee for the International Repression of Terrorism was established under the auspices of the Council of the League of Nations. The main task of the committee was to prepare a preliminary draft of an international convention on the repression of crimes committed with a political and terrorist motive.[87] At its first meeting, held in Geneva in April 1935, the committee drafted a convention that foresaw the punishment of outlawed acts directed against leading public and political figures and similar acts that threatened public safety.[88] At the second meeting, held in January 1936, the draft documents were modified based on proposals and comments made by various governments.

The participants at the first convention in April 1935 also discussed a draft international criminal code that was proposed by Pella of Italy. A proposal for establishing an international criminal court was also made, but a number of participants opposed it. Therefore, to achieve a solution, one year later in 1936, the proposal for an international criminal court was abandoned, and the issue of terrorism was discussed separately. Accordingly, the Convention for the Prevention and Punishment of Terrorism and the Convention for the Creation of an International Criminal Court were adopted in 1937. The proposed court's jurisdiction was confined to the scope of the Convention on Terrorism. Additionally, the court's establishment was made subject to the

[86] Suggestions Presented to the Council by the French Government, Appendix IV, Committee for The International Repression of Terrorism, Report to the Council on the First Session of the Committee, 1935, reprinted in ibid., pp. 269ff.

[87] Ibid., p. 270.

[88] Ibid., pp. 271–272.

terrorism convention's establishment, but the court was never established.[89] Only India ratified the Convention on Terrorism, although 19 states had signed it by May 1938. The Convention for the Creation of an International Criminal Court was signed by 13 states, none of which ratified it. It appears that "the majority of these nations were not yet willing to give up their national sovereignty to a body with compulsory jurisdiction."[90] The following observation confirms the preceding:

> The Convention for the Creation of an International Criminal Court was an effort to overcome the objections lodged against previous proposals. The court's jurisdiction was limited to a narrow range of offenses and the court was to apply municipal rather than international law. States were provided the option whether to prosecute or extradite offenders to a third party State or to the tribunal on terrorism. Nevertheless, States clearly were not willing to restrict their prosecutorial discretion and resisted recognizing the jurisdiction of an international court comprised of foreign judges who were empowered to apply alien legal doctrines.[91]

[89] It is argued that multiple world crises that erupted during the late 1930s prevented the proposed court's establishment. See Latore, "Escape Out the Back Door or Charge in the Front Door: U.S. Reactions to the International Criminal Court," p. 162.

[90] Jamison, "A Permanent International Criminal Court: A Proposal that Overcomes Past Objections," p. 423.

[91] Lippman, "Towards an International Criminal Court," p. 44.

# The Period Between World War II and the End of the Cold War

The world's failure to introduce satisfying remedies to prevent future atrocities such as those committed during World War I could surely be considered one of the leading contributors to the deaths, enormous in amount and horrifying in type that occurred during World War II. It could be argued that if some effective measure had been taken in the immediate aftermath of World War I, there would have been no appalling massacres such as the Holocaust as late as the 1940s, when the world was much more civilized in many respects but equally ignorant of large-scale crimes committed against the human race.

However, this time the world seemed to be more sensitive and responsive to atrocities, especially those committed by the Nazis. This sensitivity could be best seen in the efforts of the Allies to prosecute war criminals even before the actual end of the war.[1] In 1942, the Allies signed an agreement that created the United Nations War Crimes

[1] However, it should be noted that some were in favor of immediately executing alleged war criminals without prosecution and trials. For instance, it is argued that the British suggested that the Nazis be executed. See MacPherson, "Building an International Criminal Court for the 21st Century," p. 8, and Andreasen, "The International Criminal Court: Does the Constitution



C. Çakmak, *A Brief History of International Criminal Law and International Criminal Court*,
DOI 10.1057/978-1-137-56736-9_4

Commission.[2] This commission, composed of members from most of the Allies and chaired by Sir Cecil Hurst of the United Kingdom, was established to "set the stage for post-war prosecution."[3] Having recognized "the likelihood that justice would not be served in the national court of a nation where state policy had actively participated in the atrocities committed,"[4] it then prepared a Draft Convention for the Establishment of a United Nations War Crimes Court,[5] which was largely based on the 1937 Treaty of the League of Nations.[6] However, despite the commission's expectations, the draft convention was to a large extent subject to political rivalries and "considerations and ultimately relegated to a role far interior to that which was expected by the Allies." It could not be effective, particularly because it had little support or political power given that most of its representatives had come from governments in exile whose futures were uncertain. Moreover, to proceed with investigating and obtaining evidence of war crimes, the commission relied heavily on the Allied powers, who then failed to provide adequate staff or funds. The Allies also failed to submit necessary

---

Preclude Its Ratification by the United States?" p. 703. The British based their suggestion on the premise that "their 'guilt was so black' that it was 'beyond the scope of any judicial process.'" However, the great powers aside from Britain did not support this argument. For instance, Stalin advocated a special international tribunal for prosecuting the senior war crime suspects, namely, Hitler, his close advisers, and his top military leaders. Similarly, both the United States and France preferred the establishment of an international tribunal to prosecute war criminals. The British suggestion of summary execution was also attributed to the fear that "fair procedures would allow the accused to use the tribunal as a forum for propaganda and self-justification." Ultimately, largely because of the United States' insistence, the idea of an international criminal tribunal prevailed in this discussion. See Bassiouni, "From Versailles to Rwanda in Seventy-Five Years: The Need to Establish a Permanent International Criminal Court," p. 23.

[2] It should be noted that although it was preceded by the term United Nations, this commission had nothing to do with the United Nations that was created in 1945.

[3] Schabas, *An Introduction to the International Criminal Court,* p. 5.

[4] Jamison, "A Permanent International Criminal Court: A Proposal that Overcomes Past Objections," p. 424.

[5] "Draft Convention for the Establishment of a United Nations War Crimes Court," UN War Crimes Commission, U.N. Doc.C.50 (1), 30 September 1944. Article 1(2) of the Convention was as follows: "The jurisdiction of the Court shall extend to the trial and punishment of any person—irrespective of rank or position—who has committed, or attempted to commit, or has ordered, caused, aided, abetted or incited another person to commit, or by his failure to fulfill a duty incumbent upon him has himself committed, an offence against the laws and customs of war."

[6] Schabas, *An Introduction to the International Criminal Court,* p. 5.

information to the commission, and thus, its chair announced that it was unable to fulfill its mandate.[7]

However, after it became evident that the atrocities committed in the territories occupied by Germany were so horrifying in type and extensive in scale that they could not be overlooked and that the perpetrators could not be allowed to go unpunished, the Allies began working on collecting information on war criminals. In addition, the British government, considering the aforesaid fact, began to press the commission to proceed. This pressure was ultimately fruitful, and as a consequence, the commission managed to prepare 8,178 "dossiers" on alleged war criminals. Although the information it collected was never used in the proceedings of the international military tribunals, which will be addressed below, subsequent national prosecutions against the war criminals of World War II relied heavily on the commission's findings.[8]

Notwithstanding the fact that the Allies set aside the commission's work, they demonstrated the will and determination to achieve justice by establishing special international military tribunals that were mandated to prosecute and try suspected war criminals. It is worth noting that the governments of the United States, the United Kingdom and the Soviet Union had already declared at a 1943 Moscow conference that

> those German officers and men and members of the Nazi party who have been responsible for or have taken a consenting part in the above atrocities, massacres and executions will be sent back to the countries in which their abominable deeds were done in order that they may be judged and punished according to the laws of these liberated countries and of free governments which will be erected therein

and that "German criminals whose offenses have no particular geographical localization . . . will be punished by joint decision of the

[7] Bassiouni, "From Versailles to Rwanda in Seventy-Five Years: The Need to Establish a Permanent International Criminal Court," p. 22.

[8] Ibid., pp. 22–23.

government of the Allies."[9] The Moscow Declaration was the forerunner of the London Agreement, of which Article 1 states that "an International Military Tribunal for the trial of war criminals whose offenses have no particular geographical location whether they be accused individually or in their capacity as members of the organizations or groups or in both capacities" shall be established.[10] This time, the Provisional Government of France also joined the agreement, which annexed the Charter of the International Military Tribunal (also known and referred to as the Constitution of the International Military Tribunal).[11] Under the charter, the tribunal would have the power to try and punish those who committed war crimes within the tribunal's jurisdiction. The acts for which there would be individual criminal responsibility were classified into three groups, namely, crimes against peace, war crimes, and crimes against humanity.[12] The individual criminal responsibility would apply to all individuals, irrespective of their

[9] "A Decade of American Foreign Policy: Basic Documents, 1941–1949" (prepared by the Staff of the Committee and the Department of State) (Washington, DC: Government Printing Office, 1950), available through The Avalon Project of Yale University Law School website: http://www.yale.edu/lawweb/avalon/wwii/moscow.htm#imtmoscow.

[10] The Agreement for the Prosecution and Punishment of Major War Criminals of the European Axis, August 8, 1945, 82 U.N.T.S. 279 (London Agreement), available through The Avalon Project of Yale University Law School website available at: http://www.yale.edu/lawweb/avalon/imt/proc/imtchart.htm.

[11] Agreement for the Prosecution and Punishment of the Major War Criminals of the European Axis, August 8, 1945, Charter of the International Military Tribunal, 59 Stat. 1544, 1546, 82 U.N.T.S. 279, 284 (London Charter), available at: http://www.yale.edu/lawweb/avalon/imt/proc/imtconst.htm. Nineteen states later acceded to the Charter later.

[12] The Charter defines those acts in Article 6 as follows:

(a) Crimes Against Peace: namely, planning, preparation, initiation or waging of a war of aggression, or a war in violation of international treaties, agreements or assurances, or participation in a common plan or conspiracy for the accomplishment of any of the foregoing;
(b) War Crimes: namely, violations of the laws or customs of war. Such violations shall include, but not be limited to, murder, ill-treatment or deportation to slave labor or for any other purpose of civilian population of or in occupied territory, murder or ill-treatment of prisoners of war or persons on the seas, killing of hostages, plunder of public or private property, wanton destruction of cities, towns or villages, or devastation not justified by military necessity;
(c) Crimes Against Humanity: namely, murder, extermination, enslavement, deportation, and other inhumane acts committed against any civilian population, before or during the war; or persecutions on political, racial or religious grounds in execution of or in connection with any crime within the jurisdiction of the Tribunal, whether or not in violation of the domestic law of the country where perpetrated.

rank or official position.[13] This was a significant breakthrough given that the provision that allowed for prosecuting even heads of states could be interpreted as limiting national sovereignty. The charter also provided that each acceding state would "appoint a Chief Prosecutor for the investigation of the charges against and the prosecution of major war criminals."[14] Subsequently, the investigation teams that were appointed by the signatories began collecting evidence. The American team was the most successful in that it provided most of the documents that were used as evidence in the proceedings against the accused.[15]

The military tribunal that was established to prosecute war criminals under the London Charter indicted 24 persons, all of whom were German. Of the 22 who were prosecuted, 3 were acquitted, 12 were sentenced to death, 3 were sentenced to life imprisonment, and the rest were sentenced to terms of imprisonment ranging from 10 to 20 years. One defendant committed suicide at the end of the trial.[16] Although these trials are important and might be viewed as the achievement of at least partial justice, it is unfortunate that no Allied military personnel were indicted or tried for war crimes committed during the war.

---

[13] Article 7 of the London Charter states that "The fact that the Defendant acted pursuant to order of his Government or of a superior shall not free him from responsibility, but may be considered in mitigation of punishment if the Tribunal determines that justice so requires."

[14] Article 14 of the London Charter states,

The Chief Prosecutors shall act as a committee for the following purposes:
(a) to agree upon a plan of the individual work of each of the Chief Prosecutors and his staff,
(b) to settle the final designation of major war criminals to be tried by the Tribunal,
(c) to approve the Indictment and the documents to be submitted therewith,
(d) to lodge the Indictment and the accompany documents with the Tribunal,
(e) to draw up and recommend to the Tribunal for its approval draft rules of procedure.

Article 15 determines the duties of the Chief Prosecutors in their individual capacities:
(a) investigation, collection and production before or at the Trial of all necessary evidence,
(b) the preparation of the Indictment for approval by the Committee,
(c) the preliminary examination of all necessary witnesses and of all Defendants,
(d) to act as prosecutor at the Trial,
(e) to appoint representatives to carry out such duties as may be assigned them,
(f) to undertake such other matters as may appear necessary to them for the purposes of the preparation for and conduct of the Trial.

[15] Bassiouni, "From Versailles to Rwanda in Seventy-Five Years: The Need to Establish a Permanent International Criminal Court," p. 28.

[16] Ibid., p. 29. Detailed information about those indicted, including their names and the accusations against them, available at: http://www.yale.edu/lawweb/avalon/imt/proc/countb.htm.

Following the Nuremberg trials,[17] which were international in character, the Allies established regional courts. Subsequent to Germany's unconditional surrender, acting under the London Charter, the Allies enacted Allied Control Council Law No. 10 (CCL 10), which allowed them to prosecute Germans.[18] As with the Nuremberg trials, the trials under CCL 10 were effective.[19] Approximately 20,000 German nationals were prosecuted in the war crime tribunals that had been established by the Allies in the occupation zones.[20] Moreover, based on the council law aforementioned, the German courts continued to prosecute suspected war criminals for several decades.[21] France, Canada, and Israel also held trials to punish the perpetrators of the crimes committed during World War II. Australia and the United Kingdom, although they passed national legislation that enabled such, never brought anyone to trial in this context.[22]

---

[17] There are many works on the Nuremberg Trials. See, among others, Steven Ratner, *Accountability for Human Rights Atrocities in International Law: Beyond the Nuremberg Legacy* (Oxford: Oxford University Press, 1997); Philippe Sands (ed.), *From Nuremberg to The Hague: The Future of International Criminal Justice* (Cambridge: Cambridge University Press, 2003); W. J. Bosch, *Judgment on Nuremberg. American Attitudes toward the Major German War Crimes Trials* (Chapel Hill, NC: University of North Carolina Press, 1970); Robert E. Conot, *Justice at Nuremberg* (New York: Harper & Row, 1983); Eugene Davidson, *The Trial of the Germans, Nuremberg 1945–1946: An Account of the Twenty-Two Defendants Before the International Military Tribunal at Nuremberg* (New York: Macmillan, 1967); George Ginsburg and V. N. Kudriavtsev (eds.), *The Nuremberg Trial and International Law* (Dordrecht: Nijhoff, 1990); Sheldon Glueck, *The Nuremberg Trial and Aggressive War* (New York: Knopf, 1946); J. J. Heydecker and J. Leeb. *The Nuremberg Trial* (Cleveland: World Publishing, 1962); A. M. p. Neave, *Nuremberg: A Personal Record of the Trial of the Major Nazi War Criminals in 1945–6* (London: Hodder & Stoughton, 1978); Bradley F. Smith, *The American Road to Nuremberg. The Documentary Record 1944–1945* (Stanford: Hoover Institution Press, 1982); Telford Taylor, *The Anatomy of the Nuremberg Trials. A Personal* Memoir (New York: Knopf, 1992) and Robert K. Woetzel, *The Nuremberg Trials in International Law* (New York: Praeger, 1960).

[18] Allied Control Council Law No. 10, Punishment of Persons Guilty of War Crimes, Crimes against Peace and against Humanity, December 20, 1945, Official Gazette of the Control Council for Germany, No. 3, Berlin, January 31, 1946; reprinted in Ferencz, *Half A Century of Hope: An International Criminal Court: A Step Toward World Peace- A Documentary History and Analysis*, pp. 488ff.

[19] Bassiouni, "From Versailles to Rwanda in Seventy-Five Years: The Need to Establish a Permanent International Criminal Court," p. 29.

[20] O'Connor, "The Pursuit of Justice and Accountability: Why The United States Should Support the Establishment of an International Criminal Court," p. 942.

[21] Schabas, *An Introduction to the International Criminal Court,* p. 6.

[22] Bassiouni, "Establishing an International Criminal Court: Historical Survey," p. 55.

However, the Allies did not achieve similar success in trying Italian war criminals. Because the aforementioned council law permitted them to act as the sovereign authority in Germany only, that law did not apply to the territory of Italy; instead, Italy was subject to a surrender treaty that made possible the extradition and prosecution of war criminals.[23] However, the prosecutions foreseen in this document never took place owing to the subsequent fear of communism that became pervasive throughout Europe. Believing that the Italian fascists were prominent enemies of communism, the Allies hesitated to proceed with prosecuting or extraditing suspected Italian war criminals. As a consequence, despite the strong evidence against these suspects, and the requests to extradite these war criminals pursuant to Article 29 of the surrender treaty by the governments of Greece, Yugoslavia, Libya, and Ethiopia, in 1946, Italy refused to extradite the requested persons.[24]

However, the significance of the Nuremberg trials should not be underestimated. One can easily appreciate what was achieved in Nuremberg considering the political circumstances of the time. Affected greatly by the Nazis' atrocities, the text of the UN Charter of 1945 contained a few broad references to human rights. In other words, it was not truly a human rights document, nor was it strong enough to be binding regarding states' human rights practices. The charter was thus weak and insufficient in terms of both content and binding strength. In contrast, the Nuremberg trials, which took place at almost the same time, were very powerful. Whereas the human rights provisions of the UN Charter "were more programmatic than operational, more a program to be realized by states over time than legal rules to be applied immediately to states," what took place at Nuremberg "was concrete

[23] The Instrument of Surrender of Italy, 29 September 1943, Art. 29.

[24] It should be noted that the crimes committed by the alleged Italian war criminals were grave. The War Commission listed 750 Italian war criminals who were mainly responsible for the following: illegal use of poisonous gas against Ethiopian civilians and combatants, killing innocent civilians and prisoners of war, torture and mistreatment of prisoners, bombing ambulances, destruction of cultural property, and other violations of the laws of armed conflicts during the Italo-Abyssinian war. Moreover, the same commission obtained extensive evidence of crimes committed by the Italian suspects in Greece, Libya, and Yugoslavia during World War II. See Bassiouni, "From Versailles to Rwanda in Seventy-Five Years: The Need to Establish a Permanent International Criminal Court," pp. 30–31.

and applied: prosecutions, convictions, punishment." The prosecutions at Nuremberg were based on international customs and norms that had deep roots in international law. However, the most striking achievement of the Nuremberg trials was that they applied those customs, norms and doctrines to impose criminal punishment on individuals for committing the three crimes the London Charter covered. "The notion of crimes against the law of nations for which violators bore an individual criminal responsibility was itself an older one, but it had operated in a restricted field."[25] In other words, the trials not only applied the long-existing principle of individual criminal responsibility in a concrete and open manner but also expanded the principle's applicability. In this vein, it would not be an exaggeration to assert that the judgment delivered at the Nuremberg trials contained elements of modern international criminal law given that it declared that

> The very essence of the Charter is that individuals have international duties which transcend the national obligations of obedience imposed by the individual State. He who violates the laws of war cannot obtain immunity while acting in pursuance of the authority of the State if the State in authorizing action moves outside its competence under international law.[26]

Notwithstanding their significance as an achievement of international justice, the Nuremberg trials have been criticized for a number of reasons. One criticism refers to the content and authority of the tribunal. It is argued that the principle that states do not judge each other (*par in parem non habet iurisdictionem*) is one of the foundations of international law. This argument contends that the Nuremberg tribunal acted against the principles of the classical law of nations by trying and punishing political figures who were in fact acting on behalf of their nations.[27] In fact, the Nazis accused of having committed the crimes contained in the London Charter during the war

---

[25] Henry J. Steiner and Philip Alston (eds.), *International Human Rights in Context: Law, Politics and Morals* (Oxford: Clarendon Press, 1996), p. 99.

[26] Judgment of the International Military Tribunal for the Trial of German Major War Criminals, Nuremberg, September 30th and October 1st, 1946, available at: http://www.yale.edu/lawweb/avalon/imt/proc/judlawch.htm.

[27] Meray, *Devletler Hukukuna Giriş*, p. 590.

advocated the same view at Nuremberg. Their argument could be perfectly summarized as follows: "For what we have done only Germany can judge us. We acted in the interests of Germany alone, and only Germany has the right to decide whether we acted rightly or wrongly. It is no business of any other country what we did."[28] It is interesting to note that this argument is a good indication of states' primacy in world affairs even in the late 1940s.[29] It also demonstrates that the principle of nonintervention was so prevalent that even those who committed the gravest crimes referred to it as a panacea for what they were experiencing rather than seeking any other possible solution.

The response to this criticism also reveals the state-centric approach. The counterargument claims that there was no violation of international law in the trials because four states acted to perform a duty that should have been performed by one state, in this case, Germany. Furthermore, as the occupier forces, the Allies legally took over Germany's authority to try the suspects. Given that, they acted on Germany's behalf and proceeded with the trials.[30]

Another criticism of the Nuremberg trials is that they conflicted with the principle that there is no punishment without law. It is asserted that the crimes contained in the London Charter did not exist prior to its adoption, that is, when the alleged crimes were committed. Based on this, the argument states that the charter did not cover past acts. However, the tribunal itself declared that it had applied the rules and customs of the existing laws of nations.[31] Because war crimes were outlawed in both

---

[28] William Eldred Jackson, "Putting the Nuremberg Law to Work," *Foreign Affairs,* Vol. 25, Issue 4, 1947, p. 550.

[29] However, it should be noted that the Nuremberg tribunal rejected this argument by stating that "It was submitted that international law is concerned with the action of sovereign States, and provides no punishment for individuals; and further, that where the act in question is an act of state, those who carry it out are not personally responsible, but are protected by the doctrine of the sovereignty of the State. In the opinion of the Tribunal, both these submissions must be rejected. That international law imposes duties and liabilities upon individuals as well as upon States has long been recognized." Judgment of the International Military Tribunal for the Trial of German Major War Criminals, available at: http://www.yale.edu/lawweb/avalon/imt/proc/judlawch.htm.

[30] Meray, *Devletler Hukukuna Giriş,* p. 590.

[31] The Judgment of the Nuremberg Tribunal mentioned of the defendants objection on this matter: "It was urged on behalf of the defendants that a fundamental principle of all law—international and domestic—is that there can be no punishment of crime without a pre-existing law. 'Nullum crimen sine lege. nulla poena sine lege.' It was submitted that ex post facto punishment is abhorrent to the law of all civilized nations, that no sovereign power had made

custom and doctrine, the tribunal was authorized to prosecute the perpetrators of those crimes. Moreover, the Kellogg-Briand Pact of 1928 codified the crime of aggression. It is important to note here that 63 nations, including Germany, acceded to that pact. Moreover, this was not the only arrangement that outlawed aggression. The League of Nations repeatedly denounced aggression as criminal, and thus, the entire world was of the opinion that aggressive war was a crime.[32] More importantly, the crimes over which the tribunal was given authority were acts that were also prohibited in national jurisdictions.[33] Considering that Germany, by having acceded to the Kellogg-Briand Pact, had outlawed aggressive war, the authority of the Nuremberg tribunal is justified: "If a man plans aggression when aggression has been formally renounced by his nation, he is criminal."[34]

However, the remaining two criticisms are more important than the above. Many who criticized the trials referred to the fact that the tribunal was composed of judges who had been drawn from the Allied countries. This raised doubts and questions regarding the impartiality of the proceedings.[35] However, the Allies' preference was understandable

---

aggressive war a crime at the time the alleged criminal acts were committed, that no statute had defined aggressive war, that no penalty had been fixed for its commission, and no court had been created to try and punish offenders." However, the Tribunal refused the argument that it was directing accusations that were not codified in the pre-existing law: "it is to be observed that the maxim nullum crimen sine lege is not a limitation of sovereignty, but is in general a principle of justice. To assert that it is unjust to punish those who in defiance of treaties and assurances have attacked neighboring states without warning is obviously untrue, for in such circumstances the attacker must know that he is doing wrong, and so far from it being unjust to punish him, it would be unjust if his wrong were allowed to go unpunished. Occupying the positions they did in the government of Germany, the defendants, or at least some of them must have known of the treaties signed by Germany, outlawing recourse to war for the settlement of international disputes; they must have known that they were acting in defiance of all international law when in complete deliberation they carried out the designs of invasion and aggression. On this view of the case alone, it would appear that the maxim has no application to the present facts." Judgment of the International Military Tribunal for the Trial of German Major War Criminals. The text of the judgment is available at: http://www.yale.edu/lawweb/avalon/imt/proc/judcont.htm.

[32] Henry L. Stimson, "The Nuremberg Trial: Landmark in Law," *Foreign Affairs*, Vol. 25, Issue 2, 1947, p. 182.

[33] Meray, *Devletler Hukukuna Giriş*, pp. 591–592.

[34] Stimson, "The Nuremberg Trial: Landmark in Law," p. 184.

[35] Latore, "Escape Out the Back Door or Charge in the Front Door: U.S. Reactions to the International Criminal Court," p. 164.

given that the Leipzig tribunal that had been established after the end of World War I had failed to prosecute and convict its own nationals. It is thus quite possible that the Allies feared that this time as well, the crimes committed during the war would go unpunished.[36] The final criticism is perhaps the most important one: that only the persons from the defeated nations were prosecuted, tried and convicted; no proceeding was held against individuals from the Allied forces. This is surely a paramount shortcoming of the Nuremberg trials, particularly in consideration of international justice.

The last fact indicates that the Nuremberg tribunal was not in fact international. It is asserted that this tribunal could be viewed as a joint attempt given that it was "composed only of allied personnel and had a limited mandate to prosecute only the defeated enemy."[37] Because it was established by the Allied forces, it was not accountable to an international body. This was one of the primary reasons that the principles that had been advanced by the tribunal could not be enhanced and expanded in its aftermath. A *Foreign Affairs* article authored in 1947 foresaw this well in advance:

> It would seem especially important that the Nuremberg principles, which establish a rule of law overriding sovereignty and binding on all nations, should remain strong while the United Nations has not achieved full command of its powers. But the assizes of Nuremberg are no longer in being. The sentences have been carried out, the Tribunal has dissolved, the prosecutors have departed, and all the elaborate mechanism of justice is dispersed. The men who conceived it and made it work have all returned to their normal occupations. How, then, can we find effective means of perpetuating the Nuremberg principles so that they may operate as continuing sanctions of peace?[38]

Although the United Nations General Assembly, by adopting a resolution on 11 December 1946, affirmed the principles contained in the

[36] Meray, *Devletler Hukukuna Giriş*, p. 593.
[37] MacPherson, "Building an International Criminal Court for the 21st Century," p. 9.
[38] Jackson, "Putting the Nuremberg Law to Work," p. 551.

Nuremberg International Military Tribunal Charter and its judgment as the principles of the law of nations,[39] subsequent developments demonstrated that this affirmation did not mean much. With strong political support and will, Nuremberg could have been a precedent and prototype for a permanent criminal court. However, despite some weak attempts to create such a body, within a relatively short time, the progress made by the Nuremberg trials slowed and eventually evaporated.

The Allies, particularly the USSR, were also determined to address the war crimes committed by the Japanese. First, in response to the USSR's request, establishing the Far Eastern Commission was agreed to in December 1945.[40] The commission, which was seated in Washington, was formed of 11 states; however, the four Allied states had veto power. The commission was to transmit its directives to the Allied Council for Japan, an advisory group that was seated in Tokyo. Although the commission was established as an investigative body, its role was mainly political. In this regard, its main task was to establish a policy of Japanese occupation and to coordinate this policy in the Far East.[41] However, in addition to this function, the commission played an important role in prosecuting, trying and enforcing the sentences of the suspected war criminals, although its function ended when a treaty was signed with Japan.[42]

---

[39] Affirmation of the Principles of International Law Recognized by the Charter of the Nuremberg Tribunal, G.A. Res. 95 (I), U.N. GAOR, U.N. Doc. A/236 (1946); text available at the UN website available at: http://www.un.org/documents/ga/res/1/ares1.htm.

[40] The Commission was established by the agreement of the United Kingdom, the United States, and the Soviet Union at a meeting held in Moscow in December 1945 and held its first meeting on February 26, 1946. "Political and Legal Organizations," *International Organization,* Vol. 1, Issue 1, 1947, p. 176.

[41] The Commission was to exercise the following functions:

1. To formulate the policies, principles, and standards in conformity with which the fulfillment by Japan of its surrender obligations was to be accomplished.
2. To review, on the request of any member, any directive issued to the Supreme Commander for the Allied Powers (General Douglas MacArthur) of any of his actions involving policy decisions within the jurisdiction of the Commission.
3. To consider such matters as might be assigned to it by agreement of the participating governments.

Ibid., p. 177.

[42] Bassiouni, "From Versailles to Rwanda in Seventy-Five Years: The Need to Establish a Permanent International Criminal Court," p. 32.

On January 19, 1946, when the Nuremberg military tribunal was still in operation, US General Douglas MacArthur, as the Supreme Commander for the Allied Forces for the Pacific Theater and on behalf of the aforementioned commission, established the International Military Tribunal for the Far East (IMTFE). The charter of the tribunal[43] was approved on the same day and later amended on April 26.[44] The tribunal was empowered to try and punish Far Eastern, especially Japanese, war criminals who were "charged with offenses which include crimes against peace, conventional war crimes and crimes against humanity,"[45] the same crimes as those the defendants at the Nuremberg trials were accused of. Despite this similarity, however, and unlike the Nuremberg tribunal, the IMTFE was not based on a treaty but on General MacArthur's order. Bassiouni attributes the lack of a treaty in establishing this tribunal to US concerns about the ambitions of the Soviet Union in the Far East. Largely for this reason, each endeavor regarding the pursuit of postwar justice in the Far East was "guided by MacArthur's wishes."[46]

General MacArthur was empowered by the policy decision of the Far Eastern Commission on the Apprehension, Trial and Punishment of War Criminals in the Far East to establish an agency to investigate the war crimes committed during the war, collect and classify evidence and address other relevant matters. The members of the commission and then of the tribunal itself acted on behalf of their governments, not on their own behalf. This created a politicized commission and tribunal and also "affected the internal workings of these bodies as well as the quality of justice they administered." Procedural irregularities were frequently observed during the proceedings; the defendants were chosen on a political basis and tried in an unfair manner.[47]

[43] Charter of the International Military Tribunal for the Far East, *Trial of Japanese War Criminals* (Washington, DC: United States Government Printing Office, 1946), pp. 39–44.

[44] "Political and Legal Organizations," p. 176.

[45] Ibid.

[46] Bassiouni, "From Versailles to Rwanda in Seventy-Five Years: The Need to Establish a Permanent International Criminal Court," pp. 32–33.

[47] Ibid., pp. 33–34.

In its judgment, the tribunal ruled that Japan was guilty of waging aggressive war. The judgment cited a long series of international agreements that Japan had violated, including multiple Hague conventions.[48] All 28 defendants were found guilty. However, a few of them received light sentences. Although seven were executed, the majority were sentenced to life imprisonment.[49] Two of the defendants died during the proceedings, and the trial of one defendant was suspended on the grounds of insanity.[50] However, those who received life imprisonment did not fully serve their terms; the enforcement of their sentences was solely controlled by General MacArthur, "who had the power to grant clemency, reduce sentences, and release convicted war criminals on parole." Ultimately, each one was released by the end of the 1950s.[51]

Moreover, no domestic proceedings were held against the suspected war criminals in Japan. On November 3, 1946, Emperor Hirohito signed an Imperial Restrict that granted amnesty to all members of the Japanese armed forces who might have committed offenses during the course of the war. General MacArthur approved this action by not opposing it, although this was not publicized to avoid public opposition and criticism in Allied countries. The most important reason for this tacit approval could have been the recent promulgation of the newly devised Constitution of Japan. Furthermore, Japan passed a law that established a commission to oversee the release of convicted Japanese war criminals.[52]

The Tokyo trials were severely criticized. The critics argued that the proceedings were not fair in that some of the defendants' arguments were never examined; the judgments were based on political considerations rather than on the evidence presented; and the defendants' guilt

---

[48] "International Military Tribunal for the Far East," *International Organization,* Vol. 3, Issue 1, 1949, p. 184.

[49] Jamison, "A Permanent International Criminal Court: A Proposal that Overcomes Past Objections," p. 425.

[50] "International Military Tribunal for the Far East," p. 185.

[51] Bassiouni, "From Versailles to Rwanda in Seventy-Five Years: The Need to Establish a Permanent International Criminal Court," p. 34.

[52] For additional details, see R. John Pritchard, "The Gift of Clemency Following British War Crimes Trials in the Far East, 1946–1947," *Criminal Law Forum,* Vol. 7, Issue, 1996, pp. 37–38.

was not clearly proven. Specifically, some doubts arose about the fairness of the decisions following the proceedings.[53]

In fact, the influence of political concerns was so evident that the FEC decided on February 3, 1950, not to prosecute the Emperor of Japan as a war criminal. The underlying intent of this decision was to honor the Emperor, who had shown his intention to cooperate with the Western world.[54] In addition, the American trials conducted in the Philippines, and those conducted by the other Allies in the Far East, did not include the prosecution and punishment of crimes other than war crimes.[55]

Even the war crimes trials were not always unbiased and fair. The prosecution of General Tomoyuki Yamashita, who was convicted and executed for having committed war crimes, was exemplary in this regard. His execution is attributed to General MacArthur's desire for vengeance given that he allegedly vowed to punish the Japanese when he left the Philippines to Japanese forces. When the Allies retook the country, General Yamashita was in command but only for two or three weeks. MacArthur ordered the trial of Yamashita for committing war crimes, but there was substantial evidence that he had not actually committed the crimes for which he was being held liable. General MacArthur's order influenced the judges, who applied inappropriate legal standards that resulted in General Yamashita's conviction and execution. The military panel based its decision to convict on the notion of superior responsibility. However, it was argued that there was insufficient evidence of orders given by Yamashita to substantiate his liability for the crimes committed by his subordinates.[56]

Moreover, the fact that the tribunal's establishment was associated with General MacArthur's initiative created doubts as to whether the tribunal was international in nature. In fact, these doubts are why two of the defendants before the tribunal appealed to the US Supreme Court,

[53] Jamison, "A Permanent International Criminal Court: A Proposal that Overcomes Past Objections," pp. 425–426.

[54] Bassiouni, "From Versailles to Rwanda in Seventy-Five Years: The Need to Establish a Permanent International Criminal Court," p. 36.

[55] Ibid.

[56] Ibid., pp. 36–37.

alleging that the US High Court had jurisdiction given that the International Military Tribunal for the Far East had been established by MacArthur's order. Although the Court decided by a vote of five to four to hear the defendants' arguments, it then ruled that it had no jurisdiction over the military tribunal's cases because that court was international in nature.[57]

The tribunals that were established following the end of World War II to prosecute, try, and punish the perpetrators of wartime crimes, especially the one established in Nuremberg, were significant in the history of international criminal jurisdiction, but they did not become predecessors for more enhanced and authorized tribunals. The fact that the years following their dissolution have not witnessed serious attempts to create a permanent international criminal court could be cited as perfect proof of this observation. Moreover, "since World War II there have been many conflicts for which no international investigative or prosecutorial bodies were ever set up."[58] Although no clear and solid reason can be cited for this reluctance, as Bassiouni suggests, justice might have been "the Cold War's casualty."[59]

Of course, this does not necessarily mean that there have been no attempts to contribute to the evolution of international criminal law. However, the point that needs to be clarified is that the attempts were not particularly substantial; a Nuremberg-like tribunal was established decades after numerous incidents that needed and deserved international attention and concern.

The weak and inconclusive attempts to address international crimes have in general been made under the auspices of the United Nations, which governed the formulation and development of these attempts. However, the dominance of Cold War circumstances and states' reluctance to cooperate with the organization's endeavors obstructed the realization of eminent projects and arrangements regarding international

[57] "International Military Tribunal for the Far East," p. 186.

[58] Bassiouni, "From Versailles to Rwanda in Seventy-Five Years: The Need to Establish a Permanent International Criminal Court," pp. 38–39.

[59] Ibid., p. 39.

criminal matters. Although the UN has frequently initiated a process by which an international body could be vested with the authority to prosecute international crimes, these initiatives have in general been futile.

Initially, the UN's work to broaden the scope of international criminal jurisdiction was twofold. On the one hand, the UN attempted to adopt a Genocide Convention, pressure from civil society groups, and the horror caused by the genocidal acts of the Nazis during World War II were the main motives behind this initiative. On the other hand, the organization also engaged in activities to ensure the establishment of a permanent international criminal court.

To begin, the UN General Assembly established the International Law Commission[60] and then directed to it to formulate the Nuremberg principles. Its main tasks also included devising a Draft Code of Offenses against the peace and security of mankind.[61]

Upon its establishment, the commission was invited by the UN General Assembly to work on the "possibility of establishing an international judicial organ for the trial of persons charged with genocide or other crimes over which jurisdiction will be conferred upon that organ by international conventions,"[62] given that the preamble to the resolution recognized that "in the course of development of the international community, there will be an increasing need of an international judicial organ for the trial of certain crimes under international law."[63] The Assembly also requested that the commission "pay attention to the possibility of establishing a Criminal Chamber of the International Court of Justice."[64]

The commission began working on that matter in 1949. It appointed two rapporteurs to study the matter and to prepare and submit reports

---

[60] *Establishment of an International Law Commission*, GA Res. 174(II), UN GAOR, UN Doc. A/ 519 (1947).

[61] *Formulation of the Principles Recognized in the Charter of the Nuremberg Trial and in the Judgment of the Tribunal,* General Assembly Resolution 177(II), U.N. Doc. A/519 (1948).

[62] *Study by the International Law Commission of the Question of an International Criminal Jurisdiction,* UN General Assembly Resolution 260 B(III), U.N. Doc. A/810, December 9, 1948.

[63] Ibid.

[64] Ibid.

to the commission. The rapporteurs reviewed the major works that had been produced since the end of WWI on international criminal jurisdiction, including the 1919 Commission on the Responsibility of the Authors of the War and on Enforcement of Penalties and the 1943 UN War Crimes Commission. Upon completion their work, the rapporteurs concluded:

> That it is *desirable* to establish a judicial organ for the trial of international crimes, seems to be evidenced by all the facts, declarations, studies, proposals, recommendations, plans and decisions which have marked for a period of over thirty years the birth and growth of the idea of an international criminal jurisdiction. In fact, more than something desirable, it is a thing desired, an aspiration of Governments, institutions, conferences, jurists, statesmen and writers.[65]

The report also provided that creating an international criminal organ such as that referred to in the relevant UN General Assembly Resolution was possible. Having referred to the 1937 Geneva Convention on the trial of persons involved in terrorist acts and the two military tribunals that had been established to prosecute wartime crimes following World War II, the rapporteurs maintained that the possibility of establishing an international criminal organ of penal justice was "demonstrated by actual experience."[66]

The report made mention of national sovereignty, having considered that it was clearly related to the matter under consideration. The author of the report agreed with the assertion that such a court would mean impinging on sovereignty. However, he countered that objection "with the remark that certain crimes perpetrated by Governments or by individuals as representatives of Governments, could hardly be tried by territorial courts. Only an international court can properly try certain

---

[65] Ricardo J. Alfaro, International Law Commission, *Report on the Question of International Criminal Jurisdiction*, U.N. Doc. A/CN.4/15, reprinted in *The Yearbook of International Law Commission, Volume II*, 1950. The text could also be reached at http://untreaty.un.org/ilc/documentation/english/a_cn4_15.pdf.

[66] Ibid.

international crimes. Consequently, for the repression of crimes against peace, war crimes, crimes against humanity and genocide, an international court is essential." He also asserted that absolute sovereignty was not compatible with the organization of international order at the time because state sovereignty was "subordinated to the supremacy of international law."[67]

Special Rapporteur Emil Sanstrom also contended that an international criminal court was desirable. However, in his report, he questioned the practicality and feasibility of such a court. After having reviewed the pros and cons of an international criminal court, he concluded that "a permanent judicial criminal organ established in the actual organization of the international community would be impaired by very serious defects and would do more harm than good."[68]

As observed earlier, both rapporteurs supported establishing an international criminal court, although they were of different opinions on the practicality and usefulness of such a court. The underlying point in their approaches was the issue of national sovereignty, and once more, that notion dominated the discussion. It is important to note that even the report prepared by the commission, an institution that was at least partially free of concerns over national interests and power politics and of influence by states, referred to national sovereignty as a potential obstacle to realizing the idea concerned.

In fact, the aforementioned report's observations on sovereignty as an obstacle reflect a reality: Although independent institutions, commissions and the like prepare reports that contain novel arrangements, these rarely find acceptance in the venues in which state delegates discuss such matters, and this case was no exception.

The International Law Commission considered the report submitted by the special rapporteurs. In the report prepared by the commission that addressed multiple issues and assignments, it was stated that some

---

[67] Ibid.

[68] Emil Sandstrom, International Law Commission, *Report on the Question of International Criminal Jurisdiction,* U.N. Doc. A/CN.4/20, reprinted in *The Yearbook of International Law Commission, Volume II,* 1950. The text can also be found at http://untreaty.un.org/ilc/documentation/english/a_cn4_20.pdf.

commission members had referred to difficulties that could arise in the process of establishing an international court; the skeptics cautioned that nations would refuse to give up their sovereign rights. However, the majority contended that "while difficulties undeniably existed, they did not constitute an impossibility. If States were free to refuse to submit to an obligatory international criminal jurisdiction, they had also the power to agree thereto."[69]

After considering the matter, the commission decided that an "international judicial organ for the trial of persons charged with genocide or other crimes over which jurisdiction is conferred upon that organ by international conventions is desirable" and that it was possible to establish such an organ.[70]

The Sixth Committee of the UN General Assembly considered the commission's report, and the delegates were divided on the matter. Some were of the opinion that establishing the court that was proposed in the report was not practical in the environment of the time on the grounds that such a court would impinge upon national sovereignty; that states would refuse to surrender subjects who were accused of committing the crimes that would fall under the proposed court's jurisdiction; and that the victorious powers, following the end of the conflict, would be reluctant to submit enemy combatants to the court.

Others argued that an international criminal court would contribute to world peace and security. Some of the proponents noted that the peoples of the world had favored such a court for many years and objected to the view that such a court would be contrary to the notion of sovereignty; they argued that states' voluntary recognition of the court's jurisdiction would reflect the court's compatibility with the notion. Consequently, the UN General Assembly decided that a committee composed of members from 17 member states should meet in Geneva to prepare one or more preliminary draft conventions and

[69] Report of the International Law Commission on its Second Session, June 5–July 29, 1950, Official Records of General Assembly, 5th Session, Supplement No. 12 (A/1316), reprinted in *The Yearbook of International Law Commission, Volume II,* 1950. Also available at: http://untreaty.un.org/ilc/documentation/english/a_cn4_34.pdf.

[70] Ibid.

proposals relating to establishing an international criminal court. The assembly also requested that the Secretary-General submit to the committee one or more proposals and draft conventions that envisioned establishing such a court.[71]

The division over the desirability and practicality of this court continued in the first sessions of the Committee on International Criminal Jurisdiction. Some argued that such a court would "unavoidably become enmeshed in political conflict and controversy and would not enjoy the calm and composure required for fair minded deliberation."[72] However, the majority supported the opinion advanced by the US representative and drafted a statute for an international criminal court.[73]

The purpose for establishing the proposed court was stated in the draft statute as "to try persons accused of crimes under international law, as may be provided in conventions or special agreements among States parties to the present Statute."[74] The law to be applied by the Court was referred to as international law, including international criminal law, or national law.[75] One of the most significant provisions stated that the court should be permanent. However, the same provision provided that "sessions shall be called only when matters before it require consideration."[76]

The proposed court would have jurisdiction over natural persons only, and in the context of this jurisdiction, there would be no privilege or immunity for heads of states or those who occupied similar positions.[77] However, the court's jurisdiction would not be automatic; it could be vested with jurisdiction by states that were party to the statute, by convention, by special agreement or by unilateral declaration.[78] The

[71] UN General Assembly Resolution 489(V), 320th meeting, December 12, 1950.

[72] Lippman, "Towards an International Criminal Court," p. 76.

[73] The draft statute appears as Annex I to the Report of the Committee on International Criminal Jurisdiction, U.N. Doc. A/AC.48/4, September 5, 1951, reprinted as "United Nations: Committee on International Criminal Jurisdiction," *American Journal of International Law*, Vol. 46, Issue 1, Supplement: Official Documents, 1952, pp. 1–11.

[74] Ibid., Article 1.

[75] Ibid., Article 2.

[76] Ibid., Article 3.

[77] Ibid., Article 25.

[78] Ibid., Article 26.

logical consequence of this provision was that the Court could not act unless it was authorized by states. In this regard, the relevant provision stated, "no person shall be tried before the Court unless jurisdiction has been conferred upon the Court by the State or States of which he is a national and by the State or States in which the crime is alleged to have been committed."[79] The court's sphere of influence was further restricted by the provision that stated that it would have no jurisdiction unless it was authorized by the UN General Assembly.[80]

Also relevant to the restrictions imposed on the proposed court was how the draft statute allowed for states to initiate proceedings. Article 29 of the draft statute, which regulated access to the court, stated that only the following could initiate proceedings before the court: the UN General Assembly; any organization formed by states and authorized by the UN General Assembly; or a state that was party to the draft statute and that recognized the court's competence and jurisdiction over the offenses that were to be addressed in the proceedings.[81]

The draft statute also provided that the court might request assistance from states in performing its functions. However, the states were not obliged to provide assistance unless "any convention or other instrument in which the State has accepted such obligation" required doing so.[82] This was a clear recognition of states' privileges and prerogatives in world politics. The statute itself did not create obligations that required states to cooperate with the court. Instead, it simply reinforced the states' obligations that were incurred during their previous undertakings under international law.

The limitations that were applied to the court also included its narrow authority to enforce any convictions it imposed on the accused. The statute provided that the court's penalties were subject to the limitations "prescribed in the instrument conferring jurisdiction upon the Court."[83]

[79] Ibid., Article 27.
[80] Ibid., Article 28.
[81] Ibid., Article 29.
[82] Ibid., Article 31.
[83] Ibid., Article 32.

The court envisioned by the draft statute aforesaid was weak in terms of jurisdictional reach. It was formulated to balance "the need for an international criminal court against the interests of State sovereignty."[84] Because states that were party to the statute were not required to recognize the court's jurisdiction or cooperate with the court, "a single State would be able to frustrate prosecutions by refusing to recognize the court's jurisdiction."[85]

However, it should be noted that the committee that was charged with preparing the draft statute recognized that the text it had prepared was not final:

> The Committee does not wish to give these proposals any appearance of finality. They are offered as a contribution to a study which in the Committee's opinion has yet to be carried several steps forward before the problem of an international criminal jurisdiction, with all its implications of a political as well as a juridical character, is ripe for decision.[86]

Thus, the draft statute was subsequently forwarded to state governments as well as different legal and political units for consideration and evaluation.[87] Even some nonstate units opposed the proposed court. In 1952, the American Bar Association clearly stated its opposition to the draft statute prepared by the Committee on International Criminal Jurisdiction on the grounds that "it would be unwise to compromise the principles of territorial jurisdiction and trial by jury."[88] Eleven states also submitted critical comments on the statute.[89]

---

[84] Lippman, "Towards an International Criminal Court," p. 83.

[85] Ibid., p. 84.

[86] George A. Finch, "Draft Statute for an International Criminal Court," *American Journal of International Law,* Vol. 46, Issue 1, 1952, p. 90.

[87] It is interesting to note that some governments sought assistance from independent bodies on this matter. For instance, the US State Department sent copies of the draft statute and of the committee's report to the American Society of International Law and invited the group to consider the texts and offer comments. Ibid, pp. 90–91.

[88] Lippman, "Towards an International Criminal Court," p. 84.

[89] Australia, Chile, France, Israel, Netherlands, Norway, the Union of South Africa, the United Kingdom of Great Britain and Northern Ireland, China, and Denmark. See ibid.

The Sixth Committee considered the committee's report and the comments regarding its viability and practicality in November 1952.[90] Supporters of the court criticized the draft statute, stressing that the text was a very modest step towards establishing a permanent international criminal court that would be fully equipped to address the worst crimes. However, opponents argued that states would not be willing to abandon—even partially—their sovereign rights.[91]

The disagreements and differences between the states' positions on the proposed court were so severe that the Sixth Committee could not take any decisive steps and instead recommended postponing consideration of the report. The UN General Assembly endorsed this recommendation and requested that member states submit additional comments and views on the draft statute. A separate committee was subsequently charged with considering the previous comments along with additional comments to be submitted by states.[92] Having considered that very few states had forwarded suggestions and comments on the proposed court and that further study was needed on the question of international criminal jurisdiction, the UN General Assembly decided to appoint a committee that would "re-examine the draft statute" and submit a report on its findings to the Assembly.[93] The Assembly also realized that defining the crime of aggression was essential for reaching a solid conclusion with regard to establishing an international criminal court. For this reason, at the same session, the Assembly decided to establish a special committee of 15 members that would meet in 1953. This committee was requested to work on defining aggression and subsequently to submit draft definitions of the concept to the General Assembly.[94]

The committee that was charged with reexamining the draft statute initiated its work in July 1953. Once again, differing views clashed during

---

[90] 7th Session, GAOR C.6, at 95 (321st–328th meetings).

[91] Lippman, "Towards an International Criminal Court," p. 85.

[92] UN General Assembly Resolution 687 (VII), Seventh Session, Resolutions adopted on reports of the Sixth Committee, "International Criminal Jurisdiction," 408th meeting, U.N. Doc. 2361, December 20, 1952.

[93] Ibid.

[94] Ibid.

the debates. Some referred to the many obstacles to establishing an international criminal court. However, with the support of the majority, the committee decided to focus on preparing a report that evaluated the proposed statute. The debates were mainly about the approaches to be adopted in creating such a court, and they culminated in the decision that the best method for creating an international criminal court would be a multilateral treaty that would be adopted by an international diplomatic conference to be held under the auspices of the UN.[95]

Subsequently, the deliberations also resulted in slight modifications to the previously submitted draft statute.[96] The modified text was then submitted to the Sixth Committee. However, once again, the committee did not actively engage in the process, and it avoided confronting the difficulties that would arise from the debates over establishing such a court. During the committee's deliberations, the traditional objections were once more brought to the fore. Some argued that the international crimes that the proposed court would supposedly prosecute were adequately addressed by national courts and that even if a higher court were necessary, ad hoc tribunals would be perfectly capable of performing the task. Others referred to the international community's lack of desire for a court such as that proposed in the report.[97]

Following the debates, the committee voted to postpone considering the report and its content regarding establishing an international criminal court. The UN General Assembly agreed and decided in December 1954 to "to postpone consideration of the question of an international criminal jurisdiction until the General Assembly has taken up the report of the Special Committee on the question of defining aggression and has taken up again the draft Code of Offenses against the Peace and Security of Mankind."[98] The proposal

---

[95] Report of the 1953 Committee on International Criminal Jurisdiction, GAOR Supp. (No. 12) U.N. Doc. A/2645 (1954).

[96] Lippman, "Towards an International Criminal Court," p. 87.

[97] Ibid., p. 88.

[98] UN General Assembly Resolution 898 (IX), "International Criminal Jurisdiction," Ninth Session, 512th meeting, U.N. Doc. A/2890, December 14, 1954.

was brought up again in 1957; however, the General Assembly refused to consider it at that time, instead preferring to delay discussion.[99] The primary reason for the delay was the disagreement over the definition of the crime of "aggression."[100] This delay was virtually the end of the endeavors to create an international criminal court; the matter was not introduced to the UN's agenda until the 1970s, when studies on defining aggression as well as creating an international institution that would be vested with the power to address international crimes were undertaken.

The works on establishing an international criminal court were accompanied by the International Law Commission's works on codifying a Draft Code of Offenses against the Peace and Security of Mankind, a task, as noted earlier, that was assigned by UN General Assembly Resolution 177(II).[101] The commission immediately began its work in its first session. A special rapporteur was appointed on the subject and invited to submit a working paper to the commission in its second session. In 1950, the rapporteur submitted his report,[102] which was used by the commission as a basis for discussion. Following the consideration of the report and governments' comments and views, and following deliberations on the subject, a drafting committee of three prepared a provisional text and submitted it to the commission.[103] It endorsed the text and requested that the special rapporteur of the initial text continue working on the subject and submit a new report to the commission in its third session. Upon this request, a second draft[104] was prepared and subsequently submitted to the commission for consideration. Taking into account the report and

---

[99] UN General Assembly Resolution 1187(XII), "International Criminal Jurisdiction," Twelfth Session, 727th meeting, U.N. Doc. A/3805, December 11, 1957.

[100] The Assembly in its resolution decided to "defer consideration of the question of an international criminal jurisdiction until such time as the General Assembly takes up again the question of defining aggression and the question of a Draft Code of Offenses against the Peace and Security of Mankind." Ibid.

[101] See *footnote* 214.

[102] U.N. Doc. No. A/CN.4/25.

[103] U.N. Doc. No. A/CN.4/R.6.

[104] U.N. Doc. No. A/CN.4/44.

the draft code as well as governments' comments and observations on the report, the commission adopted a Draft Code of Offenses against the Peace and Security of Mankind.[105]

Article 2 of the draft code enumerated the acts regarded as offenses against the peace and security of mankind as follows: any acts of aggression; "any threat by the authorities of a State to resort to an act of aggression against another state"; "the preparation of the authorities of a State for the employment of armed force against another state for any purpose" other than collective or national self-defense; "the incursion into the territory of a State from the territory of another State by armed bands"; "the undertaking of encouragement by the authorities of a State of activities calculated to foment civil strife in another State"; one state's authorities' encouraging terrorist activities in another state; acts committed by a state's authorities that violate its obligations under a treaty that was adopted to ensure international peace and security through such restrictions as disarmament; acts that lead to annexing territories that belong to another state in a manner inconsistent with international law; acts committed by a state's authorities or by natural persons with the intent to destroy a national, religious, racial or ethnic group; and acts that violate the laws and customs of war.[106]

Article 3 provided that heads of states and other government officials were to be held equally responsible for committing any of the acts referred to in the code. As such, the fact that they might have been acting within the framework of their positions was not to relieve them "from responsibility for committing any of the offences" defined in the code.[107] Similarly, the code did not recognize the defense of having been a subordinate during the commission of the crime, although the person concerned was to be held responsible

[105] Draft Code of Offenses against the Peace and Security of Mankind. Reprinted in *Yearbook of International Law Commission,* Vol. II, 1951, pp. 134–137. The text reprinted in the Yearbook also included annotations and explanations on the provisions of the Code.

[106] Article 2, ibid.

[107] Article 3, ibid.

only if it had been possible for him to act contrary to superior orders.[108] The penalties for offenses were to be determined by the tribunal that had jurisdiction over the accused.[109]

The code under review was very short, with only five articles. Although it addressed war crimes and those that could be considered genocide, it contained no reference to crimes against humanity. Moreover, it did not envision or refer to an international criminal court that would have the power to prosecute the perpetrators of the offences it defined; instead, it made mention of a tribunal that would be competent to try the accused. Because the code did refer to an international tribunal, this tribunal could be a domestic court. Overall examination of the code also revealed an undue focus on the crime of aggression, which indicated that the drafters were much more concerned about the stability of interstate relations than about international crimes committed by natural persons. The code thus essentially preserved the 'sanctity' of the notion of national sovereignty. In other words, it was an important but timid step forward for international criminal jurisdiction.

The draft code was brought to the agenda of the fifth session of the General Assembly; however, shortly thereafter, it was removed from the agenda and postponed until the seventh session. The Secretary-General requested comments from governments, and 14 governments acted accordingly and submitted their views. Those views and the code itself were included in the agenda of the seventh session of the Assembly; however, once again, the Assembly decided to postpone discussion on the grounds that the International Law Commission would continue to work on the matter. In its fifth session, the commission considered the matter in 1953 and requested that the special rapporteur further study the code. Upon this request, the rapporteur prepared a third report and submitted it to the commission.[110] In this report, the rapporteur

[108] Article 4, ibid. The Article states, "The fact that a person charged with an offence defined in this Code acted in pursuant to order of his government or of a superior does not relieve him from responsibility, provided a moral choice was in fact possible to him."

[109] Article 5, ibid.

[110] "Third Report Relating to a Draft Code of Offenses against the Peace and Security of Mankind," U.N. Doc. No. A/CN.4/85.

discussed the comments and views of the governments that had responded and accordingly made modifications to the previously submitted draft code. Taking into account the modified text, the commission revised the previous code. Overall, the new text was somewhat more enhanced than the previous version. For instance, the expression "shall be punishable" was replaced with "shall be punished" to emphasize that states themselves were obliged to punish perpetrators of the offenses contained in the code. The scope of some of the paragraphs in Article 2, which specified the punishable acts, was widened to make the code more comprehensive.[111]

However, the UN General Assembly refused to consider the aforesaid code in Resolution No. 897 (IX) in December 1954.[112] The primary controversy was on the definition of aggression. The clashing views on the matter resulted in postponing consideration of the draft code until a solid approach to defining aggression could be adopted.[113] However, the work on defining aggression was never concluded, and even though the related units spent considerable effort to reach a generally acceptable definition, no substantive outcome was obtained. For this reason, there

---

[111] For additional details on the revisions to the Draft Code, see "Draft Code of Offences Against the Peace and Security of Mankind," Chapter III, Documents of the Sixth Session, including the Report of the Commission to the General Assembly, *Yearbook of the International Law Commission,* Vol. II, 1954, pp. 149–152.

[112] "Draft Code of Offences against the Peace and Security of Mankind," UN General Assembly Resolution 897(IX), 504th meeting, December 4, 1954.

[113] Ibid. The Resolution reads as follows:

> The General Assembly,
>
> *Considering* that the Draft Code of Offences against the Peace and Security of Mankind, as formulated in Chapter III of the report of the International Law Commission on the work of its sixth session, raises problems closely related to that of the definition of aggression,
>
> *Considering* that . . . the General Assembly decided to entrust to a Special Committee of nineteen Member States the task of preparing and submitting to the General Assembly at its eleventh session a detailed report on the question of defining aggression and a draft definition of aggression,

*Decides* to postpone further consideration of the Draft Code of Offences against the Peace and Security of Mankind until the Special Committee on the question of defining aggression has submitted its report.

was no codification of a Code of Offences against the Peace and Security of Mankind that was linked by the General Assembly to a definition of the notion of aggression.

The major political reason for the failures to create an international judicial system in which the perpetrators of the worst crimes would be effectively punished and future atrocities of the same kind would be prevented by the "magic" of deterrence is undoubtedly the outbreak of the Cold War. Power politics, clashing national interests, and the strong attachments to the notion of sovereignty by world government authorities became prevalent, rendering the previously mentioned attempts obsolete and meaningless. However, the technical reason is the clear disagreement on defining the notion of aggression. Whenever a proposal was brought forth to take decisive steps towards creating a system of international criminal jurisdiction, the question of how to define aggression was cited as an obstacle.[114] A brief survey of the attempts made under the auspices of the UN would demonstrate the clash over defining the notion of aggression and how this clash hindered any possible breakthroughs in advancing a system of international criminal jurisdiction.

As noted earlier in the present text,[115] on December 20, 1952, the UN General Assembly adopted a resolution that established a special committee of 15 members that was to submit to the Assembly "draft definitions of aggression or draft statements of the notion of aggression."[116] The resolution provided that the previous works of the General Assembly as well as of the International Law Commission on international criminal jurisdiction had "revealed the complexity of this question and the need for a detailed study of" more intensive and comprehensive

[114] It should be noted that the concept of aggression remained undefined until 2010, when a definition was made in the Assembly of State Parties in Kampala, Uganda. Before this, even though the International Criminal Court had been authorized to exercise jurisdiction over the crime of aggression under the Rome Statute, because the term had not been defined, the court could not proceed against perpetrators of that crime until an internationally accepted definition for the notion had been provided and inserted in the text of the statute.

[115] See footnote 247.

[116] "Question of Defining Aggression," UN General Assembly Resolution 688(VII), 408th meeting, December 20, 1952.

efforts to define the notion, including determining the various forms of aggression, the connection between aggression and international peace and security, the problems that would be raised by including this definition in the Draft Code of Offenses against the Peace and Security of Mankind, and the effect of the definition of aggression on the exercise of jurisdiction by various UN organs.[117]

A similar—in fact, almost the same—resolution was passed by the General Assembly on December 4, 1954.[118] With this resolution, the Assembly established a special committee of 20 members that would meet in 1956 and requested that it submit to the Assembly "a draft definition of aggression" upon the review and consideration of the previous efforts on the matter.[119] The committee completed its work and submitted the requested report to the Assembly.[120] The Assembly referred to the report as a "valuable work" but considered that "twenty-two additional States have recently joined the Organization and that it would be useful to know their views on the matter."[121] Therefore, it asked the Secretary-General to request the views of the new member states on the matter and to subsequently transmit the replies to the committee, which would "study the replies for the purpose of determining when it shall be appropriate for the General Assembly to consider again the question of defining aggression."[122] The Secretary-General was also requested to place the question of defining aggression on the Assembly's provisional agenda no earlier than the end of 1959.[123] However, as noted earlier, the question of defining aggression was removed from the General Assembly's agenda, and the world community remained silent on the issue until the 1970s.

---

[117] Ibid.

[118] "Question of Defining Aggression," UN General Assembly Resolution 895(IX), 504th meeting, December 4, 1954.

[119] Ibid.

[120] *Official Records of the General Assembly, 12th Session, Supp. No. 16,* U.N. Doc. A/3574.

[121] Question of Defining Aggression," UN General Assembly Resolution 1181(XII), 724th meeting, November 29, 1957.

[122] Ibid.

[123] Ibid.

The adoption of the Genocide Convention in 1948[124] was also one of the most important works within the framework of the UN's efforts to create a system of international criminal jurisdiction in the immediate aftermath of World War II. The earliest attempt to codify the Convention was UN General Assembly Resolution 96(I),[125] which provided that the crime of genocide "shocks the conscience of mankind, results in great losses to humanity in the form of cultural and other contributions" by the groups that were victimized by that crime.[126] As such, the Assembly invited member states to "enact the necessary legislation for the prevention and punishment of this crime."[127]

The Genocide Convention is significant in that it referred to a transnational court that would be vested with the jurisdiction to prosecute and punish the crime of genocide and its perpetrators. Article 6 of the Convention states that "persons charged with genocide or any of the other acts enumerated in article III shall be tried by a competent tribunal of the State in the territory of which the act was committed, or by such international penal tribunal as may have jurisdiction with respect to those Contracting Parties which shall have accepted its jurisdiction."[128] However, the Convention in effect imposes on states the obligation of preventing genocide and punishing perpetrators of that crime.[129] Article 5 of the Convention is clearer on the imposition of this obligation: "The Contracting Parties undertake to enact, in accordance with their respective Constitutions, the necessary legislation to give effect to the provisions of the present Convention, and, in particular, to provide effective penalties for persons guilty of genocide or any of the other acts

[124] Convention on the Prevention and Punishment of the Crime of Genocide (Genocide Convention), December 9, 1948, 78 U.N.T.S. 1021, approved by UN General Assembly Resolution 260(III), 179th meeting, December 9, 1948.

[125] "The Crime of Genocide," UN General Assembly Resolution No. 96(I), 55th meeting, December 11, 1946.

[126] Ibid.

[127] Ibid.

[128] Genocide Convention, Article 6.

[129] Ibid. Article 1 of the Convention provides, "The Contracting Parties confirm that genocide... is a crime under international law which they undertake to prevent and punish."

enumerated in article III."[130] In accordance with Article 7, the crime of genocide and other punishable acts under the Convention "shall not be considered as political crimes for the purpose of extradition," and states are obliged to "grant extradition in accordance with their laws and treaties in force."[131]

Therefore, what can be said of the Genocide Convention is that it is essentially weak in terms of its references to an international judicial organ that would be vested with jurisdiction over the punishable acts it covers. The Convention gives chief responsibility to states, and the reference to an international penal institution is modest. The relevant provision that refers to such an institution does not envisage its establishment; instead, it implies if such an institution is created in the future, the acts that are punishable under the Convention may be prosecuted and tried by that institution.

However, even this relatively weak document was a source of controversy during the deliberations that were held for the purpose of drafting a convention that would address the crime of genocide. This is, in fact, both interesting and shocking given that the bad memories of World War II were still fresh; there should have been an intense desire to prevent and punish the "crime of the crimes." Today, it could be thought that codifying the Genocide Convention was easy and quick, but this was not the case. Delegates of member states were eager to observe their states' national interests, and for this reason, they felt that they had to closely examine and evaluate every detail concerning the draft Convention on the Prevention and Punishment of Genocide.

As noted earlier, the efforts to address the crime of genocide began in the immediate aftermath of the end of World War II. The question was considered urgent because the experiences of the war had demonstrated that indifference towards attempts to exterminate an entire group could lead to large-scale atrocities. Therefore, at a time when the bad memories of the war were still fresh, the representatives of member states first adopted a positive and constructive approach to attempting to adopt a

[130] Ibid., Article 5.

[131] Ibid., Article 7.

multilateral treaty that addressed the crime of genocide. Initially, the UN was the venue in which those efforts took place. On November 9, 1946, the UN General Assembly forwarded a resolution drafted by Rafael Lemkin, the coiner of the term genocide, to the Sixth Committee for consideration. Cuba, India, and Panama requested a study that focused on the possibility of declaring genocide an international crime that states would have the authority to prosecute and punish.

Along with that drafted by Lemkin, the Sixth Committee considered a number of other proposals and charged a subcommittee with preparing a draft resolution based on the proposals submitted. The subcommittee's draft was adopted by the Sixth Committee on December 9, 1946, and the General Assembly adopted the resolution two days later.[132]

The Assembly continued its work on the matter by reaffirming the resolution above and declaring that "genocide is an international crime entailing national and international responsibility on the part of individuals and States."[133] In the same resolution, the Assembly also requested that the Economic and Social Council continue the work "it has begun concerning the suppression of the crime of genocide."[134]

The above suggests that the UN's response to the calls for taking effective steps to address the drafting of a Genocide Convention was swift; there were no serious and time-consuming debates during the UN's initial efforts. The most important reason for this swiftness was likely the war's impact on the world community of the time. There was a consensus on the need to establish an effective mechanism that would prevent the commission of genocidal acts. Another reason was the fact that the outcomes of the initial steps were not binding; those who were involved in these endeavors were relatively free to insert novel arrangements into their proposals that could be seen by states as impinging on national sovereignty, but such insertions did not necessarily create deadlocks during the deliberations in the bodies whose decisions were nonbinding.

---

[132] See, *footnote* 278.

[133] "Draft Convention on Genocide," U.N. General Assembly 180(II), 123rd meeting, November 21, 1947.

[134] Ibid.

However, as the issue became more concrete, the process slowed. Member states adopted a more scrutinizing approach towards the issue, which they regarded as delicate. Although the view that addressing genocide was important and warranted international concern and attention was largely shared by the member states, each of them was determined to retain their sovereignty. They were thus unduly concerned that the drafting of a Genocide Convention would be contrary to their dominant positions as agents of world politics. For this reason, the initial swiftness was replaced with a gradual and slow breakthrough that was closely monitored and controlled by states' representatives.

The initial efforts aforementioned resulted in a generally accepted proposal for a convention that would address the issue of genocide was submitted by the Secretary-General to the UN General Assembly. Under this proposal, states would be obliged to "pledge themselves to punish any offender under this Convention within any territory under their jurisdiction, irrespective of the nationality of the offender or of the place where the offence has been committed."[135] This necessarily meant that any state that was party to the convention would be required prosecute an individual who was suspected of having committed the crime of genocide, irrespective of the territory in which the punishable act was committed. If the state did not prosecute the offender, it would be obliged to surrender the suspect to an international court.

In addition to the draft proposed by the Secretary-General, another draft prepared by an ad hoc committee was considered. This one was much more modest than the previous one; it rejected the principle of universal jurisdiction and recognized the national courts as the primary authorities in proceeding against the crime of genocide. The ad hoc committee's draft stated that "persons charged with genocide . . . shall be tried by a competent tribunal of the State in the territory of which the act was committed or by a competent international tribunal."[136]

---

[135] U.N. ESCOR, art. VII, U.N. Doc. E/447 (1947) (Draft Convention on the Crime of Genocide).

[136] Ad Hoc Committee on Genocide Report to the Economic and Social Council on the Meetings of the Committee, New York, 1948, U.N. ESCOR Supp. No. 6 at U.N. ESCOR Ad Hoc Committee, art. VII.

During the discussions, some delegates opposed the concurrent jurisdiction vested in both an international court and national courts on the grounds that this would impinge upon national sovereignty. Those who dissented asserted that for this reason, a substantial number of states would not ratify the convention.[137]

The principles adopted by the ad hoc committee with regard to a Genocide Convention were then submitted to the Sixth Committee of the UN General Assembly, which accepted the draft. Although the draft broadened the role to be played by a future international criminal court, the disagreement over the need for universal jurisdiction was prevalent in the discussions.[138]

Ultimately, the Sixth Committee agreed to regard national courts as the primary agents in prosecuting and punishing the crime of genocide. Undoubtedly, the reference in the Genocide Convention was an important step forward. For this reason, the President of the General Assembly hailed its adoption, saying "the supremacy of international law has been proclaimed and a significant advance had been made in the development of international criminal law."[139] However, the failure of the international community to create the transnational court that was referred to in the convention gradually diminished its significance.

In addition to codifying the Genocide Convention, the UN also engaged in activities that mainly focused on expanding the scope of existing international treaties on war crimes. Four Geneva Conventions, all adopted in 1949, are noteworthy in that they are now regarded as the basis and backbone of international humanitarian law and customary legal rules given the many states that are party to them. The four are the Geneva Convention for the Amelioration of the Condition of the Wounded and Sick in Armed Forces in the Field (I)[140]; the Geneva Convention for the Amelioration of the Condition of Wounded, Sick

[137] Ibid., 7th meeting, U.N. Doc. E/AC.25/SR.7.

[138] 3 U.N. GAOR at art. VI, 10, U.N. Doc. A/760.

[139] 3 U.N. GAOR (179th plen. mtg) at 852 (1948).

[140] Geneva Convention for the Amelioration of the Condition of the Wounded and Sick in Armed Forces in the Field, 75 U.N.T.S. 31, *entered into force* October 21, 1950.

and Shipwrecked Members of Armed Forces at Sea (II)[141]; the Geneva Convention Relative to the Treatment of Prisoners of War (III)[142]; and the Geneva Convention Relative to the Protection of Civilian Persons in Time of War (IV).[143] The first three are amended versions of the following previously adopted ones, respectively: the Geneva Convention of 1929, for the Relief of Wounded and Sick in Armies in the Field, The Hague Convention of 1907, for the Adaptation to Maritime Warfare, and the Geneva Convention of 1929, Relative to the Treatment of Prisoners of War. The fourth convention, on the treatment of civilians in wartime, was entirely new.[144]

The four Geneva Conventions contain some common articles. Article 2 of all four conventions provides that the respective convention applies to "all cases of declared war or of any other armed conflict which may arise between two or more of the High Contracting Parties, even if the state of war is not recognized by one of them." That is, the convention still applies even if one of the parties does not recognize the state of war. Furthermore, it is noted that the conventions apply to armed conflicts that were not declared by both parties.[145] Article 3 provides that the conventions apply to conflicts that are not international. However, the respective article in each convention states the situations in which the article's underlying objective and content are to be observed. Article 7 provides that beneficiaries "may in no circumstances renounce in part or in entirety the rights secured to them" by the respective convention because "it is obvious that such persons are in no sense free to act or able to act freely."[146] The most

---

[141] Geneva Convention for the Amelioration of the Condition of Wounded, Sick and Shipwrecked Members of Armed Forces at Sea, 75 U.N.T.S. 85, *entered into force* October 21, 1950.

[142] Geneva Convention relative to the Treatment of Prisoners of War, 75 U.N.T.S. 135, *entered into force* October 21, 1950.

[143] Geneva Convention relative to the Protection of Civilian Persons in Time of War, 75 U.N.T. S. 287, *entered into force* October 21, 1950.

[144] Raymund T. Yingling and Robert W. Ginnane, "The Geneva Conventions of 1949," *American Journal of International Law,* Vol. 46, Issue 3, 1952, pp. 393–394.

[145] Ibid., p. 394.

[146] Ibid., p. 397.

important common article is the one that provides that the respective convention "shall be applied with the cooperation and under the scrutiny of the Protecting Powers whose duty it is to safeguard the interests of the Parties to the conflict," given that it should be apparent that any party to the conflict cannot be expected to follow the rules contained in the Convention.[147]

Geneva Convention (I) in many respects resembles its predecessor. In addition to articles common to all Geneva Conventions, Convention (I) contains a number of new ones. For instance, whereas the earlier version applied only to members of armed forces or other officials who were affiliated with armies, the new version extended protection to all personnel who were recognized as prisoners of war.[148]

Geneva Convention (II), also known as the Maritime Convention, is significantly different from, and in fact a replacement for, its predecessor.[149] Geneva Convention (III) on the question of prisoners of war is also a significantly improved version of the earlier codification on the same subject matter. This convention recognizes multiple categories of prisoners of war, implying much broader coverage than that contained in its predecessor. The first main category addresses traditional prisoners of war, that is, persons who fall under the control of the enemy power. In addition, considering the experiences of World War II, the conference participants elected to include persons who had been apprehended in occupied or nonbelligerent territories.[150] Overall, the new convention remarkably improves on its predecessor, extending its scope of application.[151] Geneva Convention (IV) on protecting civilians, although it is a new codification is "an extension...of earlier international rules and practices governing the treatment of alien enemies in a belligerent country and the treatment of the inhabitants of territory under

[147] Ibid., p. 397.
[148] Ibid., p. 398.
[149] Ibid., pp. 400–401.
[150] Geneva Convention relative to the Treatment of Prisoners of War, Article 4.
[151] For further details, see Yingling and Ginnane, "The Geneva Conventions of 1949," pp. 401–411.

military occupation."[152] However, the convention does not protect the nationals of any state that is not party to it.[153]

The aforementioned four Geneva Conventions were later reinforced by two additional protocols that were adopted in the 1970s and one that was adopted in 2005. Protocol (I) Additional to the Geneva Conventions of 12 August 1949, and Relating to the Protection of Victims of International Armed Conflicts[154] broadened the protection provided to civilians and restricted the means and methods used in the conduct of warfare.[155] Protocol (II) Additional to the Geneva Conventions of 12 August 1949, and Relating to the Protection of Victims of Non-International Armed Conflicts[156] provides extensive guarantees for persons who have not taken part in hostilities during non-international armed conflicts and contains rules that pertain to protecting civilians as well as to all of the means necessary for their survival.[157] Protocol (III) Additional to the Geneva Conventions of 12 August 1949,[158] and Relating to the Adoption of an Additional Distinctive Emblem, which is relatively insignificant compared with

[152] Ibid., p. 411.

[153] Geneva Convention relative to the Protection of Civilian Persons in Time of War, Article 4. Paragraph 2 reads as follows: "Nationals of a State which is not bound by the Convention are not protected by it. Nationals of a neutral State who find themselves in the territory of a belligerent State, and nationals of a co-belligerent State, shall not be regarded as protected persons while the State of which they are nationals has normal diplomatic representation in the State in whose hands they are."

[154] Protocol Additional to the Geneva Conventions of August 12, 1949, and Relating to the Protection of Victims of International Armed Conflicts (Protocol I), 1125 U.N.T.S. 3, *entered into force* December 7, 1978.

[155] *Respect for International Humanitarian Law,* Handbook prepared by some of the members of the Inter-Parliamentary Union's Committee to Promote Respect for International Humanitarian Law, the International Committee of Red Cross Publication, n.d., p. 18.

[156] Protocol Additional to the Geneva Conventions of August 12, 1949, and Relating to the Protection of Victims of Non-International Armed Conflicts (Protocol II), 1125 U.N.T.S. 609, *entered into force* December 7, 1978.

[157] *Respect for International Humanitarian Law,* p. 19.

[158] Protocol additional to the Geneva Conventions of August 12, 1949, and relating to the Adoption of an Additional Distinctive Emblem (Protocol III), available at http://www.icrc.org/ihl.nsf/FULL/615.

the first two, created an optional emblem to be used by the International Committee of the Red Cross during their work.[159]

The Geneva Conventions and its additional protocols—with over 600 articles—are extremely important in many respects. First, they are generally accepted by the world community; today, most UN member states are party to the conventions. In effect, the Geneva Conventions are regarded as international customary laws given that they are considered binding even over states that did not ratify them. For instance, the International Court of Justice, in its advisory opinion, provided that the Geneva Conventions, along with The Hague Conventions on the same subject matter, are fundamental instruments that all states are obligated to observe "whether or not they have ratified the conventions that contain them, because they constitute intransgressible principles on international customary law."[160]

Second, the conventions corrected a paramount defect that had long survived in international humanitarian law. Whereas the earlier codifications had primarily focused on the rules to be observed with reference to the belligerents in the conduct of military operations, the Geneva Conventions contain provisions that safeguard non-belligerents, including civilians and military personnel who are no longer active in the armed conflict.

However, as was the case with many multilateral treaties, implementing the Geneva Conventions was left to the discretion of the states that were party to them. In other words, although states are bound by the Geneva Conventions, no outside institution or mechanism has the power to monitor states' compliance with the conventions. As such, it

[159] Ibid., Article 4, stating, "The International Committee of the Red Cross and the International Federation of Red Cross and Red Crescent Societies, and their duly authorized personnel, may use, in exceptional circumstances and to facilitate their work, the distinctive emblem referred to in Article 2 of this Protocol." This emblem is known as the red crystal, and it was created to supplement the previously adopted two emblems, the red cross and the red crescent.

[160] Nuclear Weapons Advisory Opinion, 1996 International Court of Justice, paragraphs 75, 79 (July 8). There is evidence that states that were not party to the conventions declared that they would abide by the rules contained in them. For example, all parties to the hostilities in the Korean War agreed to follow the provisions of the conventions, even though they were not party to them. See Howard p. Levie, "History of the Law of War on Land," *International Review of the Red Cross,* Issue 838, 2000, pp. 339–350.

has been observed that states have been reluctant to incorporate the conventions or to fully comply with them. For instance, the US national courts make very few references to the Conventions.[161]

Moreover, the adoption of the Geneva Conventions cannot be attributed to states' efforts but to the efforts of civil organizations. Therefore, the credit for establishing a system of international humanitarian law should go to nonstate actors, especially the Red Cross. This organization was the leading force and impetus behind the codifications of both The Hague and the Geneva Conventions, which imposed on both states and individuals duties that they must follow during times of both war and peace. The role of states in the process was limited and, for the most part, insignificant. Their contributions to the evolution of international humanitarian law were in the form of responding to calls made by the Red Cross, participating in the conferences that were held to draft the related documents, and adhering to the conventions.

Since its foundation, the Red Cross has been dedicated to widening the scope of international humanitarian law. Its efforts have focused on the adoption of new conventions, altering based on the requirements of the time, and acting as the executive agent of their implementation. As was noted, the success achieved at The Hague Conferences was largely owing to the organization's efforts. In addition, the adoption of the Convention relating to the Treatment of Prisoners of War between the two world wars safeguarded millions of prisoners during the course of World War II.[162] Between the two wars, the committee also drafted a number of other conventions that were to be discussed in a diplomatic conference convened in 1940; however, the outbreak of the war hindered further progress on the matter.[163]

On February 15, 1945, even before the war had officially ended, the committee forwarded to governments its intention to revise the existing conventions. On receiving welcoming responses from the governments,

---

[161] David Forsythe, "1949 and 1999: Making the Geneva Conventions relevant after the Cold War," *International Review of the Red Cross,* Issue 834, 1999, pp. 277–301.

[162] Jean p. Pictet, "The New Geneva Conventions for the Protection of War Victims," *American Journal of International Law,* Vol. 45, Issue 3, 1951, pp. 462–463.

[163] Ibid., p. 463.

the committee dedicated itself to collecting relevant data and related activities. Its work lasted for 4 years, culminating in the revised conventions and entirely new drafts that were to be discussed at a diplomatic conference with the participation of government delegates.[164]

During the deliberations, the committee's input had great impact on the adoption of the conventions. The committee staff patiently and carefully collected data from the field and the places that had been affected by the war. It also managed to obtain other information from various sources, including governments, individuals, and prisoners of war.[165] In other words, the committee was prepared in all ways for the conference that resulted from its efforts.

The committee then convened the Commissions of Experts, the first of which met in Geneva in October 1945 with a very limited scope; it comprised medical commissions that had performed the duty of the examining sick and wounded during the war. The treaty provisions related to repatriating prisoners of war or accommodating them neutral countries were revised at this meeting, which was followed by the drafting of an agreement on the same subject.[166]

The second expert commission was the Preliminary Conference of National Red Cross Societies for the Study of the Conventions and of various problems related to the Red Cross. The meeting was held in Geneva between July 26 and August 3, 1946, with the participation of 145 delegates from 50 countries, who forwarded their views regarding the drafts and proposals. Accordingly, the committee devoted the following months to closely examining the input and then reorganized all data that were pertinent to the content of the conventions to be adopted.[167]

The committee then turned to governments and submitted its work to the Conference of Government Experts for the Study of the Conventions for the Protection of War Victims, held in Geneva in

---

[164] Ibid., p. 464.

[165] Ibid., p. 465.

[166] Ibid., p. 465.

[167] Ibid., pp. 465–466.

April 1947 and attended by 70 official representatives from 15 countries. The conference studied the committee's views and proposals as well as those of a number of governments and adopted a preliminary Draft Convention for the Protection of Civilians in Time of War. The opinions of the nonparticipating governments were also obtained via the committee's lead role. After consulting with major civil society organizations, including the International Union for Child Welfare and the International Labor Office, the committee completed the Draft Conventions in early 1948.[168]

The drafts were discussed at the 17th International Red Cross Conference, which was held in Stockholm in August 1948 and attended by representatives from 50 governments and 52 national Red Cross Societies. The conference endorsed the proposed draft conventions, which were then used as the sole working documents at the Diplomatic Conference that officially adopted them.[169]

The community of states and intergovernmental organizations including the UN remained silent and reluctant to make progress on establishing an international criminal court throughout the 1960s and 1970s. Moreover, there was no significant breakthrough or contribution to the international criminal legal system as a whole that could have expanded the scope of the international criminal liability of natural persons. The Convention on the Prevention and Punishment of Genocide and the four Geneva Conventions that addressed wartime atrocities in particular remain the most outstanding components of international humanitarian law during this period. The absence of an international criminal court, along with the underdeveloped international criminal system, was one of the most important sources of chaos and anarchy in the international criminal system. As a result, the Cold War, which created an anarchic and state-centric international political order, also dictated terms to the international criminal law system. Especially for this reason, in the absence of universal criminal legal jurisdiction, individual states have sought their own ways to address

[168] Ibid., p. 466.

[169] Ibid., p. 467.

individual criminal liability. The Eichmann case, which is elaborated on later in the present text, is exemplary in this regard.

However, states' reluctance to create a strong international criminal jurisdiction system does not necessarily mean that the international community as a whole was following a similar path. Although the efforts were not strong, the "unofficial" components and units of the world community made multiple attempts, even in the era of silence of the 1960s and 1970s. Essentially, "interest in an international court during this period was kept alive by numerous scholars and non-governmental organizations."[170]

In 1971, the World Peace Through Law Center organized a world conference in Belgrade in which one session was devoted to discussions on creating a permanent international criminal court. The International Criminal Court Committee also called on the UN to proceed with establishing such a court by separating it from the attempts to codify a convention or similar mechanism to define and effectively address the crime of aggression, which had been and apparently would continue to be a matter of paramount controversy among states. Professional associations and other relevant groups were also called upon to convince states to establish a permanent international court. The Belgrade World Conference resolved that "consideration should be given to the creation of a penal panel to resolve inter-State jurisdictional conflicts; hear claims involving 'special environments' over which no State is able to claim jurisdiction; and to provide an alternative forum to States which do not desire to undertake prosecutions."[171] Shortly after, another conference with remarkable attendance was held under the sponsorship of the Foundation for the Establishment of an International Criminal Court. The conference, called the Wingspread Conference, formulated a draft statute that contained a number of international punishable acts and proposed an international panel that was to be vested with jurisdiction over the crimes specified in the draft statute. However, states were given

---

[170] MacPherson, "Building an International Criminal Court for the 21st Century," p. 12.

[171] L. Kos-Rabcewicz Zubkowski, "The Creation of an International Criminal Court," in M. Cherif Bassiouni (ed.), *International Terrorism and Political Crimes* (1975), pp. 519, 521, cited in Lippman, "Towards an International Criminal Court," p. 91.

the right to choose the specific crimes concerning which the proposed panel would proceed.[172]

The only official attempt to create an international criminal court in the 1960s and 1970s was associated with adopting the International Convention on the Suppression and Punishment of the Crime of Apartheid.[173] This convention recognized apartheid as a crime against humanity[174] and also outlined a broad range of acts that fell under the definition of apartheid.[175] Individuals, members of organizations and representatives of any state, "whether residing in the territory of the State in which the acts are perpetrated or in some other State," were to be held responsible for committing the crime of apartheid, whenever they were to "commit, participate in, directly incite or conspire in the commission of the acts" mentioned in the convention or "directly abet, encourage or co-operate in the commission of the crime of apartheid."[176] Under the convention, states were obliged to work to prevent and punish the crime of apartheid.[177]

As was the case with the Genocide Convention, the Apartheid Convention referred to an international criminal court for the purpose of prosecuting the crime. Article 5 of the Convention provided that the individuals accused of having committed acts that were punishable under

[172] Ibid., pp. 523–525, cited in Lippman, "Towards an International Criminal Court," pp. 91–92.

[173] The International Convention on the Suppression and Punishment of the Crime of Apartheid, G.A. Res. 3068 (XXVIII), U.N. Doc. A/9030 (1974).

[174] Ibid., Article 1. "The States Parties to the present Convention declare that apartheid is a crime against humanity and that inhuman acts resulting from the policies and practices of apartheid and similar policies and practices of racial segregation and discrimination."

[175] Ibid., Article 2. It states that the crime of apartheid applies to, among others, the following acts: "Denial to a member or members of a racial group or groups of the right to life and liberty of person," "Deliberate imposition on a racial group or groups of living conditions calculated to cause its or their physical destruction in whole or in part," "Exploitation of the labour of the members of a racial group or groups, in particular by submitting them to forced labour," and "Persecution of organizations and persons, by depriving them of fundamental rights and freedoms, because they oppose apartheid."

[176] Ibid., Article 3.

[177] Ibid., Article 4. States that are party to the Convention are required to take any legislative and other measures necessary to suppress and prevent "any encouragement of the crime of apartheid," and if such a crime is committed, to adopt any measures necessary to prosecute, try and punish the perpetrators of the crime.

the Convention could be prosecuted and tried by a domestic court of any state that was party to the Convention or by an international criminal tribunal that was vested by states with the jurisdiction to do so.[178] However, because the court referred to in the Convention was never established, the international jurisdiction it envisaged "was never implemented."[179]

However, in 1979, the UN Commission on Human Rights took action to ensure the implementation of the Convention. The first step was to adopt a resolution charging the Ad Hoc Working Group of Experts on South Africa and the Special Committee Against Apartheid to study the matter, including the possibility of establishing an international jurisdiction as provided by the Apartheid Convention.[180] Professor M. Cherif Bassiouni, a prominent scholar of international criminal law, was appointed by the General Assembly as Expert Consultant to the Group.

Bassiouni and Professor Daniel Derby prepared a report on an international criminal court,[181] which the Ad Hoc Working Group adopted; however, it did not proceed further with regard to the report. Bassiouni and Derby authored a draft convention that was to address the crime of apartheid by establishing an international penal tribunal for the purpose of suppressing and punishing that crime.[182] The Draft Convention provided for a tribunal that would be vested with jurisdiction over violations of the Apartheid Convention, and it regarded both individuals and states, as criminally liable for acts that fell under the category of apartheid.[183] The proposed tribunal was significant because it was to be vested with universal jurisdiction with respect to the prosecution, trial, and punishment of those

---

[178] Ibid., Article 5.

[179] Bassiouni, "Establishing an International Criminal Court: Historical Survey," p. 61.

[180] G.A. Res. 34/24, U.N. Doc. A/34/618 (1979).

[181] For additional details on this endeavor, see the following article by the authors of the report, M. Cherif Bassiouni and Daniel H. Derby, "Final Report on the Establishment of and International Criminal Court for the Implementation of the Apartheid Convention and Other Relevant International Instruments," 9 *Hofstra Law Review,* Vol. 9, Issue, 1981, pp. 523.

[182] Draft Convention on the Establishment of an International Penal Tribunal for the Suppression and Punishment of the Crime of Apartheid and other International Crimes, U.N. Doc. E/CN.4/AC/22CRP.19/Rev.1 (December 10, 1980).

[183] Ibid., Article 4.

who were accused of having committed the crime of apartheid and other punishable acts under the Convention.[184]

However, as might be expected, such a novel and advanced proposal did not meet with acceptance by states. The UN did nothing further with the draft or the proposed tribunal, and it was "not... acted upon."[185] In short, "the post-war period thus failed to fulfill the promise of Nuremberg. Absent a direct demand for action, the international community was unable to release its embrace of the status quo."[186]

During the 1970s, there were other attempts that could be considered within the context of the evolution of international criminal jurisdiction and individual liability, although these were less important and significant than that aimed to codify an Apartheid Convention that included an international criminal court that would be authorized to address the crime with universal jurisdiction. These attempts focused mainly on codifying conventions related to terrorism. The first of these was the Convention for the Suppression of Unlawful Seizure of Aircraft, also known as the Hijacking Convention.[187] The Convention criminalizes acts that fall into under the category of hijacking and the commission of those acts.[188] Under the Convention, the states that are party to it are obliged to "make the offence punishable by severe penalties."[189] To this end, states that are party to the Convention and that apprehend offenders are required to either extradite them or prosecute the offenses.[190] Considering that addressing this crime requires international cooperation, the Convention also imposes obligations on states to assist each

[184] Ibid., Article 4(3).

[185] Bassiouni, "Establishing an International Criminal Court: Historical Survey," p. 61.

[186] Lippman, "Towards an International Criminal Court," p. 94.

[187] The Convention for the Suppression of Unlawful Seizure of Aircraft, 860 U.N.T.S. 105, *entered into force* October 14, 1971.

[188] Ibid., Article 1.

[189] Ibid., Article 2.

[190] Ibid., Article 7. It reads as follows: "The Contracting State in the territory of which the alleged offender is found shall, if it does not extradite him, be obliged, without exception whatsoever and whether or not the offence was committed in its territory, to submit the case to its competent authorities for the purpose of prosecution. Those authorities shall take their decision in the same manner as in the case of any ordinary offence of a serious nature under the law of that State."

other in both implementing the Convention and bringing the accused into custody and eventually prosecuting them.[191]

The second international law-related effort was the Convention for the Suppression of Unlawful Acts against the Safety of Civil Aviation,[192] which criminalized any acts that were likely to endanger the safety of an aircraft, including placing an explosive on it and held liable both offenders and their accomplices for committing crimes that were punishable under international law.[193] As was the case with the Hijacking Convention, this one also required states to make the relevant offenses severely punishable.[194] Again, states that had offenders in custody were obliged under the Convention to either extradite or prosecute them.[195]

The third effort was the Convention on the Prevention and Punishment of Crimes against Internationally Protected Persons, including Diplomatic Agents.[196] This Convention provided that heads of state, foreign affairs ministers, representatives or officials of states, or international organizations who were entitled to special protection from attack under international law were to be categorized as internationally protected persons.[197] It also listed the acts against those persons that were to be made punishable by states.[198] When such an offense was committed, the state with jurisdiction over the crime was required to extradite the offender or submit the case "without exception whatsoever and without undue delay" to "its competent authorities for the purpose of prosecution."[199]

---

[191] Ibid., Articles 6 and 8.

[192] Convention for the Suppression of Unlawful Acts against the Safety of Civil Aviation, 974 U.N.T.S. 178, entered into force January 26, 1973.

[193] Ibid., Article 1. It contains a long list of acts that could be regarded as offenses punishable under the Convention.

[194] Ibid., Article 3.

[195] Ibid., Article 7.

[196] Convention on the Prevention and Punishment of Crimes against Internationally Protected Persons, including Diplomatic Agents, GAOR 3166(XVIII), *entered into force,* February 20, 1977.

[197] Ibid., Article 1.

[198] Ibid., Article 2.

[199] Ibid., Article 7.

The fourth international law-related effort was the International Convention against the Taking of Hostages.[200] This Convention provided that acts that could be regarded as taking hostages would be punishable and that any person who committed the offense or participated as an accomplice would be liable.[201] The states that were party to the Convention were to take the necessary measures to make hostage-taking as defined in the Convention punishable under their domestic legislation.[202] The states were also required to provide any assistance with respect to prosecuting and punishing perpetrators.[203]

Although the aforementioned Conventions on various forms of terrorism called for individual criminal responsibility for perpetrators of related punishable offenses, none of them referred to an international criminal court that would be established for the purpose of prosecuting and punishing the offenses. In other words, enforcing the Conventions was left entirely to the states, and there were no sanctions for states that did not comply with the provisions of the Conventions. Moreover, it should be noted that adopting these Conventions was relatively simple because their regulations were not particularly controversial with respect to national sovereignty.

Arguably, a much more important codification from the 1970s than the four terrorism conventions aforementioned was the Convention on the Non-Applicability of Statutory Limitations to War Crimes and Crimes against Humanity.[204] It filled a significant void in international humanitarian law because the previous instruments that had been

---

[200] International Convention against the Taking of Hostages, G.A. Res. 146 (XXXIV), U.N. Doc. A/34/46 (1979), *entered into force* June 3, 1983.

[201] Ibid., Article 1.

[202] Ibid., Article 2.

[203] Ibid., Article 11. It reads as follows: "States Parties shall afford one another the greatest measure of assistance in connexion with criminal proceedings brought in respect of the offences set forth in article 1, including the supply of all evidence at their disposal necessary for the proceedings."

[204] Convention on the Non-Applicability of Statutory Limitations to War Crimes and Crimes Against Humanity, G.A. res. 2391 (XXIII), U.N. Doc. A/7218 (1968), *entered into force* November 11, 1970.

created to impose individual criminal responsibility on those who committed war crimes contained no provisions regarding statutory limitations. Considering this shortcoming and that "war crimes and crimes against humanity are among the gravest crimes in international law," and recognizing the need to affirm "the principle that there is no period of limitation for war crimes and crimes against humanity, and to secure its universal application," the Convention provided that no statutory limitations would apply to war crimes or crimes against humanity "whether committed in time of war or in time of peace."[205] It also imposed obligations on states to adopt any measures "necessary to ensure that statutory or other limitations shall not apply to the prosecution and punishment of the crimes referred to" and directed that "where they exist, such limitations shall be abolished."[206]

A later attempt was made to reaffirm the above-mentioned Convention. The General Assembly adopted the Principles of International Co-Operation in the Detection, Arrest, Extradition and Punishment of Persons Guilty of War Crimes and Crimes against Humanity[207] in 1973 to ensure that the perpetrators of war crimes and crimes against humanity would not go unpunished. The resolution declared that the respective crimes "shall be subject to investigation and the persons against whom there is evidence that they have committed such crimes shall be subject to tracing, arrest, trial and, if found guilty, to punishment."[208] It also provided that although states had the right to prosecute and punish their own nationals for war crimes and crimes against humanity,[209] they were to cooperate through bilateral and multilateral treaties to prevent the commission of these crimes[210] and to "assist each other in detecting, arresting and

---

[205] Ibid., Article 1.

[206] Ibid., Article 4.

[207] Principles of International Co-Operation in the Detection, Arrest, Extradition and Punishment of Persons Guilty of War Crimes and Crimes against Humanity, G.A. res. 3074 (XXVIII), U.N. Doc. A/9030/Add.1 (1973).

[208] Ibid., paragraph 1.

[209] Ibid., paragraph 2.

[210] Ibid., paragraph 3.

bringing to trial persons suspected of having committed such crimes and, if they are found guilty, in punishing them."[211]

However, although the two attempts aforementioned are noteworthy steps in the evolution of international humanitarian law, their effectiveness and legitimacy rested upon the willingness of states to cooperate and comply with their provisions.

[211] Ibid., paragraph 4.

# From the End of the Cold War to the Present

It has been a fashion among students of international relations and international law, as well as strategists, analysts, and pundits of all types, to refer to the end of the Cold War as a significant historical turning point, the beginning of an abrupt and remarkable transformation in world politics, and a clear departure from the previous international political and economic order. Numerous terms were coined in the context of adequately explaining this new tendency. Among others, perhaps the most popular were "the new world order," "globalization," "global governance," "interdependency," "hegemony," and so forth.

However, although these have been useful for the most part, as far as progress on international criminal jurisdiction is concerned, the situation has been business as usual for some time. It can be argued that the end of Cold War would have facilitated the development of international criminal law if the notorious atrocities had not occurred in the former Yugoslavia and in Rwanda. Although significantly easing the tension between the two major power blocks contributed greatly to the evolution of various branches of international law, including international human rights law, states remained the primary authorities to implement international criminal laws.



C. Çakmak, *A Brief History of International Criminal Law and International Criminal Court*,
DOI 10.1057/978-1-137-56736-9_5

Of course, this does not necessarily mean that there have been no attempts to improve the reach and scope of international criminal jurisdiction. However, the important point that needs to be emphasized here is that there is no clear evidence that these attempts could be attributed to the ease in tensions between the two major blocks that had dominated world politics for a significant period of time. Instead, the needs that technological advances brought to the fore were the primary impetus for states' efforts to invoke at least some elements of international criminal jurisdiction.

In particular, the revolutionary changes in communication technology, although they were beneficial in many respects, had a great impact on transforming the characteristics of crime. Committing certain crimes became much easier owing to the ease of the communication and travel. The new conditions created an environment in which terrorists and international criminal organizations could conduct their activities across the continents, superseding the theory and practice of sovereignty and border protection. Territorial criminal jurisdiction no longer applied to these types of crimes because the criminals' ease of movement made it impossible for any specific state to prosecute and punish the perpetrators of crimes committed within its territory.

Extraterritorial jurisdiction, which allowed any state to extend its jurisdiction beyond its territory to prosecute an individual whom it deemed responsible for committing a crime within its territory proved to be problematic, and the practice of extradition was also not successful.[1] The failure of the aforementioned methods occasionally resulted in unlawful attempts to bring criminals to trial. For example, whereas the United States practiced the method of abduction, at least some scholars legitimized assassination in the absence of an effective method for ensuring the prosecution of those who were accused of committing international crimes.[2] As a result, states were compelled

[1] Lippman, "Towards an International Criminal Court," pp. 94–95.

[2] Ibid., p. 95. Lippman gives an example: Louis Rene Beres, "Iraqi Crimes and International Law: The Imperative to Punish," *Denver Journal of International Law and Policy,* Vol. 21, Issue 2, 1992, p. 335.

to cooperate and subsequently establish international criminal jurisdiction that would make possible the prosecution and punishment of such criminals.

Thus marks the beginning of the developments that were closely related to international criminal jurisdiction and that coincided with the end of the Cold War. First, nation-states' law enforcement bodies sought cooperation by entering into various cooperative agreements and other means of collaboration. However, these attempts did not change the existing system of international criminal law. Although there were calls to create an international criminal court,[3] "the problem of establishing an effective enforcement regime remained."[4]

Concurrently, the UN also involved itself in the process once again, recognizing the need to address the growing concern over the negative impact of transnational crimes. However, this time, "the focus was not on war crimes and genocide, but on terrorism and narcotics trafficking."[5] This is exactly why both the United States and the Soviet Union supported establishing an international tribunal that could address such crimes as terrorism and drug trafficking. The Soviet Union, however, insisted that the proposed court's jurisdiction be confined to crimes in

---

[3] For example, Bassiouni, referring to the need for an international criminal court that in particular could address such transnational crimes as terrorism, drug trafficking and the like, made his call in the following fashion: We no longer live in a world where narrow conceptions of jurisdiction and sovereignty can stand in the way of an effective system of international cooperation for the prevention and control of international and transnational criminality. If the United States and the Soviet Union can accept mutual verification of nuclear arms controls, then surely they and other countries can accept a tribunal to prosecute not only drug traffickers and terrorists, but also those whose actions constitute such international crimes as aggression, war crimes, crimes against humanity and torture... The permanency of an international criminal tribunal acting impartially and fairly irrespective of whom the accused may be is the best policy for the advancement of the international rule of law and for the prevention and control of international and transnational criminality... It is unconscionable at this stage of the world's history, and after so much human harm has already occurred, that abstract notions of sovereignty can still shield violators of international criminal law or that the limited views and lack of vision and faith by government officials can prevent the establishment of such an important and needed international institution. The time has come for us to think and act in conformity with the values, ideals and goals we profess. M. Cherif Bassiouni, "The Time has Come for an International Criminal Court," *Indiana International and Comparative Law Review*, Vol. 1, Issue 1, 1991, pp. 33–35.

[4] Lippman, "Towards an International Criminal Court," p. 96.

[5] MacPherson, "Building an International Criminal Court for the 21st Century," p. 12.

the category of terrorism.[6] A number of states joined the United States and the USSR in supporting the creation of such a court.[7] In 1989, under the leadership of the Prime Minister of Trinidad and Tobago, 17 Caribbean and Latin American states expressed their support for an international court and subsequently requested that the General Assembly proceed with considering the possibility of creating a permanent international criminal court that would have jurisdiction over drug trafficking crimes.[8]

The UN's response to states' requests for further consideration of establishing an international tribunal with jurisdiction over narcotics trafficking and related crimes was swift. First, in 1988, the UN General Assembly invited the International Law Commission to continue its work on drafting a Code of Crimes against the Peace and Security of Mankind,[9] a task that had been off the table for decades. Then, in 1989, it also requested that the International Law Commission prepare a report on the possibility of international criminal jurisdiction for prosecuting people who committed crimes related to drug trafficking.[10]

At the same time, the International Institute of Higher Studies in Criminal Sciences, an NGO, in cooperation with the United Nations Crime Prevention Branch and the Italian Ministry of Justice, charged a committee of experts with preparing another draft statute. The committee, chaired by Professor Bassiouni, submitted the draft statute, which in fact was based on the draft proposal he had submitted in 1981, to the Eighth United Nations Congress on Crime Prevention and the Treatment of

[6] Ibid., p. 13.

[7] However, it should be noted that the majority of states, especially Western countries, opposed the creation of such a court at that time. See Sharon A. Williams, "The Rome Statute on the International Criminal Court: From 1947–2000 and Beyond," *Osgoode Hall Law Journal*, Vol. 38, Issue 2, 2000, p. 303.

[8] Ibid., p. 13.

[9] "Draft Code of Crimes against the Peace and Security of Mankind," UN General Assembly Resolution 43/164, 43rd Session, 76th meeting, December 9, 1988.

[10] "International Criminal Responsibility of Individuals and Entities Engaged in Illicit Trafficking of Narcotic Drugs Across National Frontiers and Other Transnational Criminal Activities: Establishment of an International Criminal Court with Jurisdiction over Such Crimes," UN General Assembly Resolution 44/39, 44th Session, 72nd meeting, December 4, 1989.

Offenders.[11] The Eighth Congress recognized the need for an international criminal court and partially endorsed the proposal.[12] However, it ceased further consideration of the draft statute, so that once more, the attempt to create an international criminal court became fruitless.

However, the International Law Commission (ILC) continued its efforts, discussed the details of a possible international criminal tribunal, and subsequently decided to continue the discussions along with the 1991 Draft Code of Crimes.[13] The ILC's additional efforts that then led to the adoption of the Rome Statute are discussed below. The early 1990s are important in terms of the evolution of international criminal law because two ad hoc international criminal tribunals with broad authority were created to effectively address the massive killings in the former Yugoslavia and in Rwanda. These two institutions were, of course, not on the agendas of global policy-makers; however, the circumstances dictated taking action.

The tragedy in the former Yugoslavia began in early 1991, shortly after its dissolution. Within a very short time, the breakup process proved to be violent, seriously affecting the security of millions of civilians. During the civil war, the commission of atrocities ranging from plain killings to torture to death in various forms and from forced migration to systematic rapes, which were employed by the Serbians in particular as a means of humiliation and ethnic cleansing, was all too apparent, but the world community preferred not to intervene for a long time. In particular, the European states did not want the United States to get involved in the matter, which they saw as a European question, and so European actors made the effort to achieve resolution.[14]

---

[11] "Draft Statute: International Criminal Tribuna," U.N. GAOR, 45th Sess., U.N. Doc. A/Conf. 144/NGO.7 (1990).

[12] Report of the Eighth United Nations Congress on the Prevention of Crime and the Treatment of Offenders, U.N. GAOR, 45th Sess., U.N. Doc. A/Conf. 144/28 (1990), cited in Bassiouni, "From Versailles to Rwanda in Seventy-Five Years: The Need to Establish a Permanent International Criminal Court," pp. 55–56.

[13] Report of the International Law Commission, U.N. GAOR, 46th Sess., U.N. Doc. A/46/10 (1991).

[14] The events in the former Yugoslavia gained broad publicity largely because they were "occurring in Europe, which had twice endured World Wars. The Western powers could not ignore what was occurring in their back yard, as they might have had it been happening elsewhere." MacPherson, "Building an International Criminal Court for the 21st Century," p. 13.

However, all attempts by the European institutions and individual actors were great failures and disappointments.

Eventually, the UN Security Council decided to engage with the question, even though a deadlock could have caused serious damage to the organization and negatively affected its legitimacy as the overseer of global peace and security. On September 25, 1991, the Council acknowledged the seriousness of the problem and expressed its concern that "the continuation of this situation constitutes a threat to international peace and security."[15] Although it supported the efforts led by the European states, it also decided that "all States shall, for the purposes of establishing peace and stability in Yugoslavia, immediately implement a general and complete embargo on all deliveries of weapons and military equipment to Yugoslavia until the Security Council decides otherwise following consultation between the Secretary-General and the Government of Yugoslavia."[16]

However, this attempt neither sufficed to end the conflict nor alleviated the violence. For this reason, the Council took an additional step and reminded the warring parties that they were obliged under international humanitarian law to observe the provisions of the Geneva Conventions of 1949 and that any persons who committed or ordered the commission of grave breaches of the Conventions were to be held individually responsible.[17] The warning was ineffective, and numerous reliable reports continued to submit evidence of widespread atrocities of various types, most of them falling into the category of grave breaches of international humanitarian law. On August 13, 1992, the Council, referring to the practice of "ethnic cleansing," strongly condemned the violations of international humanitarian law within the territory of the former Yugoslavia.[18] With the same resolution, it also decided that "all parties and others concerned in the former Yugoslavia, and all military

[15] UN Security Council Resolution S/RES/713 (1991).

[16] Ibid., para 6.

[17] UN Security Council Resolution S/RES/764 (1992), para. 10.

[18] United Nations Security Council Resolution 771 (Concerning Information on Violations of International Humanitarian Law in the Territory of the Former Yugoslavia), S.C. res. 771, U.N. Doc. S/RES/771 (1992), para. 2.

forces in Bosnia and Herzegovina, shall comply with the provisions of the present resolution, failing which the Council will need to take further measures under the Charter."[19]

Further, on October 6, 1992, the Security Council decided to establish a Commission of Experts to investigate and collect evidence of the atrocities committed during the civil war.[20] The resolution adopted for this purpose set the commission's mandate as follows:

> [The Security Council] *Requests* the Secretary-General to establish, as a matter of urgency, an impartial Commission of Experts to examine and analyse the information submitted pursuant to resolution 771 (1992) and the present resolution, together with such further information as the Commission of Experts may obtain through its own investigations or efforts, of other persons or bodies pursuant to resolution 771 (1992), with a view to providing the Secretary-General with its conclusions on the evidence of grave breaches of the Geneva Conventions and other violations of international humanitarian law committed in the territory of the former Yugoslavia.[21]

The Commission of Experts' work culminated in 65,000 pages of documents, over 300 hours of video records, and 3,300 pages of analysis.[22] All of this information was appendixed to the commission's final report[23] and submitted to the then-established tribunal's prosecutor.

However, it should be noted that the commission's work was not easy, even though it was established under the UN's sponsorship. It received no UN funding, which it greatly needed to carry out the field investigation; ultimately, it had to seek external resources to complete its work. In preparing its report, the commission also had to rely

---

[19] Ibid., para. 7.

[20] United Nations Security Council Resolution 780 (Establishing a Commission of Experts to Examine and Analyze Information Submitted Pursuant to Resolution 771), S.C. res. 780, U.N. Doc. S/RES/780 (1992).

[21] Ibid., para. 2.

[22] Bassiouni, "From Versailles to Rwanda in Seventy-Five Years: The Need to Establish a Permanent International Criminal Court," p. 40.

[23] Final Report of the Commission of Experts Established pursuant to Security Council Resolution 780 (1992), U.N. SCOR, 47th Sess., Annex, U.N. Doc. S/1994/674 (1994); Annexes to the Final Report, U.N. SCOR, 47th Sess., U.N. Doc. S/1994/674/Add.2 (1994).

on information and data provided by the International Human Rights Law Institute of DePaul University in Chicago, directed by Professor Bassiouni.[24] The report contains, in general terms, the following conclusions:

> Reports received and investigations conducted by the Commission indicate that the level of victimization in this conflict has been high. The crimes committed have been particularly brutal and ferocious in their execution. The Commission has not been able to verify each report; however, the magnitude of victimization is clearly enormous.
>
> The Commission finds significant evidence of and information about the commission of grave breaches of the Geneva Conventions and other violations of international humanitarian law which have been communicated to the Office of the Prosecutor of the International Tribunal.
>
> ... The practices of "ethnic cleansing," sexual assault and rape have been carried out by some of the parties so systematically that they strongly appear to be the product of a policy. The consistent failure to prevent the commission of such crimes and the consistent failure to prosecute and punish the perpetrators of these crimes, clearly evidences the existence of a policy by omission. The consequence of this conclusion is that command responsibility can be established.
>
> The Commission is shocked by the high level of victimization and the manner in which these crimes were committed, as are the populations of all the parties to the conflict. The difference is that each side sees only its own victimization, and not what their side has done to others.[25]

The commission's work was a real success. However, as the field investigations were being conducted, the commission became a genuine threat to the prospect of a political settlement, a resolution very much desired by the leading powers in world politics, including the United States and the EU. Because the evidence and information collected by the commission substantiated the large-scale commission of crimes that

[24] Bassiouni, "From Versailles to Rwanda in Seventy-Five Years: The Need to Establish a Permanent International Criminal Court," p. 41.

[25] Ibid., Part V. General Conclusions and Recommendations.

warranted international criminal prosecution before an international penal tribunal, there was no room left to negotiate with possible criminals. For this reason, "it became politically necessary to terminate the work of the Commission while attempting to avoid the negative consequences of such a direct action."[26]

Subsequently, although the Security Council did not terminate the commission's work,[27] various measure forms were taken to prevent its working effectively. Bassiouni, who witnessed this obstruction firsthand as the Chairman of the Commission, explains it as follows:

> An administrative decision was taken—probably at the behest, but certainly with the support of, some of the Permanent Members—leaving no legal trace of the deed. Thus, the Chairman was administratively notified that the Commission should end its work by April 30, 1994. When the Commission's mandate was terminated, it still had over $ 250,000 in a trust fund and had not yet completed its Final Report. Between April 30 and December 31, 1994, the Chairman completed the Final Report and the Annexes and then continued to work until July 1995 to see that they were published by the United Nations.[28]

The reason the Security Council, at least some of its members, wanted to terminate the commission's work is somewhat unclear, but the question becomes more relevant considering that the Council elected to establish an international criminal tribunal to address the atrocities being committed in the former Yugoslavia. Shortly after the commission submitted its interim report,[29] in its Resolution 808 (1993), the Council decided

[26] Bassiouni, "From Versailles to Rwanda in Seventy-Five Years: The Need to Establish a Permanent International Criminal Court," p. 41.

[27] S.C. Res 827, U.N. SCOR, 48th Sess., at preamble, U.N Doc. S/RES/827 (1993). It states, "the Commission of Experts established pursuant to resolution 780 (1992) should continue on an urgent basis the collection of information relating to evidence of grave breaches of the Geneva Conventions and other violations of international humanitarian law as proposed in its interim report."

[28] Bassiouni, "From Versailles to Rwanda in Seventy-Five Years: The Need to Establish a Permanent International Criminal Court," p. 42.

[29] Interim Report of the Commission of Experts Established pursuant to Security Council Resolution 780 (1992), U.N. SCOR, 48th Sess., Annex, at 20, U.N. Doc. S/25274 (1993).

that "an international criminal tribunal shall be established for the prosecution of persons responsible for serious violations of international humanitarian law committed in the territory of the former Yugoslavia since 1991."[30]

Under that resolution, the Secretary-General was requested to submit to the Council a report on the subject of the possibility of creating such an international tribunal as envisaged in the resolution within 60 days.[31] Accordingly, the Secretary-General prepared the requested report, in which a draft statute for the tribunal and detailed commentaries on its content was provided.[32] In general terms, the Secretary-General's proposal contained a recommendation that the Security Council establish an international criminal tribunal in connection with its authority under Chapter VII of the UN Charter to prevent threats to international peace and security.[33] The Security Council approved the proposed statute without change and adopted Resolution 827, by which the tribunal was established.[34] The resolution also mandated full cooperation from

[30] S.C. Res. 808, U.N. SCOR, 48th Sess., U.N. Doc. S/RES/808 (1993). The Council determined that the situation in the former Yugoslavia constituted a threat to international peace and security and thus required effective action to "put an end to such crimes and to take effective measures to bring to justice the persons who are responsible for them." Accordingly, the Council expressed its agreement that "the establishment of an international tribunal would enable this aim [addressing the situation in the former Yugoslavia] to be achieved and would contribute to the restoration and maintenance of peace."

[31] Ibid., preamble.

[32] Report of the Secretary-General pursuant to paragraph 2 of Security Council Resolution 808 (1993), U.N. SCOR, 48th Sess., U.N. Doc. S/25704 (1993).

[33] Ibid.

[34] S.C. Res 827, U.N. SCOR, 48th Sess., at preamble, U.N Doc. S/RES/827 (1993). The Council decided

> to establish an international tribunal for the sole purpose of prosecuting persons responsible for serious violations of international humanitarian law committed in the territory of the former Yugoslavia between 1 January 1991 and a date to be determined by the Security Council upon the restoration of peace and to this end to adopt the Statute of the International Tribunal annexed to the above-mentioned report.

Ibid., paragraph 2. The Council also requested that the Secretary-General give the tribunal judges, once they had been elected, "any suggestions received from the States for the rules of procedure and evidence." Ibid., paragraph 3.

all states[35] and urged "States and intergovernmental and non-governmental organizations to contribute funds, equipment and services to the International Tribunal, including the offer of expert personnel."[36] The tribunal entered into force on May 25, 1993.[37] Subsequently, its judges were elected on September 15, 1993, and the prosecutor assumed the office on August 15, 1994.[38]

---

[35] Ibid., paragraph 4, which states,

> all States shall cooperate fully with the International Tribunal and its organs in accordance with the present resolution and the Statute of the International Tribunal and that consequently all States shall take any measures necessary under their domestic law to implement the provisions of the present resolution and the Statute, including the obligation of States to comply with requests for assistance or orders issued by a Trial Chamber.

[36] Ibid., paragraph 5.

[37] However, it should be noted that establishing the tribunal was not without controversy; there was not a firm consensus on the matter. For instance, not all of the permanent members of the Security Council favored the action. The opposing members were of the view that such a tribunal would be "potentially disruptive of negotiations for a political settlement of the conflict." Some insisted that the tribunal should be established under the auspices of the General Assembly, not under the control of the Security Council. Some also proposed that a multilateral treaty be accorded for the purpose of establishing the tribunal. Although the minority favored a permanent international criminal court, "the political advantages of controlling ad hoc institutions by the Security Council prevailed." See, Bassiouni, "From Versailles to Rwanda in Seventy-Five Years: The Need to Establish a Permanent International Criminal Court," p. 44.

[38] The tribunal that was established for the purpose of prosecuting the crimes committed in the former Yugoslavia drew significant attention and interest from academics. As a result, many works have appeared on the matter. See, among others, George H. Aldrich, "Jurisdiction of the ICTY," *American Journal of International Law*, Vol. 90, Issue 1, 1996, pp. 64–69; Louise Arbour, "The International Tribunals for Serious Violations of International Humanitarian Law in the Former Yugoslavia and Rwanda," *McGill Law Journal*, Vol. 46, Issue 1, 2000, pp. 195–201; Louise Arbour and Aryeh Neier, "History and Future of the International Criminal Tribunals for the Former Yugoslavia and Rwanda," *American University International Law Review*, Vol. 13, Issue 6, 1998, pp. 1495–1508; M. Cherif Bassiouni and Peter Manikas, *The Law of the International Criminal Tribunal for the Former Yugoslavia* (Irvington-on-Hudson, NY: Transnational Publishers, 1996); Morten Bergsmo, "International Criminal Tribunal for the Former Yugoslavia: Recent Developments," *Human Rights Law Journal*, Vol. 15, 1994, pp. 405–410; Gideon Boas, "Creating Laws of Evidence for International Criminal Law: The ICTY and the Principle of Flexibility," *Criminal Law Forum*, Vol. 12, Issue 1, 2001, pp. 41–90; Anne Bodley, "Weakening the Principle of Sovereignty in International Law: The International Criminal Tribunal for the Former Yugoslavia," *New York University Journal of International Law and Politics*, Vol. 2, 1998, pp. 417–471; Matthew M. DeFrank, "ICTY Provisional Release: Current Practice, a Dissenting Voice, and the Case for a Rule Change," *Texas Law Review*, Vol. 80, Issue 6, 2002, pp. 1429–1463.

Under Article 1 of its statute, the tribunal was to "have the power to prosecute persons responsible for serious violations of international humanitarian law committed in the territory of the former Yugoslavia since 1991 in accordance with the provisions of the present Statute."[39] The statute provided that individuals, including heads of states, would be held criminally responsible for the commission of acts over which the tribunal had jurisdiction.[40] The tribunal's general jurisdiction covered grave breaches of the Geneva Conventions of 1949,[41] violations of the laws or customs of war,[42] genocide,[43] and crimes against humanity.[44] The court was to exercise concurrent jurisdiction with domestic courts,[45] although, it enjoyed supremacy over the latter.[46] The statute provided that an independent prosecutor "be responsible for the investigation and prosecution of persons responsible for serious violations of international humanitarian law."[47] Under the statute, the prosecutor was to act independently and conduct his or her duties as a separate organ of the tribunal. The independence of the prosecution was further reinforced by the affirmation that "he or she shall not seek or receive instructions from any Government or from any other source."[48] However, the prosecutor

[39] Article 1 of the Statute of the International Tribunal, annexed to Report of the Secretary-General pursuant to paragraph 2 of Security Council Resolution 808 (1993).

[40] Ibid., Article 7. Article 7(1) states, "A person who planned, instigated, ordered, committed or otherwise aided and abetted in the planning, preparation or execution of a crime referred to in articles 2 to 5 of the present Statute, shall be individually responsible for the crime." Heads of states were not immune to prosecution by the tribunal in accordance with Article 7(2): "The official position of any accused person, whether as Head of State or Government or as a responsible Government official, shall not relieve such person of criminal responsibility nor mitigate punishment."

[41] Ibid., Article 2.

[42] Ibid., Article 3.

[43] Ibid., Article 4.

[44] Ibid., Article 5.

[45] Ibid., Article 9(1): "The International Tribunal and national courts shall have concurrent jurisdiction to prosecute persons for serious violations of international humanitarian law committed in the territory of the former Yugoslavia since 1 January 1991."

[46] Ibid., Article 9(2): "The International Tribunal shall have primacy over national courts. At any stage of the procedure, the International Tribunal may formally request national courts to defer to the competence of the International Tribunal in accordance with the present Statute and the Rules of Procedure and Evidence of the International Tribunal."

[47] Ibid., Article 16(1).

[48] Ibid., Article 16(2).

was to be appointed by the Security Council,[49] which was likely to affect the independence of the office.

Nevertheless, the statute granted the prosecutor broad authority, vesting the position with the power to initiate investigations and decide "whether there is sufficient basis to proceed."[50] The prosecutor's power under the statute also included questioning suspects, victims and witnesses, collecting "evidence and . . . conduct[ing] on-site investigations."[51] He or she could proceed further, preparing "an indictment containing a concise statement of the facts and the crime or crimes with which the accused is charged under the Statute."[52] However, the statute required the prosecutor to submit the indictment to the trial chamber for review, with further action subject to the chamber's approval of the indictment.[53]

The statute provided that the tribunal's decisions on convictions were to be upheld by the majority of the trial chamber judges.[54] Although the tribunal was international, the statute required that the penalties to be imposed on the criminals be determined based on the tribunal's "recourse to the general practice regarding prison sentences in the courts of the former Yugoslavia."[55] However, the possibility that pardons might be granted to the convicted[56] appeared to be a paramount defect in the statute.

---

[49] Ibid., Article 16(3): "The Prosecutor shall be appointed by the Security Council on nomination by the Secretary-General. He or she shall be of high moral character and possess the highest level of competence and experience in the conduct of investigations and prosecutions of criminal cases."

[50] Ibid., Article 18(1): "The Prosecutor shall initiate investigations ex-officio or on the basis of information obtained from any source, particularly from Governments, United Nations organs, intergovernmental and non-governmental organizations. The Prosecutor shall assess the information received or obtained and decide whether there is sufficient basis to proceed."

[51] Ibid., Article 18(2).

[52] Ibid., Article 18(4).

[53] Ibid., Article 19(1).

[54] Ibid., Article 23(2).

[55] Ibid., Article 24(1).

[56] Ibid., Article 28:

> If, pursuant to the applicable law of the State in which the convicted person is imprisoned, he or she is eligible for pardon or commutation of sentence, the State concerned shall notify the International Tribunal accordingly. The President of the International Tribunal, in consultation with the judges, shall decide the matter on the basis of the interests of justice and the general principles of law.

It should be noted that the creation of the tribunal was a remarkable step forward in the context of improving international criminal jurisdiction. It, at least partially, ended the tradition of impunity for war crimes and other serious violations of established and well-respected international legal norms, and it ascertained and fortified the end of that impunity to heads of states, who had long been granted privileges under diplomatic customs and international legal rules, including not being prosecuted. The tribunal's establishment ensured that "the question is no longer whether leaders should be held accountable, but rather how can they be called to account."[57] However, perhaps the most important and noteworthy achievement of the tribunal was the indictment of a head of state, Slobodan Milosevic, by the prosecutor, on the grounds that he had committed crimes that warranted international criminal prosecution while he was in power.

Notwithstanding its achievements, the tribunal was impaired by substantial deficiencies that could be referred to in the context of how political considerations once again prevailed and negatively affected the process. The first was its subordination to the UN Security Council, where the major powers are entitled to proceed with their own agendas and in accordance with their own interests and considerations. As a general rule, an international criminal tribunal, as a judicial organ, has to be independent of political influence and other external pressures.

In theory, the independence of the Yugoslavia tribunal was ensured by the appointment of an independent prosecutor. The tribunal's statute openly stated that the prosecutor should have the power to proceed independent of political pressure. Although a number of the statute's articles affirmed the prosecutor's, the position's appointment by the UN Security Council could have been questioned with regard to the tribunal's fairness.

The tribunal's financial independence from the Security Council was considered additional support for the argument that it was not controlled by the Council. Article 32 of the statute states that "the expenses of the International Tribunal shall be borne by the regular budget of the United Nations in accordance with Article 17 of the Charter of the

[57] "Bringing Justice to the Former Yugoslavia the Tribunal's Core Achievements," http://www.un.org/icty/cases-e/factsheets/achieve-e.htm.

United Nations."[58] However, although this provision at first glance appears to have ensured the tribunal's independence, the matter was in fact open to controversy. Prof. Bassiouni contends that the case should have been just the opposite:

> If the Security Council had funded the Tribunal through its peacekeeping budget, the Tribunal would not have needed to go through the various stages of the General Assembly's budget procedures. At that time the General Assembly's budget was severely reduced, and as a result the Tribunal has been inadequately funded since its inception. The exercise of administrative and financial control over the Tribunal by U.N. headquarters' personnel subordinates important decisions concerning personnel, travel, and witness protection to New York. These arrangements hamper, delay, and frustrate the work of the Tribunal, particularly the investigatory and prosecutorial efforts.[59]

What is more important is that the Tribunal remained inactive for one year after its establishment because no prosecutor was appointed until 1995. The Security Council's engagement was already prolonged, considering that the atrocities had begun in 1991 and the Council's consideration of the matter began in 1993. Furthermore, neither the government of Serbia and Montenegro nor the Bosnian Serb de facto government recognized the tribunal's competence. Of course, they did not cooperate with the investigations and indictments of the accused.[60] However, despite their uncooperative attitudes, no effective measures were taken against the two governments for the purpose of ensuring the apprehension of the war criminals. As a result of this reluctance, "once again the pursuit of a political settlement prevail[ed] over justice."[61]

However, despite the politicized process in which the tribunal for war crimes committed in the former Yugoslavia was established, it later

[58] Article 32 of the Statute of the International Criminal Tribunal for Former Yugoslavia.

[59] Bassiouni, "From Versailles to Rwanda in Seventy-Five Years: The Need to Establish a Permanent International Criminal Court," p. 44.

[60] Ibid., p. 45.

[61] Ibid.

benefited the establishment of the International Criminal Tribunal for Rwanda (ICTR).[62] The lessons learned from the experience helped the International Criminal Tribunal for the Former Yugoslavia (ICTY) serve as a precedent for the ICTR.[63] In other words, the Rwanda tribunal was established by the UN Security Council "on the strength" of the ICTY experience.[64] The influence of this strength was so substantial that, as

[62] For details and comprehensive analyses of the ICTR, see, among others, the following: Howard Adelman and Astri Suhrke, *The Path of a Genocide: The Rwanda Crisis from Uganda to Zaire* (New Brunswick, NJ: Transaction Publishers, 1999); Payam Akhavan, "Beyond Impunity: Can International Criminal Justice Prevent Future Atrocities?" *American Journal of International Law*, Vol. 95, Issue 1, 2001, pp. 7–31; Amnesty International, *Rwanda: The Hidden Violence: "Disappearances" and Killings Continue* (New York: Amnesty International, 1998); Amnesty International, *Rwanda: Ending the Silence* (New York: Amnesty International, 1997); Amnesty International, *Rwanda: Crying Out for Justice* (New York: Amnesty International, 1995); Louise Arbour, "History and Future of the International Criminal Tribunals for the Former Yugoslavia and Rwanda," *American University International Law Review*, Vol. 13, Issue 6, 1998, pp. 1495–1508; Michael Barnett, *Eyewitness to a Genocide: The United Nations and Rwanda* (New York: Cornell University Press, 2002); Stuart Beresford, "In Pursuit of International Justice: The First Four-Year Term of the International Criminal Tribunal for Rwanda," *Tulsa Journal of Comparative & International Law*, Vol. 8, Issue 1, 2000, pp. 99–132; Evelyn Bradley, "In Search for Justice: A Truth and Reconciliation Commission for Rwanda," *Journal of International Law and Practice*, Vol. 7, Issue 2, 1998, pp. 129–158; Christina M. Carroll, "An Assessment of the Role and Effectiveness of the International Criminal Tribunal for Rwanda and the Rwandan National Justice System in Dealing with the Mass Atrocities of 1994," *Boston University International Law Journal*, Vol. 18, Issue 2, 2000, pp. 163–200; Rocco P. Cervoni, "Beating Plowshares Into Swords: Reconciling the Sovereign Right to Self-determination with Individual Human Rights Through an International Criminal Court: The Lessons of the Former Yugoslavia and Rwanda as a Frontispiece," *St. John's Journal of Legal Commentary*, Vol. 12, Issue 2, 1997, pp. 477–534; Erin Daly, "Between Punitive and Reconstructive Justice: The Gacaca Courts in Rwanda," *New York University Journal of International Law and Politics*, Vol. 34, Issue 2, 2002, pp. 355–396; Adama Dieng, "International Criminal Justice: From Paper to Practice: A Contribution from the International Criminal Tribunal for Rwanda to the Establishment of the International Criminal Court," *Fordham International Law Journal*, Vol. 25, Issue 3, 2002, pp. 688–707.

[63] Legal Advisor to the International Criminal Tribunals for Former Yugoslavia and Rwanda Payam Akhavan stated that "the Rwanda Tribunal was established because of the precedential effect of the Yugoslav Tribunal." Payam Akhavan, "The International Criminal Tribunal for Rwanda: The Politics and Pragmatics of Punishment," *American Journal of International Law*, Vol. 90, Issue 3, 1996, p. 501.

[64] Bassiouni, "Establishing an International Criminal Court: Historical Survey," p. 57. Some scholars contend that the UN Security Council's swifter action in the case of Rwanda could be attributed to the success of ICTY. For instance, MacPherson argues that "the Security Council felt compelled to do the same the following year when faced with ever-greater ethnic violence and death in Rwanda," and subsequently "established a tribunal to deal with that situation." MacPherson, "Building an International Criminal Court for the 21st Century," p. 14.

one observer succinctly observed, "it is questionable whether the Rwanda Tribunal would have been established without the Yugoslav precedent."[65] When the atrocities in Rwanda began, the international community already had the experience of the ICTY to address the new situation. Therefore, with this experience at hand, it was easier and swifter for the international institutions with the primary responsibility for maintaining international peace and security to take effective actions regarding the genocidal acts and other atrocities that were being committed in Rwanda.

The tension and rift that had long been influential between the major tribes of Rwanda[66] became a horrifying conflict shortly after the murder of the Rwandan President in an aircraft crash, heralding one of the worst genocidal campaigns of the century.[67] The UN Security Council's response was relatively swift considering that the first serious step was taken on May 17, 1994, roughly a month later than the aircraft crash of April 1994.[68] With Resolution 918 (1994), the UN Security Council decided that "all States shall prevent the sale or supply to Rwanda by their national or from their territories or using their flag vessels or aircraft of arms and related material of all types, including weapons and ammunition, military vehicles and equipment, paramilitary police equipment and spare parts."[69]

---

[65] Shraga and Zacklin, "The International Criminal Tribunal for Rwanda," *European Journal of International Law,* Vol. Issue p.

[66] It is asserted that the conflict between the Hutus and the Tutsis was an unavoidable part of daily life in Rwanda ever since the Tutsi royal family was overthrown in 1959. Massive atrocities were committed in 1959, 1963, 1966, and 1973, and nearly annually beginning in 1990. Ibid., p.

[67] For a brief historical survey of the tension between the tribes and ethnic groups as well as the campaign of genocide, see, for example, the following: Alexandra A. Miller, "From the International Criminal Tribunal for Rwanda to the International Criminal Court: Expanding the Definition of Genocide To Include Rape," *Pennsylvania State Law Review,* Vol. 108, Issue 1, 2003, pp. 350–357 and Beresford, "In Pursuit of International Justice: The First Four-Year Term of the International Criminal Tribunal for Rwanda," pp. 100–104.

[68] In fact, the President of the Security Council condemned all beaches of international humanitarian law in Rwanda on April 30, 1994, three weeks later than the beginning of the atrocities. Statement by the President of the UN Security Council, UN Doc. S/PRST/1994/21, April 30, 1994.

[69] UN Security Council Resolution 918 (1994), UN Doc. S/RES/918, May 17, 1994, at paragraph 13.

Subsequently, the Secretary-General prepared a comprehensive report on the situation in Rwanda in which he observed that "the magnitude of the human calamity that has engulfed Rwanda might be unimaginable but for its having transpired. On the basis of evidence that has emerged, there can be little doubt that it constitutes genocide, since there have been large-scale killings of communities and families belonging to a particular group."[70] The commission of the crime of genocide was also admitted and referred to as a matter of concern by Security Council Resolution 925 (1994).[71]

This was followed by Resolution 935 (1994), in which the Council requested that the Secretary-General establish an impartial commission to examine and analyze the information it received or obtained through its own investigations, "with a view to providing the Secretary-General with its conclusions on the evidence of grave violations of international humanitarian law committed in the territory of Rwanda, including the evidence of possible acts of genocide."[72] The commission's mandate was further expanded by the Secretary-General to study the possibility of an international criminal panel to be vested with the authority to prosecute the accused.[73]

On October 4, 1994, the Commission of Experts submitted an interim report to the Secretary-General[74] that concluded that the Rwandan conflict was non-international. It further reported that based on the evidence and information it had collected, both parties to the conflict had seriously violated the rules and norms set by various instruments of international humanitarian law.[75] The commission also found evidence that Hutus had carried out genocidal acts against the Tutsi minority,[76] and suggested that those who were responsible for the crimes

[70] Report of the Secretary-General on the Situation in Rwanda, UN Doc. S/1994/640 (1994), para. 36.

[71] UN Security Council Resolution, 925 (1994), UN Doc. S/RES/925 (1994), June 8, 1994.

[72] UN Security Council Res. 935, U.N. SCOR, 49th Sess., U.N. Doc. S/RES/935 (1994).

[73] Report of the Secretary-General on the Establishment of the Commission of Experts pursuant to paragraph 1 of Security Council Resolution 935 (1994), UN Doc. S/1994/879 (1994).

[74] Preliminary Report of the Independent Commission of Experts, U.N. Doc. S/1994/1125 (1994).

[75] Ibid.

[76] Ibid.

committed during the course of conflict "be brought to justice before an independent and impartial international criminal tribunal."[77]

The Secretary-General endorsed the recommendation to bring the perpetrators before an international tribunal, and this endorsement was submitted to the Security Council in a report on October 6, 1994.[78] The Commission of Experts also submitted its final report to the Secretary-General on November 29, 1994,[79] after the tribunal had been established.

Although the two reports constituted the legal grounds for the Tribunal that was established to address the international crimes being committed in Rwanda, and, in particular, the first had resulted in establishing the Tribunal itself, the Commission of Experts was criticized as a nearly complete failure. Unlike the commission appointed through ICTY, this commission was given a limited mandate, an indication of the UN's unwillingness to substantiate the commission of large-scale atrocities. Moreover, the commission was unable to conduct detailed investigations because it only had four months for the work, "which was not long enough for the Commission to effectively fulfill its investigatory mandate." Furthermore, it had no financial or technical means to pursue its mandate. As a result, "the three-man Commission spent a total of one week in the field, and conducted no investigations. Its report was patterned on the Final Report of the Commission of Experts for the Former Yugoslavia, but necessarily lacked the thoroughness of the latter. The Rwanda Commission Report was based on reports made by other bodies, and other media and published reports."[80] The practical consequence was thus that the International Criminal Tribunal for Rwanda had little information on or evidence to substantiate the

---

[77] Ibid.

[78] Progress Report of the Secretary-General on the United Nations Assistance Mission for Rwanda, U.N. Doc. S/1994/1133 (1994). Keeping in mind the commission's preference regarding the international tribunal, the Secretary-General's report did not contain any specific recommendation but left the matter to the Security Council's discretion.

[79] Final Report of the Independent Commission of Experts established in accordance with Security Council Resolution 935 (1994), U.N. Doc. S/1994/1405 (1994).

[80] Bassiouni, "From Versailles to Rwanda in Seventy-Five Years: The Need to Establish a Permanent International Criminal Court," p. 46.

charges directed against the individuals who were allegedly responsible for committing the various international crimes.

Following the commission's report, the UN Security Council adopted Resolution 955 (1994) on November 8, 1994, by which it established an international tribunal for the purpose of prosecuting the international crimes being perpetrated in Rwanda.[81] Having determined that the situation in Rwanda "continue[d] to constitute a threat to international peace and security," and believing that "the establishment of an international tribunal for the prosecution of persons responsible for genocide and the other above-mentioned violations of international humanitarian law [would] contribute to ensuring that such violations [were] halted and effectively redressed," the Council decided "to establish an international tribunal for the sole purpose of prosecuting persons responsible for genocide and other serious violations of international humanitarian law committed in the territory of Rwanda and Rwandan citizens responsible for genocide and other such violations committed in the territory of neighbouring States, between 1 January 1994 and 31 December 1994."[82] With this resolution, the Council also required states to cooperate on this matter[83] and called upon all other international actors, including intergovernmental and nongovernmental organizations, to make contributions to facilitate the tribunal's work.[84] The tribunal's statute was appendixed to the text of the resolution.

---

[81] S.C. Res. 955, U.N. SCOR, 49th Sess., U.N. Doc. S/RES/955 (1994).

[82] Ibid.

[83] The relevant provision reads as follows: the UN Security Council decided that

> all States shall cooperate fully with the International Tribunal and its organs in accordance with the present resolution and the Statute of the International Tribunal and that consequently all States shall take any measures necessary under their domestic law to implement the provisions of the present resolution and the Statute, including the obligation of States to comply with requests for assistance.

Ibid., paragraph 2.

[84] The relevant provision is as follows: the Council urged "States and intergovernmental and non-governmental organizations to contribute funds, equipment and services to the International Tribunal, including the offer of expert personnel." Ibid., paragraph 3.

The statute provided that the tribunal would have temporal jurisdiction over any pertinent prosecutable crimes,[85] and the tribunal's jurisdiction authorized it to prosecute crimes of genocide[86] and crimes against humanity.[87] Because the conflict in Rwanda was characterized as non-international, the statute included no provision regarding violations of the laws and customs of war or the rules and norms of the 1949 Geneva Conventions as they applied to international conflicts.[88] However, the statute provided that violations of the common articles of the 1949 Geneva Conventions and the 1977 Additional Protocol II were to be prosecuted.[89]

Under the statute, individuals responsible for committing the crimes referred to in it were to be criminally liable.[90] The tribunal's jurisdiction applied to Rwandan citizens only and was only exercisable within the territory of Rwanda.[91] As was the case with the ICTY, the ICTR also provided for concurrent jurisdiction with domestic courts.[92] The remaining articles also greatly resemble the corresponding articles from the ICTY statute.

Some referred to the ICTR as an example of success. For example, Stuart Beresford, Associate Legal Officer for the ICTY, argued that

---

[85] Statute of the International Criminal Tribunal for the Prosecution of Persons Responsible for Genocide and Other Serious Violations of International Humanitarian Law Committed in the Territory of Rwanda and Rwandan Citizens Responsible for Genocide and Other Such Violations Committed in the Territory of Neighbouring States, between January 1, 1994 and December 31, 1994, annexed to S.C. Res. 955 (1994). Article 1:

> The International Tribunal for Rwanda shall have the power to prosecute persons responsible for serious violations of international humanitarian law committed in the territory of Rwanda and Rwandan citizens responsible for such violations committed in the territory of neighbouring States, between 1 January 1994 and 31 December 1994, in accordance with the provisions of the present Statute.

[86] Ibid., Article 2.

[87] Ibid., Article 3.

[88] Bassiouni, "Establishing an International Criminal Court: Historical Survey," p. 47.

[89] Ibid., Article 4.

[90] Ibid., Article 6.

[91] Ibid., Article 7.

[92] Ibid., Article 8.

"although it has essentially operated in the shadow of the Yugoslavia Tribunal since its inception, the achievements the Tribunal has made in the pursuit of international justice has enabled it to take its own place in the chronicles of the development of international humanitarian law." He attributes this success to the support provided by the international community to the tribunal.[93]

However, the dissenting opinions consider a number of points. First, the tribunal was not a true success because it was, in fact, the government of Rwanda that had demanded its establishment,[94] and as the negotiations over the terms of the tribunal proceeded, the disparities between the government's expectations and the Council's intentions became apparent. The Rwandan government favored an institution with broadly defined jurisdiction, whereas the Council intended a very narrow scope in terms of both the prosecutable crimes and the territory where the tribunal would be able to exercise its jurisdiction in addition to the scope of the penalties that could be imposed upon the criminals. For example, the Rwandan government wanted to include the death penalty in the possible penalties, but the Council was opposed.[95]

---

[93] Beresford, "In Pursuit of International Justice: The First Four-Year Term of the International Criminal Tribunal for Rwanda," p. 132.

[94] Statement Dated 28 September 1994 on the Question of Refugees and Security in Rwanda, U. N. SCOR, 49th Sess., U.N. Doc. S/1994/1115 (1994), cited in Madeline H. Morris, "The Trials of Concurrent Jurisdiction: The Case of Rwanda," *Duke Journal of Comparative and International Law,* Vol. 7, Issue 2, 1997, p. 353.

[95] Bassiouni, "From Versailles to Rwanda in Seventy-Five Years: The Need to Establish a Permanent International Criminal Court," p. 48.

# Review and Analysis

One could infer many conclusions from the evolution of international criminal law as surveyed earlier. However, the following are highlights and should not be considered representative or reflective of the full picture:

1. The study of the history of international criminal law clearly demonstrates that all components of the international community, including nation-states, always showed interest in establishing strong, concrete institutions and mechanisms for the general purpose of ensuring the prosecution and punishment of criminals who had committed what were deemed to be crimes under international law and the particular purpose of creating a permanent international penal tribunal with universal jurisdiction to address preventing the commission of the aforementioned types of crimes or, in the case of their commission, punishing the perpetrators.

   Moreover, this interest was not peculiar to the twentieth century, when the commission of such international crimes as genocide, crimes against humanity, and war crimes was widespread and more



C. Çakmak, *A Brief History of International Criminal Law and International Criminal Court*,
DOI 10.1057/978-1-137-56736-9_6

influential and damaging than ever. In fact, the desire for an overarching body of enforcement is nearly as old as humanity itself, although the evidence available at hand only permits us to trace this interest to several centuries ago.

Yet, even the limited search facilities and capabilities are sufficiently indicative of the fact that the idea, and even desire, to maintain international order and achieve justice by holding responsible those individuals who commit the worst crimes and bringing them before an impartial international penal body has always existed.

2. However, it should be noted that although one could easily prove the perpetual existence of the above-mentioned interest, it is also true that the most substantial and concrete attempts to transform this interest into solid measures were made after serious global events that had affected the international community as a whole. Needless to say, the world wars are exemplary in this regard.

Although many examples could be cited as proofs for the aforementioned argument, a number are noteworthy. The Hagenbach case, referred to by some as the first international trial, is surely the first. The commission of atrocities that deeply wounded the conscious of international society led to an outcry even as early as the fifteenth century, when wars and, of course, the deaths associated with them, were seen as inevitable.

The second is the first proposal for a permanent international criminal court by Gustave Moynier. Although previously he was not in favor of such an institution, the horrifying outcome of the Franco-Prussian War changed his mind. Furthermore, although it is not possible to speculate that he would not have advanced this proposal in the absence of such a concrete reason, it is very likely that he was affected by the war.

The end of World War I (WWI) saw a much more intense and solid interest in creating an international penal institution for the purpose of prosecuting the persons responsible for committing crimes during the war. The absence of such an institution was strongly felt, and a promising enthusiasm emerged soon after the end of the war.

Similarly, World War II was preceded by serious attempts to prevent the future commission of crimes that were similar to those committed during WWI. This time, the attempts resulted in more visible and concrete outcomes such as the Nuremberg trials and the UN's adoption of the principles that were set during those trials as a guide for future reference.

3. However, the revival of the international community's interest in establishing an international criminal tribunal following the global wars was never sufficient to achieve satisfactory results. Despite the enthusiasm and numerous attempts made in this context, once the horrifying impact of the war lost its strength, the attempts and enthusiasm were immediately replaced with reluctance and ignorance.

   Moynier's proposal was never seriously taken into consideration, and over time, it has become a courageous yet unfruitful attempt that is today referred to by students of international criminal law with respect and admiration. As a consequence, it took its place in history only as the first proposal for an international criminal court.

   The attempts to prosecute, try, and punish the perpetrators of the international crimes committed during WWI also failed in that the prosecutions never took place. Although the establishment of an international tribunal was envisaged even during the war, the individuals who were responsible for the war crimes for the most part went unpunished. The excitement and determination to achieve justice that were prevalent during the ward lost their impact, and soon after the wounds caused by the war had healed, that passion was left to the slow passage of time.

   With some exceptions, the immediate aftermath of WWII witnessed nearly the same developments. While the war was still being fought, voices from Great Britain, France, and the United States stated a determination to punish the perpetrators of the crimes committed during the war. These declarations were promising in that the nations' determination indicated that this time, the perpetrators would not go unpunished. However, only a few of those perpetrators were brought before competent tribunals, and, moreover, only a few of those who were brought to justice were in fact found guilty of war crimes and other international crimes.

4. The reluctance of the international community and the lack of will to address the commission of such serious crimes as genocide and war crimes led to the reiteration of the past atrocities. It is interesting to note that although there has been substantial progress in many fields,

the situation concerning civil casualties during wars has not improved significantly. Although the international political order has over time improved markedly, it became apparent that this order could not prevent the occurrence of large-scale atrocities; genocides and killing campaigns were witnessed even as late as the 1990s.

However, this time, the primary outlets for committing atrocities were not interstate wars. Whereas previous large-scale atrocities had been committed during wartime, following the end of WWII, internal conflicts and repressive regimes were the major sources of killings and other violations.

As the cases of Chile, Cambodia, and Argentina demonstrate, repressive governments could easily be brutal to even their own subjects on the grounds of political opposition. It should be noted that the brutalities committed by these governments against their own nationals occurred despite the existence of numerous international legal documents that obliged states to protect their own subjects. In the absence of an effective enforcement mechanism, however, these instruments proved to be useless in those cases.

Exactly, the same could be said for the genocidal campaigns that were initiated nearly simultaneously in the former Yugoslavia and Rwanda. In those cases as well, the victimized groups were affected by internal conflicts.

5. Upon the examination of the evolution of international criminal law and individual criminal responsibility, the question of why there has always been reluctance to address the commission of large-scale atrocities, even in the presence of a strong desire for and interest in creating an international mechanism for this purpose, becomes relevant and even necessary. Although this might seem to be a contradiction, in fact there is a simple and clear explanation for it. States have always been more concerned about preserving their sovereignty in world politics than in engaging in such international problems as genocides and war crimes.

   As the earlier survey demonstrates, on countless occasions, states have shown that they were interested in prosecuting and punishing people who commit international crimes only to the extent that their engagement would not negatively affect their prerogatives as sovereign units.

Thus, it is evident that sovereignty has been the key to understanding states' ineptness and sometimes indifference in addressing the question of international criminal jurisdiction. In particular, the objections raised by states' representatives during the UN's deliberations against the proposals for an international legal order with universal jurisdiction over prosecuting and punishing the perpetrators of the worst crimes are noteworthy in this regard.

It is clear that states have regarded any institution with the authority to prosecute and punish individuals regardless of their nationality or the territory where they are apprehended as a threat to and intrusion on international order based on the mutual recognition of territorial sovereignty. States have been especially concerned regarding individual criminal responsibility, which was seen as individual states' domain. In other words, although states have tended to act flexibly on some matters, they wanted the question of prosecuting criminals to remain at their sole discretion.

6. However, it should also be noted that despite the states' resistance to establishing an effective system of international criminal jurisdiction on the grounds that such an attempt would substantially damage the nation-state's dominant position in world politics, numerous successes have been achieved. In other words, although states could have managed to retain their sovereign positions at least to some extent, they had to make concessions in response to the demands voiced by the large masses of the international community.

Therefore, the progress that was made over the centuries cannot be overlooked because the current, permanent international criminal court is partly the culmination of that progress. The attempts made in the late nineteenth century served as a basis for later efforts. The experience accrued during the immediate aftermath of WWI should have contributed to the idea of creating an international penal tribunal for the purpose of addressing the massacres of civilians during the war. It could be argued that in the absence of previously codified legal documents and adopted principles, such an idea could not even have been voiced. The same could be said for the developments after the end of WWII. The experiences of Nuremberg and Tokyo Trials borrowed a great deal from the past, and in this vein, one could easily find numerous references in the Nuremberg process as a whole to the previously adopted principles and documents.

Similarly, one cannot underestimate the significance of the Nuremberg trials despite their numerous deficiencies. Although they have remained forgotten for nearly five decades, they were the point of departure in addressing the genocides and other international crimes that were perpetrated in Rwanda and the former Yugoslavia.

7. However, given that nation-states have consistently demonstrated strong attachment to the notion of national sovereignty and the principle of nonintervention in the internal matters of other sovereign states when the question of a universal criminal jurisdiction has been deliberated, it is not possible to attribute the above-discussed incremental developments and partial achievements to sovereignty-based international order. Rather, the insistence and patience of civil society actors better explain international society's gains with regard to the evolution of international criminal law and individual criminal accountability.

   The involvement of private actors, ranging from outstanding individuals with no organizational attachments to internationally recognized nongovernmental organizations, in the processes of codifying the instruments of international criminal law reflect the influence of civil society on the development of a more individual-oriented order. The contributions of and input from various civil society organizations regarding all stages of treaty-making pursuant to international criminal law, including preparation, drafting, revising and codifying, are therefore what we should consider the determinative if not sole factors in creating what could be called a partially successful system of international criminal jurisdiction.

   Once more, it should be recalled that the first proposal for an international criminal court was made by an individual, Gustave Moynier of the Red Cross. The Hague Conventions of 1899 and 1907, the predecessors of modern international humanitarian law, were attended by hundreds of civil society organizations. Raphael Lemkin is today still remembered and respected for his tireless efforts to coin the term genocide and for the recognition of that crime of as punishable under international law, and many more examples could be mentioned in this regard. However, one final one might be sufficient: without Bassiouni's perseverance and the attempts he made in his individual capacity despite consistent obstruction in the forms of bureaucratic and financial obstacles created by the UN, which resulted in a vast amount of evidence that substantiated the claims that international crimes were being committed in the former Yugoslavia, it cannot be said that the ICTY would have succeeded.

8. However, notwithstanding the extensive involvement of civil society actors in the debates on universal criminal jurisdiction, their influence has proven to be limited. This is reflected in the failure to create a permanent international penal institution vested with the power to prosecute individuals who commit the worst crimes regardless of their nationality or where they were apprehended. Because of the limited influence and pressure exerted by the 'outside' actors, nation-states have for the most part been able to shape outcomes according to their own positions and agendas.

   Of course, the aforementioned argument is not intended to deny the significant contributions of civil society. However, the point that needs to be underlined is that the achieved success has often not been in proportion to civil society's levels of participation in the deliberations. They have had limited access to treaty-making processes and relatively little influence on the delegates of nation-states, and, most importantly, their recommendations have frequently been rejected, sometimes with no explanation.

   The best explanation for the limited influence described aforementioned is the uncoordinated efforts led by various civil society actors. They have often failed to agree on a commonly acceptable agenda and thus to create a joint platform for coming together to develop coordinated efforts that could have an impact on states' delegates.

9. The historical survey aforementioned demonstrates that the question of international criminal jurisdiction has been addressed using differing approaches by different actors and institutions at different stages. Although the matter was initially discussed in multilateral conferences, in the later stages, intergovernmental organizations such as the League of Nations and the UN were included in the process. Although multilateral conferences have also been used, the

UN has been the primary actor and venue in discussing and addressing the issue since its creation.

The creation of the UN facilitated developing a more comprehensive international criminal law because under the previous 'system', gathering states together had proven to be difficult. To discuss an issue that was relevant to international criminal jurisdiction, a lengthy and painstaking procedure had to be followed. Therefore, states nearly always had to be convinced, often by civil society actors. However since its creation, the UN has been the primary venue for the pertinent discussions. Over time, a pattern formed with regard to engaging in any current issue that was relevant to international criminal accountability. The general pattern is as follows:

First, the issue is taken up by the UN General Assembly, which typically appoints a special committee to further review and study the matter and then submit to the Assembly a report summarizing its work and recommendations. The Assembly then includes the Secretary-General in the process. The matter is discussed in an Assembly session where it considers the recommendations in the special committee's report. The representatives of governments recommend revisions to the proposal and then, if an agreement is reached, the proposal becomes reality.

In more serious situations that need to be urgently addressed, the Security Council typically takes the lead, acting in accordance with its mandate to maintain world peace and security. In these situations, the initiative is left nearly entirely to the Council, and such secondary actors as the special committees, the General Assembly, the Secretary-General, and even states other than those with permanent seats on the Council assume the role of assisting the Council in its work.

10. However, while UN organs that act relatively free of political considerations, such as the International Law Commission (ILC), have tended to be progressive with regard to the question of international criminal jurisdiction, others, especially the UN Security Council, have often prioritized political consequences rather than achieving justice when addressing the issue at hand. In other words, the Council's involvement in problems with a specifically international criminal law component has in general been politically motivated.

Even though the commission of genocide was evident in the cases of both Rwanda and the former Yugoslavia, the Council was evasive in approaching both situations. In both cases, political considerations appear to have been prevalent in the UN Security Council's actions. For the permanent members, the political stability in the regions where the incidents had occurred was more important than pursuing justice.

Similarly, the ILC has, in general, made proposals concerning particular aspects of international criminal law in which it set relatively advanced principles. However, when those proposals were considered in the relevant organs where the influence of national interests was evident, these proposals were either rejected or significantly altered so that their novel arrangements lost their power and likely impact.

# Part II

## Forming the International Criminal Court

# Developments Leading to the Establishment of the ICC Prior to the Rome Conference

Initial attempts to create a permanent International Criminal Court (ICC) in the 1990s were made by the International Law Commission (ILC). However, the ILC's concrete efforts and subsequent proposals were weakened by the UN General Assembly, which, rather than calling for a multilateral diplomatic conference, decided to establish an ad hoc committee that would be charged with studying the issue further. This was especially shocking and disappointing for a select group of NGOs that had been following the deliberations concerning creating an ICC. Realizing that their efforts would once again be halted, these NGOs chose a new strategy, and the idea of forming a coalition of NGOs was the outcome of this decision.[1] The NGOs' involvement in the process gave rise to the strong and decisive efforts to create a permanent court.

The idea of a permanent ICC was revived in the early 1990s. The ILC assumed the role of drafting a generally acceptable statute for a

[1] Glasius, "Expertise in the Cause of Justice: Global Civil Society Influence on the Statute for an International Court," p. 145.



C. Çakmak, *A Brief History of International Criminal Law and International Criminal Court*,
DOI 10.1057/978-1-137-56736-9_7

permanent court. In 1992, a working group that adopted the basic parameters for a draft statute was created under the auspices of the commission.[2] Both the commission and the UN General Assembly endorsed the work of the working group in 1992.[3]

The working group submitted its report, which provided a draft statute for an International Criminal tribunal, to the commission in 1993.[4] The ILC forwarded the report to the General Assembly for consideration and comment without adopting the text.[5] The 1993 draft statute was generally compatible with the approach that had been adopted in 1992, "but with a number of modifications and refinements and with much further detail."[6] The General Assembly noted the draft statute "with appreciation," and invited the Commission to continue its work "as a matter of priority." The Assembly also expressed its anticipation of a final draft at its 1994 session.[7]

In 1994, considering the comments made in the Sixth Committee and the forwarded comments and views from a number of states and other bodies, the ILC adopted a Draft Statute for an International Criminal Court. Although the draft "followed closely the proposals of the working group as reconstituted in 1994," "there were important refinements and modifications to the 1993 draft."[8] The commission also recommended that a diplomatic conference be conveyed to discuss

---

[2] Report of the International Law Commission on the Work of its Forty-fourth Session, UN GAOR, 47th Session, Supp. No. 10, UN Doc. A/47/10 (1992).

[3] UN General Assembly Resolution No. 47/33, UN GAOR, 47th Session, Supp. No. 49, paragraphs 4–6, UN Doc. A/47/49 (1992).

[4] Report of the Working Group on the Question of an International Criminal Jurisdiction, in Report of the International Law Commission on the Work of its Forty-fifth Session, UN GAOR, 48th Session, Supp. No. 10, UN Doc. A/48/10 (1993).

[5] James Crawford, "The ILC Adopts A Statute for an International Criminal Court," American Journal of International Law, Vol. 89, Issue 2, 1995, p. 405.

[6] Ibid., pp. 405–406.

[7] UN General Assembly Resolution No. 48/31, UN GAOR, 48th Session, Supp. No. 49, UN Doc. A/48/49 (1993).

[8] Crawford, "The ILC Adopts A Statute for an International Criminal Court," p. 406. It was argued that the 1994 ILC draft statute "was complex, and it was geared towards producing a court that would operate on a restrictive consent basis with strict Security Council control." Sharon A. Williams, "The Rome Statute on the International Criminal Court: From 1947–2000 and Beyond, *Osgoode Hall Law Journal*, Vol. 38, Issue 2, 2000, p. 309.

establishing an international criminal court. However, rather than calling on states to convene a diplomatic conference, the General Assembly decided to create an ad hoc committee to review the draft.[9]

That committee submitted its report in 1995.[10] Because "there was consensus that the Draft Statute needed further work,"[11] in 1995, the UN General Assembly established a committee to consider the ILC's 1994 draft statute for a permanent ICC.[12] The committee was charged with "preparing a widely acceptable consolidated text of a convention for an international criminal court as a next step towards consideration by a conference of plenipotentiaries."[13] It convened its first two sessions and submitted its reports to the General Assembly in 1996.[14]

The UN General Assembly reaffirmed the committee's mandate and decided that the committee would meet for four more sessions "in order to complete the drafting of a widely acceptable consolidated text of a convention, to be submitted to a diplomatic conference," and that "a diplomatic conference of plenipotentiaries [would] be held in 1998, with a view to finalizing and adopting a convention on the establishment of an international criminal court."[15] The Assembly also urged extensive participation in the committee "by the largest number of States so as to promote universal support for an international criminal court."[16] In its

[9] UN General Assembly Resolution No. 5046 (L), 50th Session, Official Records, Supp. No. 49, UN Doc. A/5249 (1997).

[10] Report of the Ad Hoc Committee on the Establishment of an International Criminal Court, adopted 6 Sept. 1995, U.N. GAOR, 50th Session, Supp. No. 22, UN Doc. A/50/22 (1995).

[11] Nanda, "The Establishment of a Permanent International Criminal Court: Challenges Ahead," pp. 415–416.

[12] Report of the International Law Commission, U.N. GAOR, 49th Session, Supp. No. 10, U.N. Doc. A/49/10 (1994).

[13] UN GAOR 50/46, 50th Session, UN Doc. A/RES/50/46 (1995).

[14] Report of the Preparatory Committee on the Establishment of an International Criminal Court, adopted September 13, 1996, UN GAOR, 51st Session, Supp. No. 22, UN Doc. A/51/22, Vol. I (1996); Report of the Preparatory Committee on the Establishment of an International Criminal Court, adopted September 13, 1996, UN GAOR, 51st Session, Supp. No. 22A, UN Doc. A/51/22, Vol. II (1996).

[15] UN General Assembly Resolution on the Establishment of an International Criminal Court, UN Doc. A/51/627, December 17, 1996.

[16] The UN General Assembly Resolution No. 51/207, UN GAOR, 51st Session, Supp. No. 49, UN Doc. A/51/49 (1996).

Resolution 52/160, the General Assembly further requested that the Secretary-General "prepare the text of the draft rules of procedure of the Conference, to be submitted to the Preparatory Committee for its consideration and for recommendations to the Conference."[17]

Subsequently, four more PrepComI sessions were held.[18] At the third session, the committee chose to continue its discussions in two informal working groups that were open to all states: a working group that focused on the definitions of crimes and a working group for the general principles of criminal law and penalties.[19] At its last session, the PrepComI agreed to conduct its work on the following subjects: procedural matters, composition and administration of the court, establishing the court and its relationship with the United Nations, applicable law, *ne bis in idem*, jurisdictional issues, and enforcement.[20] At its 57th meeting, the committee adopted the reports submitted by the working groups,[21] and on April 3, 1998, the committee adopted the text of a draft statute on establishing an international criminal court[22] and the draft final act.[23] Pursuant to UN General Assembly Resolution 52/160, the committee also adopted the draft rules of conference procedure at its 61st meeting on April 3, 1998.[24] In addition, it also "took note of the draft organization of work prepared by the Secretariat and decided to transmit it to the Conference."[25]

---

[17] Establishment of an International Criminal Court, The UN General Assembly Resolution No. 52/160, UN GAOR 52nd Session, U.N. Doc. A/RES/52/160, adopted December 15, 1997.

[18] The PrepComI met February11–21, August 4–15 and December 1–12, 1997, and from March 16 to April 3, 1998.

[19] Hall, "The Third and Fourth Sessions of the UN Preparatory Committee on the Establishment of an International Criminal Court," p. 126.

[20] Report of the Preparatory Committee on the Establishment of an International Criminal Court, U.N. Doc. A/CONF.183/2, April 14, 1998.

[21] Ibid.

[22] Report of the Preparatory Committee on the Establishment of an International Criminal Court, U.N. Doc. A/CONF. 183/2/Add. 1, April 14, 1998, pp. 2–168.

[23] Ibid., pp. 168ff.

[24] Report of the Preparatory Committee on the Establishment of an International Criminal Court, U.N. Doc. A/CONF.183/2, April 14, 1998.

[25] Ibid., paragraph 14.

At the same meeting, the committee agreed to submit to the conference the draft statute for the International Criminal Court, the Draft Final Act of the United Nations Diplomatic Conference of Plenipotentiaries on the Establishment of an International Criminal Court, the draft rules of procedure for the United Nations Diplomatic Conference of Plenipotentiaries on the Establishment of an International Criminal Court, and the draft organization of work of the United Nations Diplomatic Conference of Plenipotentiaries on the Establishment of an International Criminal Court.[26]

The preparatory committee completed its official business on April 14, 1998. As mandated by the UN General Assembly, the committee was able to produce a text to be discussed at the upcoming conference, and thus in that respect, it was a success. This success notwithstanding, many contentious issues still needed to be addressed effectively. The draft statute, the most important document the committee forwarded to the conference, contained 116 articles with approximately 1,700 brackets, which indicated areas of contention and disagreement.[27] From another perspective, it could be asserted that the PrepComI sessions were not particularly successful in the sense that instead of a consolidated text, it "produced a report compiling various proposals, so that when delegates arrived in Rome, virtually every major issue was open for debate."[28]

The ILC produced a draft statute for further deliberation. This draft was extensively discussed in reports published by expert NGOs. Although numerous works fell under this category, only some of the prominent ones are referred to here. One of the fundamental reasons for the abundance of these works was that the idea of creating an ICC had become concrete because the ILC had adopted a draft statute. As such, there was a clear framework for discussion whose boundaries had been determined by that statute. Another reason is that the expert NGOs had allowed them to

---

[26] Ibid., paragraph 15.

[27] Van der Vyver, "Civil Society and the International Criminal Court," p. 425.

[28] David Davenport, "The New Diplomacy," *Policy Review,* Issue 116, 2002–2003, p. 24.

create substantial documents. Among the prominent documents produced in this period, the first is Amnesty International's (AI's) position paper regarding a permanent ICC, which was released in October 1994.[29]

The report openly acknowledges the positive aspects of the statute; that is, it provides that the court will have jurisdiction over serious crimes; states will have to submit to the court's jurisdiction for the crime of genocide; the statute excludes the death penalty and so on. However, despite those aspects, the report contended that the draft statute proposed by the court far exceeded expectations and that substantial revisions should be made to the statute to achieve a fair and effective ICC.[30]

The report suggests that the court should have jurisdiction over a broad range of crimes whose clear definitions should be provided by the statute. States should clearly state that they will acknowledge the court's jurisdiction regarding the core crimes. Although the report recognizes a possible role for the Security Council in relation to the court's exercising its jurisdiction, it demands that this role be limited to the Council's obligations under Chapter VII of the UN Charter. The report also urges ensuring the prosecutor's independence and ensuring that the prosecutor is able to independently proceed with investigating or prosecuting the crimes under the court's jurisdiction.[31]

The Third Position[32] Paper of the International Commission of Jurists (ICJ) on the ICC that was released in August 1995[33] is also

[29] Amnesty International, *Establishing A Just, Fair and Effective International Criminal Court* (Amnesty International: AI Index: IOR 40/05/94, 1994). A slightly revised and updated version of this report was later published in 1995: *Time for a Permanent International Criminal Court* (Amnesty International: AI Index: IOR 40/04/95, 1995).

[30] Ibid., p. 4.

[31] Ibid., pp. 5–8.

[32] This is the fourth document produced by the ICJ on the ICC. The first three are "Towards Universal Justice," June 1993, Christian Tomuschat, "A System of International Criminal Prosecution is Taking Shape,"

*Review of the International Commission of Jurists,* Vol. 50, 1993, pp. 56–70, and "ICJ Campaign for the Establishment of the International Criminal Court", published in February 1995.

[33] International Commission of Jurists, "The Third ICJ Position Paper on the International Criminal Court," August 1995.

one of the earlier documents to refer to NGO demands that were pertinent to the ICC. In this fairly long and detailed 83-page report, the ICJ stresses that the initial steps taken by the ad hoc committee appointed by the UN General Assembly to help create an ICC were positive and constructive. However, despite this generally positive view, the ICJ provided detailed comments and suggestions that were relevant to various aspects of the Court as proposed by the draft statute. Although the ICJ agreed with the ad hoc committee's work, and the provisions of the draft statute on most issues, for a number of subjects, it stated its objections and suggested alternatives. For example, the ICJ argued that requiring a high number of ratifications for the court to be entered into force would unnecessarily delay its operation.[34]

The report clearly states that ICJ strongly favored a permanent institution; however, it supports that the Court should meet only when necessary.[35] In relation to crimes that were prosecutable by the court, ICJ believed that it was essential to clearly define the crimes that would under the proposed court's jurisdiction.[36] In particular, it argued that the sub-crimes that would be cited as crimes against humanity needed to be clearly stated.[37] However, it also argued in the report that the crime of aggression should not be included in the crimes that would be covered by the statute that established a permanent ICC because of the draft statute's suggestion regarding the determination of the act of aggression. The draft provided that this task was to be performed by the Security Council, but the ICJ opposed this suggestion on the grounds that it would negatively affect the court's functions.[38]

The report also supported the complementarity principle that was contained in the Revised Draft Statute. That is, the ICJ favored the primacy of national courts in prosecuting the crimes under the ICC's jurisdiction.[39] Despite this unusual stance—given that most NGOs, in

[34] Ibid., p. 5.
[35] Ibid., p. 8.
[36] Ibid., p. 17.
[37] Ibid., p. 20.
[38] Ibid., p. 18.
[39] Ibid., p. 28.

strong contrast to this position, consistently expressed their preference for the court's primacy over national jurisdictions—the ICJ clearly advocated that the proposed court should have inherent jurisdiction over all crimes covered by the statute.[40] However, the report once again slightly contrasted with the overall stance of civil society concerning the "opt-out" regime, recognizing states' rights to express reservations. The ICJ argued that allowing such reservations would be the better approach.[41]

However, the ICJ did draw attention to the limited scope of the complaint mechanism and argued that it should be expanded so that individuals and NGOs could lodge complaints with the court.[42] It also suggested alterations to the draft statutes provisions that limited the Court's ability to exercise its jurisdiction. The ICJ argued that states should be able to submit complaints without conditions concerning matters they may have consented to.[43] In a similar vein, the ICJ also objected to the draft statute's emphatic reference to the UN Security Council, especially regarding the crime of aggression.[44] With regard to the applicable penalties, the report criticized the revised statute for its failure to provide clarity on the sentences to be imposed by the court. The ICJ stressed that the penalties should be clearly defined and that the Court should have sole discretion in determining the sentences.[45]

A brief review of the ICJ report shows that it adopted a realistic approach. Although it contained some comments that were inconsistent with the general stance of the other NGOs, the court that was envisioned in this report was not inferior. Moreover, it should also be noted that the final statute adopted at the end of the Rome Conference greatly resembles the one advocated in the ICJ report, indicating that the report was prepared realistically and that the ICJ's experience

[40] Ibid., pp. 31–32.
[41] Ibid., p. 34.
[42] Ibid., p. 37.
[43] Ibid., p. 39.
[44] Ibid., p. 43.
[45] Ibid., p. 61.

regarding the ICC was substantial. Overall, the report was coherent, realistic, and balanced.

Another major position paper that reflected the views of the NGO sector was released by the Lawyers Committee for Human Rights (LCHR) in August 1996.[46] Overall, the paper states that the committee supported limiting the scope of the court's jurisdiction to a set of core crimes. Stressing that the court had to be independent if it were to be credible, the LCHR believed that the court should have inherent jurisdiction over all crimes contained in the statute. The committee also argued that both the prosecutor and individuals should be allowed to lodge complaints before the court. Lastly, although it raised no objections to the competence of any national legal systems in addressing the core crimes under the Court's jurisdiction, the committee urged that the determination of whether the national authorities could or could not address a particular issue concerning the commission of the relevant crimes should come from the Court itself.[47]

A joint report prepared by the Committee on International Law and the Committee on International Human Rights of the Association of the Bar of the City of New York[48] also provided useful insight on the proposed ICC. Although it welcomed the progress that had been made in relation to creating the ICC, the report refers to certain deficiencies in the draft statute. For example, it was argued in the report that the draft did not state how the court would be financed.[49]

The report also offered recommendations for possible consideration during the creation of the ICC. According to the report, the court's initial subject matter should be limited to genocide, war crimes, and crimes against humanity; it also objected to the states' consent approach

---

[46] *Establishing an International Criminal Court: Major Unresolved Issues in the Draft Statute: A Position Paper* (New York: The Lawyers Committee for Human Rights, 1996).

[47] Ibid., pp. 1–35.

[48] *Report on the Proposed International Criminal Court* (New York: The Committee on International Law, and The Committee on International Human Rights of The Association of the Bar of the City of New York, 1996).

[49] Ibid., p. 30.

that was provided in the draft statute on the grounds that it could negatively affect the Court's exercising its jurisdiction and that it should therefore be replaced. The report also opined that the prosecutor should have the power to initiate an investigation or prosecution and, lastly, that the Security Council's role in relation to the court's functioning should not include the power to block its operation.[50]

In the same year, AI prepared a report that drew attention to the challenges ahead for the UN PrepComI,[51] which was scheduled to convene soon. The author of the report, Christopher Keith Hall, an AI legal advisor, noted that although the steps taken towards creating the ICC were by all means significant, historical experience had taught that the momentum could be easily lost amid objections and concerns related to preserving national sovereignty and amid strong references and attachments to national interests and noninterference in internal affairs. To this end, he noted that "the result of the last attempt nearly half a century ago by the General Assembly to establish a permanent international criminal court suggest[ed] that" the world community needed to be cautious yet determined on the issue of creating an ICC.[52]

He provided solid reasons for his warning:

> Despite the broad support for the establishment of a permanent court of some sort, many governments at the Ad Hoc Committee and the Sixth Committee advocated changes in the 1994 draft statute which would weaken the court.[53]

Referring to probable obstructions by at least some state delegates that would diminish the role and efficiency of the prospective court, Hall urged that the preparatory committee secure the prosecutor's authority to initiate independent investigations and prosecutions, the court's

---

[50] Ibid., p. 30.

[51] Christopher Keith Hall, *Challenges Ahead for the United Nations Preparatory Committee Drafting a Statute for a Permanent International Criminal Court* (AI Index: IOR 40/03/96, 1996).

[52] Ibid., p. 2.

[53] Ibid., p. 3.

authority to bring suspects before it when states could not take the necessary steps, definitions of core crimes, and fair trial guarantees.[54]

It was observed during the period between the adoption of the ILC's draft statute for an ICC in 1994 to the inauguration of the Rome Conference that at least some of the NGOs that had produced technical documents, including reports, briefs, and position papers, were organizations that focused on legal issues and that had high levels of expertise and knowledge on various aspects of international humanitarian and criminal law; the American Bar Association (ABA) was one of these. The ABA released a report in 1998 that contained detailed recommendations for the future Court.[55]

The report provided that the court's initial jurisdiction should be limited to three core crimes—genocide, war crimes, and crimes against humanity—that the Court should be able to exercise its jurisdiction over those crimes without needing any further authorization and that this jurisdiction should not negatively affect the status or role of national jurisdictions; that is, it should complement rather than replace national judicial systems.[56] However, it should also be noted that although the report urged protecting national sovereignty, it also recognized the role of the UN Security Council in issues relating to international security and further stated that "The UN Security Council, states parties to the ICC treaty, and, with appropriate safeguards, the ICC Prosecutor should be permitted to initiate proceedings."[57]

---

[54] Ibid., pp. 4–19.

[55] *ABA Resolution* (Washington, DC: American Bar Association, 1998).

[56] Ibid., p. 2.

[57] Ibid., p.3. The report also recommends "the establishment of a permanent International Criminal Court (ICC) by multilateral treaty in order to prosecute and punish individuals who commit the most serious crimes under international law," and that the US Government should continue to "play an active role in the process of negotiating and drafting a treaty establishing the ICC." P. 1.

# The Rome Conference

## The Overall Situation at the Outset of the Conference: Little Hope, Much Skepticism, Many Challenges

The decision, made at the end of the process by which an ad hoc committee and six preparatory committee meetings had been held, to convene a multilateral conference to discuss the issue of creating an International Criminal Court (ICC) with a permanent seat and inherent power to address the most egregious crimes was surely a huge success. Yet, at the outset of the conference, a number of unresolved issues still caused a great deal of skepticism over the prospect of the court as envisioned by the civil society actors.

The first major challenge was the ambiguous and contentious text that to be discussed at the conference. The PrepComI sessions were able to achieve tremendous progress over the draft statute that had been originally proposed by the International Law Commission (ILC). However, it was not a package deal, and it contained many controversial articles. The text at hand before the conference was inaugurated was 173 pages long, with 116 articles, and approximately 1,300 brackets "for optional



C. Çakmak, *A Brief History of International Criminal Law and International Criminal Court*,
DOI 10.1057/978-1-137-56736-9_8

provisions and word choices," a fact that indicates the difficulty that lay ahead not only for those who were involved in the process for the first time but also for those who had participated in the ad hoc and PrepComI sessions and were familiar with the subject.[1] For this reason, as the President of the Conference—Philippe Kirsch—and John T. Holmes noted at the beginning of the conference, "the task awaiting the negotiators was daunting" and that "within the time available, the conference could not have possibly resolved the outstanding issues systematically."[2] Therefore, virtually all that could be said immediately before the inauguration of the conference was that it was easy "to be intimidated by the range and scope of the disagreements."[3]

The most visibly contentious issues in the proposed text to be negotiated at the Rome Conference included "the question of whether the Court can apply the death penalty; on whether the Security Council has pre-eminent authority over the Court or not; and on how much jurisdiction the ICC prosecutor has to initiate investigations."[4] In addition to these relatively secondary issues, it was even still unclear that the "entire areas of criminal activity may or may not appear before the Court."[5] The contentious issues also included the three specific categories of crimes—crimes committed against UN personnel, terrorism, and drug trafficking were all bracketed and are likely to be dropped from the negotiations at the Rome Conference.[6] Given the large number of

[1] M. Cherif Bassiouni, "Negotiating the Treaty of Rome on the Establishment of an International Criminal Court," *Cornell International Law Journal*, Vol. 43, Issue 2, 1999, p. 446.

[2] Philippe Kirsch and John T. Holmes, "The Rome Conference on an International Criminal Court: The Negotiating Process," *American Journal of International Law*, Vol. 93, Issue 1, 1999, p. 5. Kirsch and Holmes assert that the number of the brackets were about 1,400.

[3] "The Case for an International Criminal Court," *On the Record ICC*, Vol. 1, Issue 1, June 15, 1998, available at: http://www.advocacynet.org/news_view/news_59.html.

[4] Farhan Haq, "Bracket-busting Time Begins," *Terra Viva*, Issue 1, June 15, 1998, p. 1.

[5] Ibid.

[6] Ibid. However, it should be noted that especially Trinidad-Tobago, which put forward the proposal that triggered the ICC process in 1989, insisted that the final statute contains provisions to make drug trafficking a prosecutable crime before the court. On the first day of the conference, the Attorney-General of Trinidad-Tobago made a speech in which he invited the delegates to "reintroduce drug trafficking into the jurisdiction of the International Court." See "Forget the Square Brackets, Go Back to Square One, Urges Trinidad and Tobago," *On the Record ICC*, Vol. 1, Issue 2, June 16, 1998, available at: http://www.advocacynet.org/news_view/news_75.html.

issues that remained unresolved, "few could have expected the five-week session to conclude in agreement."[7]

The ambiguities and uncertainties in the text essentially reflect the varying and often conflicting prior positions of the participant states. Although they decided to take part in the conference, the states did not have a commonly shared view on the nature and features of the future court. Of course, the disagreements were recognized as natural, and the negotiating process was all about resolving them; otherwise, there would have been no need for a conference. However, the major distinct options available before the conference were so conflicting that reconciliation between them seemed to be nearly impossible.

In principle, there appeared to be agreement among the participating delegates that a permanent ICC should be created by the end of the conference. However, the court that was envisioned and desired by, for instance, the United States, and the court desired by Germany were completely different. It was already evident that the permanent members in the UN Security Council in particular were strongly against a powerful court and would seek "the least common denominator."[8]

For instance, even though it had clearly stated its full support for creating a permanent ICC, prior to the conference, China still remained "wary on issues that may erode the principle of national sovereignty it so jealously guards."[9] However, the strongest position was held by the United States, which ardently stated its opposition to strong, independent court that would not be under UN Security Council control. The US administration began its tactics to exert maximum pressure on the participant delegates even before the

[7] David Davenport, "The New Diplomacy," *Policy Review*, Issue 116, 2002–2003, p. 25. Human Rights Watch report reads as follows: "The Diplomatic Conference began on June 15 amid great uncertainty. Given the large number of disputed provisions throughout the "consolidated" draft text, there was widespread concern that the delegates would be unable to finish the work in the five weeks allocated." Human Rights Watch World Report 1999, Special Issues and Campaigns: International Criminal Court, available at: http://www.hrw.org/worldreport99/special/icc.html.

[8] Ramesh Jaura, "Legal Experts on ICC Compromise Yes, Clout No," *Terra Viva*, Issue 1, June 15, 1998, p. 3.

[9] Anioaneta Bezlova, "China Keeps Wary Eye on Interference by Tribunal," *Terra Viva*, Issue 2, June 16, 1998, p. 3.

inauguration of the conference. In early April, Pentagon authorities met with military attachés from the embassies in Washington to make the American view known to other states.[10]

The United States also particularly opposed a strong prosecutor with broad authorities to initiate investigations and prosecutions on the grounds that such "a politicized prosecutor" might target the US personnel who were assuming tasks under the auspices of UN peacekeeping missions. As a consequence of this skeptical position, the US "tabled proposals that would make it virtually impossible for the ICC to take up any case without getting prior permission from the UN Security Council, where the United States exercises a veto."[11] In an effort to prevent the creation of a court that was not favored by the United States, the Pentagon lobbied NATO member countries, and a number of key political figures from the United States explicitly stated that the United States would not endorse a call for an independent court with a powerful prosecutor.[12]

Overall, with the exception of the United Kingdom, the permanent members of the Security Council constituted a strong block with a commonly shared approach regarding the court they favored. As Kirsch and Holmes observed, their solidarity was clear in two major areas: the envisioned control of the Security Council over the court and the exclusion of nuclear weapons from the court's jurisdiction. They also wanted "the jurisdiction of the court and its exercise to be carefully circumscribed."[13]

However, it should be noted that the United States and the other permanent Security Council members were not the only countries that expressed their opposition at the beginning of the Rome Conference to the court that was envisions by the civil society actors. Many nonaligned governments were reluctant to support a powerful court, which they

[10] Human Rights Watch World Report 1999, Special Issues and Campaigns: International Criminal Court.

[11] "The Case for an International Criminal Court."

[12] Ibid.

[13] Kirsch and Holmes, "The Rome Conference on an International Criminal Court: The Negotiating Process," p. 5.

conceived of as undermining national sovereignty.[14] More importantly, it was reported soon before the inauguration of the conference that China and Pakistan were pursuing a common policy to organize and lead a nonaligned movement against an institution with broad authorities and jurisdiction.[15]

The nonaligned governments, that is, Mexico, India, Pakistan, and Egypt, although they were "extremely suspicious of the Security Council and insisted on the inclusion of nuclear weapons among weapons prohibited by the statute," generally "espoused positions that were similar to those of the P-5, in advocating a court whose powers would be relatively restricted."[16] In addition to these two main opposition camps, there were also other countries and groups of countries that fell in neither category but still opposed a strong and powerful court. For instance, the member states of the Arab League adopted a policy to limit the court's authority to address war crimes and crimes against humanity committed during internal armed conflicts and strongly opposed a statute with gender-friendly provisions.[17] There were also salient disagreements over relatively minor issues. For instance, whereas some states insisted on including terrorism and regional drug trafficking in the court's jurisdiction, others argued that those should be left to national authorities.[18]

The issue of including aggression in the crimes that would be prosecutable by the future court was another area of contention. Some states favored its inclusion, whereas others opposed it on the grounds that it was too difficult to define the crime. It should also be noted that the controversy over the crime of aggression was marked by the individual positions of countries from one of the major blocks that opposed the

[14] "The Case for an International Criminal Court."

[15] Jaura, "Legal Experts on ICC Compromise Yes, Clout No," p. 3.

[16] Kirsch and Holmes, "The Rome Conference on an International Criminal Court: The Negotiating Process," p. 5.

[17] Human Rights Watch World Report 1999, Special Issues and Campaigns: International Criminal Court.

[18] Kirsch and Holmes, "The Rome Conference on an International Criminal Court: The Negotiating Process," p. 5.

overall block position. For instance, Russia and Germany, two leading players from two major camps at the conference, the like-minded group (LMG) and the P5 group, shared the same view on including crime of aggression in the final statute.[19]

The trigger mechanism also revealed distinct positions. Supporting states favored automatic jurisdiction, which would ensure that the court could address cases under its established jurisdiction without requiring consent from any other party. However, a number of states were of the opinion that the court should obtain authorization from interested parties before taking action.[20]

The broad-based alliance established between the NGOs and the LMG constituted the camp against those who strongly opposed an independent and effective court.[21] Although they were never able to adopt a coherent and commonly shared position on the projected ICC, the members of the LMG had a decisive impact on the negotiations. Despite the vast differences between the members, the existence of the group "served to generate and legitimize support for a strong ICC."[22]

In addition, the European Union, most of whose members were also in the LMG, expressed clear support for a powerful court. At the beginning of the Rome Conference, the President of the European Council declared a number of important principles that the member states had committed to abide by. These principles generally supported an institution that was quite similar to those that had been advocated by the global civil society actors:

> The Council held that the Court should be universal and effective yet be complementary to national jurisdictions. In principle it should be an

[19] "The Case for an International Criminal Court."

[20] Kirsch and Holmes, "The Rome Conference on an International Criminal Court: The Negotiating Process," p. 5.

[21] Ibid., p. 5. Pace notes that NGOs and the LM countries, both of which have adopted a list of principles to be followed at the conference, "were prepared to tackle the challenges of Rome together." William R. Pace, "CICC NGO Papers," Workshop on International Criminal Accountability, Social Science Research Council, November 6–7, 2003, Washington, DC.

[22] Human Rights Watch World Report 1999, Special Issues and Campaigns: International Criminal Court.

> independent institution yet in relationship with the United Nations. Its prosecutor should be independent from governments. Additionally, the crimes under its jurisdiction should include genocide, crimes against humanity and war crimes, and the crime of aggression to the extent that the Security Council's role in the maintenance of international peace and security would not be compromised. Moreover, war crimes should cover both international and internal armed conflicts as well as gender-related crimes. The Security Council should have a right of referral to the Court in situations where crimes under the Court's jurisdiction may have been committed.[23]

The NGOs in particular repeatedly declared that they strongly and vehemently supported a court with broad powers that could act independent of any superior body.[24] In his opening statement at the first day of the Rome Conference, William Pace, who had convened the NGO Coalition for an International Criminal Court (CICC), openly stated that civil society actors would strongly reject a court as proposed and favored by the actors who wanted it to be a weak institution:

> The issue is whether the majority of nations will galvanize the political will to resist those nations not ready for this court, who will attempt to block the adoption of a strong treaty, or who will attempt to create a weak and powerless court which would be subject to the control or veto of the most powerful nations, or which would require the consent of the nations whose leaders, as the Secretary-General acknowledged, are often the ones who have committed these crimes. Such a court, described by a major world leader of a country which should know as an "alibi" court, is unacceptable to global civil society, to NGOs.[25]

---

[23] Nicolaos Strapatsas, "The European Union and Its Contribution to the Development of the International Criminal Court," *Revue de Droit Universite de Sherbrooke*, Vol. 33, Issue 2, 2002/2003, p. 406.

[24] The editorial of the first issue of *Terra Viva,* a magazine that was published throughout the conference under the sponsorship of the NGO coalition read as follows: "The issue now at stake in Rome is global governance, and civil society is determined to play its part in creating an International Criminal Court that is not just another ritual but an effective instrument of check and balance." "Editorial: It's All about Governance," *Terra Viva*, Issue 1, 15 June 1998, p. 2.

[25] William Pace, "Awful and Awesome Responsibility Stands In Front of Us. We Cannot Fail," Statement at the Official Opening Plenary Session, *The International Criminal Court Monitor,* Special Issue 2, June 16, 1998, p. 1.

On the same day, the NGOs that were committed to establishing an independent and powerful court declared the basic principles of the institution they favored. These principles are significant because they addressed the coalition's goals that were to be pursued during the full course of the conference. Whether the objectives on the list were achieved would tell much about the coalition's success rate. In other words, if the final statute to a great extent resembled the one envisioned by these principles, then it would be apparent that the NGOs had been highly successful at the Rome Conference.
The principles read as follows:

1. The ICC should have the broadest possible jurisdiction over the most serious crimes under international law, such as genocide, war crimes, and crimes against humanity. Its jurisdiction must include crimes committed in non-international armed conflicts and crimes against humanity committed in peacetime.
2. The ICC should have automatic ("inherent") jurisdiction over genocide, war crimes and crimes against humanity. This means that a state accepts the court's jurisdiction over these crimes by ratifying the ICC treaty.
3. The ICC should be able to exercise universal jurisdiction over genocide, war crimes, and crimes against humanity in keeping with established rules of international law. No state consent should be required as a condition for the exercise of this jurisdiction.
4. The ICC should complement national criminal justice systems. The ICC should be able to exercise jurisdiction when it determines that national criminal justice systems have failed to carry out their primary responsibility for bringing to justice individuals who commit crimes within the court's jurisdiction.
5. The ICC should have an independent prosecutor who is empowered to initiate proceedings on his or her own. The prosecutor should be able to initiate proceedings based on information from any source, with appropriate safeguards.
6. The ICC should be able to perform its tasks free from the interference of any political body, including the UN Security

Council and states. Although the Security Council should be able to refer situations to the ICC, it should not be able to delay or stop ICC investigations or prosecutions.

7. All states, including their courts and officials, should be obliged to comply without delay with any ICC orders and requests at all stages of proceedings.
8. The ICC should ensure suspects and accused persons the highest international standards of fair trials and due process at all stages of proceedings. The court should scrupulously adhere to international fair trial standards if justice is to be served and to be seen to be served.
9. The ICC should ensure justice for the victims of international crimes, including women and children, and should ensure that all aspects of its work take gender concerns into account.
10. No reservations should be permitted to the ICC treaty.
11. The ICC should have long-term and secure funding.[26]

The declared list of principles was undersigned by ten leading NGOs on the coalition steering committee. However, this should not be misleading because the principles were prepared in consultation and cooperation with the coalition members and eventually agreed upon by the steering committee.[27] In other words, not only the undersigned NGOs but also those represented in the coalition endorsed the principles in an attempt to reflect the coherent and united stance of the civil society actors regarding the ICC. It should also be noted that the declaration of principles was not meant to serve as a limiting factor on the individual NGOs' activities in their respective areas.[28] That is, as they remained free to take action in pursuit of their goals, they declared their commitment to the commonly shared principles.

[26] "Basic Principles for an Independent Effective and Fair International Criminal Court," *The International Criminal Court Monitor*, Special Issue 2, June 16, 1998, pp. 2–3.

[27] Pace, "CICC NGO Papers," Workshop on International Criminal Accountability, Social Science Research Council, November 6–7, 2003, Washington, DC.

[28] "Campaigners Launch a Broadside," On the Record ICC, June 16, 1998, available at: http://www.advocacynet.org/news_view/news_75.html.

However, it should be noted that the overall situation in the first week of the conference was rather pessimistic. In such an environment, there was little hope that the conference would produce a final text that could be the basis for an effective and fair ICC. Hence, there was every reason to speculate that the stated objectives of the global civil society actors were merely part of a utopian approach.

Even one week after the inauguration of the conference, the two main categories of delegates posed a great challenge before any progress had been made:

> those with some knowledge of the Draft Statute's text, either from their previous participation in the Ad Hoc Committee or the PrepCom or from their own study; and those who had little or no knowledge of the text. The former, who constituted only about one-tenth of the delegates, were optimistic; the latter were not, and they initially expressed concerns and raised questions that had been previously debated (and in some cases even settled) by the PrepCom. With this difficult beginning, it seemed unlikely that the Conference would have a promising outcome. By the second week, some delegates started to speculate about the need for a second Diplomatic Conference, or Rome II.[29]

The pessimistic situation prevailed even into the second week.[30] One particular reason can be mentioned for the inability to make substantial progress: the disparities between the delegates of the developed countries and those of the developing ones. Whereas the developed countries had sent well-equipped delegates with broad information and knowledge on the particular subjects of international criminal law, in general terms, the delegates from developing countries had limited competence. In addition, the delegates from the developed countries enjoyed the advantage of having broad discretion, which allowed one to adopt positions within a broad range of available options. Conversely, the developing countries'

[29] Bassiouni, "Negotiating the Treaty of Rome on the Establishment of an International Criminal Court," p. 450.
[30] Ibid., p. 451.

delegates had to rely on constantly changing instructions from their home countries.[31]

However, despite the initial setback, significant progress was made by the end of the conference. It is amazing to see the dramatic differences between the originally proposed 1994 ILC document and the final text that was adopted at the end of the Rome Conference. That the latter is much improved over the 1994 ILC draft clearly marks the success and influence of the civil society organizations throughout the negotiations in Rome.

The statute's drafters designed the court to be established as a permanent institution.[32] However, it would sit only when requested.[33] Article 4(1) of the ILC statute stated that the proposed court "shall act when required to consider a case submitted to it."[34] Under this statute, the court would have jurisdiction over the crime of genocide,[35] the crime of aggression,[36] serious violations of law and customs applicable in armed conflicts,[37] crimes against humanity,[38] and crimes "which, having regard to the conduct alleged, constitute exceptionally serious crimes of international concern."[39]

However, as proposed by the statute, the court would have automatic jurisdiction over the above crimes, with the exception of the crime of

---

[31] Ibid., pp. 456–457.

[32] Draft Statute for an International Criminal Court, Report of the International Law Commission, U.N. GAOR, 49th Sess., Supp. No. 10, at 43, U.N. Doc. A/49/10 (1994), Article 4(1). (hereinafter the 1994 ILC Draft Statute).

[33] However, it should be noted that based on the increase in the court's workload, the President of the court could request that the states convert the court's status to full time by a resolution. Bradley E. Berg, "The 1994 I.L.C. Draft Statute for an International Criminal Court: A Principled Appraisal of Jurisdictional Structure," *Case Western Reserve Journal of International Law,* Vol. 28, Issue 2, 1996, p. 226. He further noted that the contradiction between the permanent character of the court and the fact that it would proceed only when requested "reflects a compromise between the virtues of permanency and the practical expectation that, at least initially, the Court would not be sufficiently busy to necessitate a full-time structure."

[34] The 1994 ILC Draft Statute, Article 4(1).

[35] The 1994 ILC Draft Statute, Article 20(a).

[36] The 1994 ILC Draft Statute, Article 20(b).

[37] The 1994 ILC Draft Statute, Article 20(c).

[38] The 1994 ILC Draft Statute, Article 20(d).

[39] The 1994 ILC Draft Statute, Article 20(e).

genocide. Article 22 of the draft statute provides that a state that was party to the statute could accept the court's jurisdiction by a declaration.[40] Under the same article, the declaration "may be of general application, or may be limited to particular conduct or to conduct committed during a particular period of time,"[41] and "may be made for a specified period."[42]

Hence, being party to the statute would not create automatic obligations for the state with respect to the crimes under its jurisdiction. To this end, the statute established two separate jurisdictional regimes. Under the first regime of inherent (or automatic) jurisdiction, a state that was party to the Genocide Convention that became party to the statute "accept[ed] the court's jurisdiction with respect to that crime without any further consent requirements." The second regime envisioned a jurisdictional mechanism based on state consent.[43] That the proposed court was to be vested with inherent jurisdiction with regard to the crime of genocide is a clear recognition of "the universal acknowledgement of genocide as a part of jus cogens, the widely ratified status of the Genocide Convention, and particularly, the Convention's express contemplation of an international criminal court for this offense."[44]

Under the second regime, the court could proceed with investigation of prosecution in relation to situations under its jurisdiction only if "both the state which has custody of the accused (the custodial state) and the state on whose territory the crime was committed (the territorial state) have agreed to the court's jurisdiction with respect to the crime involved."[45]

In addition to the restrictions by which the court and the prosecutors would be bound regarding exercising the court's jurisdiction over the

---

[40] The 1994 ILC Draft Statute, Article 22 (1).

[41] The 1994 ILC Draft Statute, Article 22 (2).

[42] The 1994 ILC Draft Statute, Article 22 (3).

[43] Jelena Pejic, "Creating a Permanent International Criminal Court: The Obstacles to Independence and Effectiveness," *Columbia Human Rights Law Review*, Vol. 29, Issue 2, 1998, p. 320.

[44] Berg, "The 1994 I.L.C. Draft Statute for an International Criminal Court: A Principled Appraisal of Jurisdictional Structure," p. 230.

[45] Ibid., p. 321.

crimes contained in the statute, neither entity would be free to initiate investigations. Under the statute, only states and the Security Council could initiate the investigation process. Article 23 of the statute provided that the court would have jurisdiction over a situation if that situation was referred to by the Security Council.[46] The Council was also recognized the absolute authority by the statute with regard to the crime of aggression:

> A complaint of or directly related to an act of aggression may not be brought under this Statute unless the Security Council has first determined that a State has committed the act of aggression which is the subject of the complaint.[47]

Regarding states' authority to refer a situation to the Court, the statute provided that any state that was to both the Genocide Convention and the statute could lodge a complaint with the prosecutor alleging the commission of the crime of genocide.[48] Therefore, in the case of genocide, under the statute, no further requirement was sought.[49] With respect to the crimes under the court's jurisdiction other than genocide, in order to be authorized to refer a situation to the prosecutor, a state had to have already accepted the court's jurisdiction with respect to the crime that was relevant to that situation.[50]

The prosecutor as designed under the 1994 draft statute would not have broad discretion to proceed with situations that were referred to it. Article 26 provided that the prosecutor was to initiate investigation of situations that were referred to it by the Security Council unless he or she "conclude[d] that there [was] no possible basis for a prosecution under this Statute and decide[d] not to initiate an investigation."[51] The

[46] The 1994 ILC Draft Statute, Article (23)(1).
[47] The 1994 ILC Draft Statute, Article (23)(2).
[48] The 1994 ILC Draft Statute, Article (25)(1).
[49] Pejic, "Creating a Permanent International Criminal Court: The Obstacles to Independence and Effectiveness," p. 324.
[50] The 1994 ILC Draft Statute, Article (25)(2).
[51] The 1994 ILC Draft Statute, Article (26)(1).

warrants and subpoenas required to open an investigation were to be issued by the President upon the request of the prosecutor.[52]

If the prosecutor concluded that there was sufficient evidence to proceed with an investigation, he or she should file an indictment with the Registrar.[53] The indictment would be subject to review by the President, which, after determining that the evidence submitted was sufficient for opening an investigation, "shall confirm the indictment and establish a trial chamber."[54] If the President did not agree with the prosecutor with regard to the need to initiate an investigation, he was to inform the complainant state or the Security Council depending on the nature of the situation and the party that referred it.[55] After it was confirmed that "there is probable cause to believe that the suspect may have committed a crime within the jurisdiction of the Court"[56]; and "the suspect may not be available to stand trial unless provisionally arrested,"[57] the President was also authorized to issue warrants for the provisional arrest and transfer of the accused.

A brief review of the court that was envisioned in the 1994 ILC draft statute implies that the penal institution it would create was a weak one whose function would have to depend on the consent and willingness of states to cooperate. In other words, the "central theme of the Statute" was state consent, and it was designed as an institution that would be closely affiliated with the UN.[58] However, it was observed that even such a weak and state-friendly court would not be welcomed by the majority of states:

> States, however, are uneasy about granting jurisdiction prospectively to a new court. As a result, the Draft Statute is riddled with provisions that

[52] The 1994 ILC Draft Statute, Article (26)(3).
[53] The 1994 ILC Draft Statute, Article (27)(1).
[54] The 1994 ILC Draft Statute, Article (27)(2).
[55] The 1994 ILC Draft Statute, Article (27)(3).
[56] The 1994 ILC Draft Statute, Article (28)(1)(a).
[57] The 1994 ILC Draft Statute, Article (28)(1)(b).
[58] Berg, "The 1994 I.L.C. Draft Statute for an International Criminal Court: A Principled Appraisal of Jurisdictional Structure," p. 226.

> would eviscerate this otherwise significant grant of jurisdiction and make prospective declarations relatively meaningless. Cases would be inadmissible when they are of insufficient gravity, the accused has been tried for the offense in a national court, a state has investigated and a decision not to prosecute is well-founded, or a state is investigating and there is no reason for the court to take immediate action.[59]

The analogy established by the one commentator between the court proposed by the ILC draft statute and the International Court of Justice[60] connotes that the penal institution the statute provided for would have been ineffective, given that the ILC had for the most part remained a failure and a great disappointment.

Furthermore, even though the draft statute did not explicitly acknowledge the Security Council's role with regard to addressing the international crimes it covered, the court that would be created under the statute would in fact have concurrent jurisdiction to be exercised in conjunction with the Security Council. This is especially true with regard to the crime of aggression. Although the statute provided that individuals accused of committing that crime could be held responsible, exercising jurisdiction over those individuals would strictly depend on the Security Council's prior determination that an act of aggression had been committed by a state.[61] In addition, "domestic courts would continue to have judicial jurisdiction over every international crime."[62]

The narrow jurisdiction vested by the statute in the court was the result of the skeptical attitude of states during the negotiations towards a supranational body that would be charged with overseeing the international criminal regime. The practical consequence of this stance was as follows:

---

[59] Bryan F. MacPherson, "Building an International Criminal Court for the 21st Century," *Connecticut Journal of International Law,* Vol. 13, Issue 1, 1998, pp. 30–31.

[60] Berg, "The 1994 I.L.C. Draft Statute for an International Criminal Court: A Principled Appraisal of Jurisdictional Structure," pp. 226–227. According to Berg, both courts would have to exercise what could be called limited "ceded jurisdiction," which refers to the dependence on state consent.

[61] Ibid., p. 228.

[62] Ibid., p. 228.

> Both the Draft Statute and the position taken by many states in the negotiations reflect an extremely myopic vision of the contribution that an international criminal court could make toward a more stable and just world order. The focus has been on only one factor of the criminal justice equation, that of increasing the likelihood that those accused of international crimes will be effectively prosecuted. Although every effort is being made to ensure that the court will itself administer justice fairly, the superiority of an international tribunal over national courts in furthering the second factor of the criminal justice equation, that of providing fair, unbiased trials, has received scant recognition.[63]

Instead, the states' prerogatives, and their privileges stemming from the worldwide recognition of national sovereignty, were strictly observed and preserved. States were granted broad discretion with regard to the court's functioning, which was in fact designed to be subordinate to the states' consent and will. Additionally, where the states' consent was not required or sought, the statute would recognize the role of the UN Security Council in maintaining global justice. The statute provided that when the Council was involved, no further prerequisite would be required for further action. In this regard, the court provided by the statute had great resemblance to the ad hoc tribunals created under the control of the Security Council.[64] Moreover, whether the court would be competent to address the issue in question or a separate, ad hoc, international tribunal would be established was at the Council's discretion.[65]

The relatively weak and flawed court proposed in the 1994 ILC statute was replaced with a much more enhanced and effective one at the end of the Rome Conference, where global civil society actors had a determinative impact. Although the scope of the crimes covered by the Rome Statute appears to be narrower than that of the draft statute, the ICC was given broad discretion in exercising jurisdiction over those

[63] MacPherson, "Building an International Criminal Court for the 21st Century," p. 29.

[64] Berg, "The 1994 I.L.C. Draft Statute for an International Criminal Court: A Principled Appraisal of Jurisdictional Structure," p. 230.

[65] Ibid., p. 231.

crimes. Unlike the draft statute, the Rome Statute provided that the prosecutor could act on his or her own with regard to addressing a situation that fell under the court's jurisdiction. In other words, even if the states or the Security Council did not refer a situation to the court, the prosecutor, with no prior consent or authorization from third parties, could proceed.

As for the nature of the court's jurisdiction, the Rome Statute significantly differed from the draft statute. Whereas the draft recognized inherent jurisdiction only with regard to the crime of genocide, the ICC had automatic jurisdiction over the crimes under the Rome Statute, requiring no state authorization in order to exercise its jurisdiction.

# Negotiations at the Rome Conference

The discussions at Rome Conference revolved around three major issues and aspects that were relevant to the future court. The first was the issue of trigger mechanism and the court's jurisdiction, which was closely related to the fairness and effectiveness of the future court in that if the states or the UN Security Council had been given determinative roles in submitting cases before the Court, it would have been an "alibi" court. Most issues that were relevant to the issue of jurisdiction had already been resolved even before the inauguration of the conference. For instance, there was wide agreement that the court would admit cases related to acts committed after its entrance into force. Although some NGOs—although not a large number—insisted that the court should be able to act retroactively, as was the case with the previously established ad hoc tribunals in Nuremberg, Tokyo, the Hague, and Tanzania, this proposal did not find support.[1]

As for the personal jurisdiction, there was also general agreement that the court should only try natural persons, although some proposals were

[1] Marlies Glasius, *The International Criminal Court: A Global Civil Society Achievement* (London and New York: Routledge, 2006), p. 61.



C. Çakmak, *A Brief History of International Criminal Law and International Criminal Court*,
DOI 10.1057/978-1-137-56736-9_9

voiced to ensure that the International Criminal Court (ICC) would be able to exercise jurisdiction over nonstate entities. Subject-matter jurisdiction was somewhat contentious, but it was not unduly serious. In a very short time, an agreement emerged that the court should have jurisdiction over the most serious crimes, that is, genocide, crimes against humanity, and war crimes. The only serious disagreement was over the inclusion of the crime of aggression, although this did not cause disruptive gaps between the relevant parties' positions. Although there were various other proposals for including crimes such as drug trafficking, terrorism, and other related crimes, they never met with substantial support.[2]

However, in regard to the options on the trigger mechanisms by which the court and its prosecutor could establish cases, conflicting views have emerged. Because the basic tenets of the trigger mechanism were closely related to the principle of national sovereignty and non-intervention, states' delegates were concerned with the issue and attempted to determine useful stand points:

> Delegations were prepared to consider the inclusion of a broad range of crimes, if the jurisdiction of the court was limited, for example, by requiring state consent on a case-by-case basis or by permitting states to opt in or opt out of certain crimes. Conversely, the possibility of automatic jurisdiction upon ratification, or of a system close to universal jurisdiction, provoked some delegations to argue for a limited range of crimes, narrower definitions and higher thresholds. The permissibility or not of reservations also had an impact on positions.[3]

[2] Ibid., pp. 61–62. Both the NGOs and the states' delegates were opposed to extending the court's jurisdiction beyond the most serious crimes to include the proposed crimes. Even the most discontent voice at the conference, the United States, joined the majority camp in that opposition. The United States remained particularly opposed to including terrorism because it did not want to endanger its own policy of having suspected terrorists extradited to US authorities, and this same argument applied to the other proposed crimes. In other words, the United States wanted to remain the sole authority that would address those crimes and did not want ICC involvement. "The US in a Bind over Terrorism," *Terra Viva,* Issue 5, June 19, 1998, p. 3.

[3] Kirsch and Holmes, "The Rome Conference on an International Criminal Court: The Negotiating Process," p. 6.

The contentious issues regarding the trigger mechanisms included: would any state's ratification of the statute state mean that it automatically accepted the court's jurisdiction or would additional instruments be required for the court to take action? Or, would the states have the opportunity to choose whether to accept the Court's competence for some crimes but not others? Would the states have the opportunity to accept the court's jurisdiction for a limited period of time only, or would they be bound by their commitment to accepting the court's permanent jurisdiction based on their ratification of the statute?

More important than the aforementioned questions, however, was how investigations and prosecutions would be initiated under the court's jurisdiction. In other words, who would be authorized to refer cases to the court prosecutor? Would the court be authorized to proceed on its own against a suspect of a crime under its jurisdiction? Or would only states and the UN Security Council have the authority to refer cases to the court and request that the prosecutor take further action? What would be the role of the prosecutor? Would he be able to trigger the investigation and the prosecution process, or would he be subject to preconditions? How those issues would be resolved would have determined the nature and quality of the court to a great extent. Hence, most discussions were allocated to those thorny issues during the course of the conference.

Proposals Discussed at the Rome Conference:

The ad hoc committee and PrepComI meetings produced some useful texts that would be discussed by the delegates who had participated in the conference. Especially with regard to the few important issues, there were proposals that claimed to resolve the contentious points. These issues were, of course, the extent of the prosecutor's authority, the framework within which the prosecutor would enjoy said authority, the trigger mechanisms, and the scope of the court's jurisdiction. As might be expected, states were unwilling to turn over their sovereign rights to a supranational body, whereas civil society actors favored a strong court with the broadest authority to address the most egregious crimes. Although all participating countries had previously expressed their support for establishing the court, their views greatly differed on whether it would be designed as an international body that was superior to the states' systems or subordinate to power politics.

At the conference, the Committee of the Whole considered a number of options in the draft statute that had been adopted at the last PrepComI session. In general terms, those options were the German Proposal, the United Kingdom Proposal, the Korean Proposal, the opt-in regime, the case-by-case consent regime, and the US Proposal. These proposals "ranged from inherent universal jurisdiction for the ICC proposed by Germany and a broad jurisdictional basis at one end of the spectrum, to the restrictive mandatory consent of all interested states proposed by some delegations at the other."[4]

The German proposal departed from the premise that "if states individually have a legitimate basis at international law to prosecute the core crimes . . . on account of universal jurisdiction, then the ICC should have the same capacity as contracting states."[5] It was reported that "the German delegation vigorously supported universal jurisdiction, noting that under current international law all States may already exercise universal jurisdiction for genocide, crimes against humanity, and war crimes."[6]

Hence, the proposal implied that the states that were party to the statute, by virtue of their having become party, would recognize the only rights they had under international law to the ICC.[7] The proposal was deemed "to be appropriate for a permanent international criminal court being founded for the good of the international community of states as a whole."[8]

[4] Sharon A. Williams, "The Rome Statute on the International Criminal Court: From 1947–2000 and Beyond," *Osgoode Hall Law Journal,* Vol. 38, Issue 2, 2000, pp. 312–313.

[5] Proposal of Germany, A/AC.249/1998/DP.2, 1998. The proposal further reads: "There is no reason why the ICC—established on the basis of a Treaty concluded by the largest possible number of States—should not be in the very same position to exercise universal jurisdiction for genocide, crimes against humanity, and war crimes in the same manner as the contracting Parties themselves . . . By ratifying the Statute of the ICC, the States Parties accept in an official and formal manner that the ICC can also exercise criminal jurisdiction with regard to these core crimes. This means that, like the Contracting States, the ICC should be competent to prosecute persons which have committed one of these core crimes, regardless of whether the territorial State, the custodial State, or any other State has accepted the jurisdiction of the Court."

[6] Susan Hannah Farbstein, "The Effectiveness of the Exercise of Jurisdiction by the International Criminal Court: The Issue of Complementarity," *European Centre for Minority Issues,* Working Paper No. 12, 2001, p. 54.

[7] Williams, "The Rome Statute on the International Criminal Court: From 1947–2000 and Beyond," p. 313.

[8] Ibid., p. 315.

The United Kingdom proposal[9] provided for a jurisdictional regime based on "the in-built safeguard of complementarity."[10] The proposal also required that both the custodial state and the state where the crime occurred accept the court's jurisdiction by becoming states that were party to the statute if the situation had been referred to the court by a state or when the prosecutor chose to initiate a prosecution on his or her own.[11] However, this proposal was largely objected to on the grounds that "obtaining consent from both these States would be difficult, and the proposal was eventually amended by removing the custodial State requirement."[12]

The South Korean Proposal[13] was "a compromise position."[14] It did not favor the inherent universal jurisdictional regime contained in the German proposal. In simple terms, it favored a court that would be "as effective as possible" and require state consent once, at the time the state in question became party to the statute.[15] The option also required that one of the following states become party to the statute in order for the court to be authorized to exercise its jurisdiction: the territorial state, the custodial state, the accused's state of nationality, or the victim's state of nationality.[16] The proposal reads:

> Those who favor the concept of inherent jurisdiction overlook the fact the proposed Court is a treaty body to be created through the consent of the States.
>
> It is State consent that justifies the jurisdictional link between States Parties to the Statute and the Court. Forgoing any precondition to the

---

[9] The United Kingdom Proposal, U.N. Doc. A/AC.249/WG.3/DP.1.

[10] Williams, "The Rome Statute on the International Criminal Court: From 1947–2000 and Beyond," p. 316.

[11] Ibid., p. 317.

[12] Farbstein, "The Effectiveness of the Exercise of Jurisdiction by the International Criminal Court: The Issue of Complementarity," p. 57.

[13] The Proposal of the Republic of Korea, U.N. Doc. A/CONF.183/C.1/L.6, (June 18, 1998).

[14] Williams, "The Rome Statute on the International Criminal Court: From 1947–2000 and Beyond," p. 317.

[15] Ibid., p. 317.

[16] Farbstein, "The Effectiveness of the Exercise of Jurisdiction by the International Criminal Court: The Issue of Complementarity," p. 56.

> exercise of jurisdiction would run a risk of rendering the acceptance of the Court's jurisdiction meaningless... The adherents to the State consent regime also fail to recognize that the requirement of State consent at two distinct stages—acceptance and exercise—would render the Court ineffective due to this jurisdictional hazard. For the Court to be as effective as possible, State consent should be called for once, when a State becomes party to the Statute. Otherwise, it would deprive the Court of the predictability of its function by granting States a de facto right of veto to determine whether the Court is able to exercise jurisdiction.[17]

The proposal was presented by the Koreans following the growing opposition to the German proposal, which called for inherent jurisdiction. Although the Korean proposal received wide support, many states opposed it on the grounds that it contained "a type of universal jurisdiction." Even some states that favored the inherent jurisdiction regime showed hesitance towards the Korean proposal's suggested regime.[18]

The state "opt-in" proposal required a state's additional consent after it became party to the statute. As was suggested in the 1994 ILC draft statute, this additional consent could be expressed at the time of ratification or at a later stage. The gist of the proposal was that "before the ICC could assume jurisdiction, as many as five states potentially would have had to have consented to the exercise of jurisdiction by the court over the crime in question: the custodial state, the territorial state, the state that had requested extradition of the person from the custodial state, unless the request was rejected, the state of nationality of the accused and the state of nationality of the victim."[19] It is evident that under this proposal, the court would have been less able and competent than states to address the crimes under its jurisdiction. If the court had been established as envisioned

[17] U.N. Doc. A/CONF.183/C.1/L.6.

[18] Farbstein, "The Effectiveness of the Exercise of Jurisdiction by the International Criminal Court: The Issue of Complementarity," p. 57.

[19] Williams, "The Rome Statute on the International Criminal Court: From 1947–2000 and Beyond," p. 318.

in this proposal, ratification by states would have meant little because "States could remove a case from consideration by the Court when politically expedient."[20]

Under the case-by-case consent proposal, in order for the ICC to exercise its jurisdiction, state consent would have been sought for the specific cases. This implies that the court would have to be authorized by the relevant states to proceed with investigation or prosecution. As was the case with the opt-in regime, ratification would mean little under the case-by-case consent regime.[21] It should be noted that the courts as designed under both the opt-in and case-by-case consent regimes were "alibi" courts, which had been referred to by William Pace. In practice, those courts would not have been effective and would have been destined to remain symbolic.

The same could, for the most part, be said for the US proposal, which called for a jurisdictional regime based on "consent from both the territorial State and the State of nationality of the accused in cases where the Security Council did not trigger the Court's jurisdiction."[22] That proposal also held that the ICC's jurisdiction should not be extended to the nationals of nonstates on the grounds that this would constitute a violation of the Vienna Convention on the Law of Treaties. Throughout the conference, the United States "made it clear that it could not adhere to a text that allowed for United States forces operating abroad to be brought even conceivably before the ICC, even where the United States had not become a party to the statute." In case of the adoption of a final text it would object to, the United States also indirectly threatened that "this would derogate from its ability to act as a major player in multinational humanitarian and peacekeeping operations."[23]

---

[20] Farbstein, "The Effectiveness of the Exercise of Jurisdiction by the International Criminal Court: The Issue of Complementarity," p. 57.

[21] Williams, "The Rome Statute on the International Criminal Court: From 1947–2000 and Beyond," p. 318.

[22] Farbstein, "The Effectiveness of the Exercise of Jurisdiction by the International Criminal Court: The Issue of Complementarity," p. 58.

[23] Williams, "The Rome Statute on the International Criminal Court: From 1947–2000 and Beyond," p. 319.

## Discussions on the Crimes Proposed for the Court's Jurisdiction

As already noted, there was little disagreement over which crimes the court should have jurisdiction over, even at the beginning of the conference. Both government delegations and civil society actors were largely of the opinion that the court should only have the authority to prosecute the most heinous crimes, that is, the crime of genocide, crimes against humanity, and war crimes. However, it was already evident at the inception that the definitions of these agreed-upon crimes would be areas of contention between the delegations and the NGOs.

It should also be noted that some governments and NGOs expressed discontent over the largely agreed-upon crimes that would be covered by the final statute. For instance, although there was agreement on including genocide and similar crimes for which there were already international legal instruments that took precedence over states' jurisdictions, including the crime of aggression did not find the same large-scale support.[24] Although some favored its inclusion, others objected to it on the grounds that it was difficult to define the crime. There was disagreement even between the members of the same negotiating group. For instance, speaking on behalf of the European Union at the conference, British minister Tony Lloyd said that the final statute should include "the properly defined" crime of aggression.[25]

Conversely, however, some NGOs explicitly opposed extending the court's jurisdiction to cover the crime of aggression. Some even argued that such a move would jeopardize the court's effectiveness and its future ability to address the worst crimes. For instance, a representative of the Canadian Network for an ICC said:

---

[24] The inclusion of the crime of aggression in the language of the final statute was not a priority even for the CICC because there was "no consensus among NGOs on the matter." See Alejandro Kirk, "High Noon," *Terra Viva,* Issue 23, July 15, 1998, p. 2.

[25] "Campaigners Launch a Broadside," *On the Record ICC,* Vol. 1, Issue 2.

> As international human rights law evolves, we are progressively civilising international relations. However, it's a stage by stage process. These negotiations may not be able to establish a relationship between the UN Security Council and the ICC that would allow the Court to prosecute the crime of aggression on a consistent and reliable basis.[26]

Other NGOs remained neutral, expressing no opinion on the matter. For instance, in the brief it submitted during the conference, the International Commission of Jurists, while declaring that "it is essential for the court to have jurisdiction over the three core crimes, i.e., genocide, war crimes and crimes against humanity," also made it clear that it did not take any "position on the inclusion of the crime of aggression or the definition of this crime."[27]

However, this was not the contentious issue, that is, including the crime of aggression or not. The real issue at the Rome Conference was about the content of the largely agreed-upon crimes. Although there was consensus that the court should be able to prosecute and try the perpetrators of the crime of genocide, crimes against humanity, and war crimes, state delegates sought ways to extremely limit the content of the covered crimes, and thus the scope of the court's jurisdiction, by narrowing the definitions of the crimes.

The crime of genocide was the most easily defined during the Rome negotiations. There was consensus and solidarity among the state delegates as well as NGOs that the 1948 Genocide Convention should be the basis for the definition of the crime that would be included in the final text of the statute. That convention was already the most authoritative document with regard to the crime of genocide, so there was no need for alternative approaches.

However, the same did not apply to the other crimes: war crimes and crimes against humanity. One leading reason for the great disagreement

---

[26] "Aggression Splits the Rome Conference," *On the Record ICC,* Vol. 1, Issue 5, available at http://www.advocacynet.org/news_view/news_78.html.

[27] International Commission of Jurists, "Definition of Crimes," ICJ Brief No. 1 to the UN Diplomatic Conference of Plenipotentiaries on the Establishment of an International Criminal Court, Rome June15–July 17, 1998, p. 2.

over the definitions of those crimes was the lack of authoritative documents in the relevant fields. Although there were a number of international legal instruments regarding war crimes, they contained substantial differences. In addition, as states sought ways to ensure the adoption of text with lower standards than those in the Geneva Conventions, NGOs attempt to include a definition that would comprise situations beyond those stated in the Conventions. As for crimes against humanity, the gap was even broader between the positions taken by states' delegates and those of the NGOs.

Unlike with the crime of genocide and war crimes, no authoritative text provided a useful definition that could serve as a point of departure at the conference. The only definition had been provided in the Nuremberg Charter. However, the delegates who participated in the conference made "a concerted attempt to weaken the existing definition of crimes against humanity, as the Rome conference embarks on a detailed review of the draft ICC statute." With their attempts, these governments aimed to link crimes against humanity with armed conflict, and possibly only international armed conflicts.[28] Some governments also attempted to raise the threshold for this crime and proposed that in order for the court to be able to proceed with cases involving those crimes, the relevant cases should include both "systematic" and "widespread" commission of the acts. In an attempt that alarmed NGOs, India even proposed removing disappearances from the definition of crimes against humanity.[29]

In contrast, while states were attempting to narrow the scope of the crimes of humanity, civil society actors made efforts to ensure that the court would have jurisdiction over a number of crimes against humanity. For instance, in early July, NGOs called for the recognition of murder, extermination, forced disappearances, torture, rape, forced prostitution,

[28] For instance, Arab states proposed linking crimes against humanity to international conflicts only. Obviously, this proposal would have weakened the court's ability to address the commission of atrocities during internal conflicts, rebellions, and other similar incidents. See "Attempt Begins to Water Down Crimes Against Humanity," *On the Record ICC*, Vol. 1, Issue 4, available at: http://www.advocacynet.org/news_view/news_77.html.

[29] Ibid.

forced sterilization, forced pregnancy and other sexual crimes, deportation or forcible internal transfer of populations, arbitrary detention, slavery, sexual slavery, political, racial or religious persecution, and other inhumane acts as crimes against humanity, or war crimes where appropriate.[30]

In an effort to make determinative contributions to defining crimes against humanity, the International Commission of Jurists submitted a brief at the conference that urged the delegates to consider the Charters for the Nuremberg and Tokyo Tribunals, the Draft Code of Crimes Against the Peace and Security of Mankind prepared by the International Law Commission, and the Statutes for the International Tribunals for the Former Yugoslavia and for Rwanda, as well as the existing conventions that regulated certain particular crimes that could fall under the category of crimes against humanity to reach a clear definition.[31]

The initial discussions on the definition of crimes against humanity were held in the Committee of the Whole on June 17. In addition to the controversies over which acts should be included, two additional debates caused serious tensions during the deliberations. Whereas some countries argued that crimes against humanity could be committed during times of peace, others insisted that only acts committed during wars should be considered crimes against humanity.[32] Another serious disagreement was on whether the criteria of "widespread" and "systematic" should be required to substantiate the crime or if just one of the criteria would be sufficient to proceed. Its suggested wording was to add "and" or "or" depending on the result. Observing that it would be difficult to apply, one delegate proposed removing "widespread" from the text. However, the proposal was not taken into consideration.[33]

---

[30] "NGO Alliance Backs Widening List of Crimes," *Terra Viva,* Issue 17, July 7, 1998, p. 1.

[31] International Commission of Jurists, "Definition of Crimes," ICJ Brief No. 1 to the Rome Diplomatic Conference, p. 12.

[32] Phyllis Hwang, "Defining Crimes against Humanity in the Rome Statute of the International Criminal Court," *Fordham International Law Journal,* Vol. 22, Issue 2, 1998, p. 496. Some even argued that only crimes committed during international wars should be put under the court's jurisdiction.

[33] Ibid., p. 496.

There was no official debate over the definition of crimes against humanity until June 22. This time, the discussions were held in the working groups. The controversy over whether the criteria of "widespread" and "systematic" would be required together dominated the deliberations.[34] Two additional states proposed deleting "widespread." The debate was further heated by additional controversies on the meanings of the terms. In an effort to distinguish rare incidents from "widespread" ones, the delegates generally contended that "widespread" would refer to a crime that involved a "multiplicity of persons" or a "massive" attack. Delegates also held that "systematic" would indicate "some degree of planning, pattern, coordinated activity, or scheme."[35] It was reported that the US delegation provided a definition of "systematic" as follows: "attack that constitutes or is part of, or in furtherance of, a preconceived plan or policy, or repeated practice over a period of time."[36]

Although the delegates were making progress on the matter, there emerged a consensus over "the exclusion of a nexus between crimes against humanity and armed conflict, amid the opposition of China, which was later joined by Turkey." Whether a reference to a "civilian population" should be included in the definition was also debated; in the end, a compromise was reached after the British proposal, which provided that "planning by a government or organization should be an additional criteria [*sic*]."[37]

On July 1, the Canadian delegation introduced a compromise package on the definition of crimes against humanity. The proposal reads as follows:

> (1) For the purpose of the present Statute, a crime against humanity means any of the following acts when knowingly committed as part of a widespread or systematic attack against any civilian population . . .

---

[34] Ibid., p. 496.

[35] Ibid., p. 497.

[36] NGO Coalition for an International Criminal Court (Definitions Team), Informal Report of June 23, 1998 (1998), cited by Hwang, "Defining Crimes against Humanity in the Rome Statute of the International Criminal Court," at p. 497, footnote 237.

[37] Ibid., p. 498.

(2) For the purpose of paragraph 1: (a) "attack against any civilian population" means a course of conduct involving the commission of multiple acts referred to in paragraph 1 against any civilian population, pursuant to or knowingly in furtherance of a governmental or organizational policy to commit those acts.[38]

However, the compromise proposal did not find broad support from government delegations, and the previous controversies over the nexus between crimes against humanity and war crimes and the debate over the terms "widespread" and "systematic" persisted. Although two major meetings—one informal and one associated with the efforts of the working group—no significant progress was made on a generally acceptable definition.[39]

However, the most ardent opposition to the Canadian proposal came from the NGOs, following the debates. Although they welcomed the first paragraph of the definition, which sought only one of the two criteria to substantiate the crime, they strongly criticized the second paragraph on the grounds that it was actually "an ill-disguised attempt to reintroduce these criteria as cumulative."[40]

In light of the strong objections, the subsequent attempts markedly altered the definition provided in the Canadian proposal. In the end, the following definition was agreed on:

(1) For the purpose of the present Statute, a crime against humanity means any of the following acts when committed as part of a widespread or systematic attack against any civilian population and with knowledge of the attack.

(2) For the purpose of paragraph 1: (a) "attack against any civilian population" means a course of conduct involving the multiple commission of acts referred to in paragraph 1 against any civilian

[38] Canadian Delegation, Background Paper on Some Jurisprudence on Crimes Against Humanity (July 1, 1998), cited in ibid., at footnote 239.

[39] Ibid., p. 498.

[40] Ibid., p. 499.

> population, pursuant to or in furtherance of a State or organizational policy to commit such attack.[41]

The final definition contains at least four significant alterations to the one provided in the Canadian proposal. First, the expression "commission of multiple acts" was replaced by "multiple commission of acts." Second, the latter definition removed the requirement of double knowledge, which made substantiating the crime more difficult. Thus, the definition in the final statute ensured that the prosecutor and the court judges could more easily reach agreement on whether a crime against humanity had been committed. Third, the requirement on the evidence of policy became a "policy to commit such an attack" instead of a "policy to commit acts." Fourth, the entity sought behind the planned policy was now the state, not the government.[42]

Negotiations over war crimes did not cause as serious controversies as those over crimes against humanity. Overall, what could be said is that individual governments rather than blocks of alliances occasionally made their positions known by other delegates. These positions were marked by special circumstances and the needs of the relevant governments. Because these proposals did not have broad bases, they did not cause serious clashes.

For instance, Great Britain stated its opposition to including the use of land mines in the list of war crimes that would be prosecutable under the final statute. The British proposal provided that states that were party to the statute should have the discretion to opt out if the issue came up in the future.[43] However, it should also be noted that major negotiating groups rarely adopted positions on the scope and definition of war crimes. For instance, the nonaligned movement made vigorous attempts to "include nuclear weapons on any list of prohibited weapons,

---

[41] Rome Statute, Article 7.

[42] Hwang, "Defining Crimes against Humanity in the Rome Statute of the International Criminal Court," p. 502.

[43] "Britain Opposes Inclusion of Landmines as War Crime to Defend UK Nuclear Program," *On the Record ICC,* Vol. 1, Issue 16, July 9, 1998, available at: http://www.advocacynet.org/news_view/news_88.html.

the use of which would constitute a crime under the International Criminal Court (ICC) Statute."[44] And of course, the NGOs made efforts to ensure a high standard for war crimes. For instance, NGOs and individual activists pushed the delegates at the conference to ensure the inclusion of nuclear weapon use as a war crime under the ICC statute, amid the ardent opposition of the United States and an explicit statement that such an inclusion would make American ratification impossible.[45]

The final statute for the most part relied on the previous codifications on war crimes, especially the most authoritative documents on those types of crimes, namely, the Geneva Conventions. Although the final statute did not contain any innovations in terms of definitions of war crimes, the practical consequence of the statute's inclusion of war crimes was that the court would have the ability to serve a means to consolidate humanitarian and human rights law, which had long existed as separate bodies of law. It was commented that if it functioned properly, the court could possibly humanitarian law and human rights law, which had been "historically distinct in their form, domain of application, and subjects."[46]

---

[44] "Non-Aligned Nations Target Nukes," *Terra Viva,* Issue 10, June 26, 1998, p. 1.

[45] "Definition of Crimes: Nuclear Cloud Over War Crimes Debate," *On the Record ICC,* Vol. 1, Issue 12, July 3, 1998, available at: http://www.advocacynet.org/news_view/news_85.html.

[46] Audrey I. Benison, "War Crimes: A Human Rights Approach to a Humanitarian Law Problem at the International Criminal Court," *Georgetown Law Journal,* Vol. 88, Issue 1, 1999, p. 143.

# Debates on Inherent or Preauthorized Jurisdiction

At the beginning of the conference, the International Committee of the Red Cross urged the delegations in Rome to adopt a statute that would not provide a jurisdictional regime based on state consent; otherwise, the president of the committee warned, the Geneva Conventions would have been seriously weakened.[1] However, it soon became clear that the governments were not willing to give up on state consent so easily. The United States in particular appeared very eager on this matter from the very beginning. In addition to state consent, the United States also favored a regime that would rely on the extensive functioning of the UN Security Council. Soon France, another permanent member of the UN Security Council, had aligned itself with the American position.[2] At the inception

[1] "State Consent Could Weaken the Geneva Conventions Warns Red Cross Chief," *On the Record ICC*, Vol. 1, Issue 3, June 17, 1998, available at: http://www.advocacynet.org/news_view/news_76.html.

[2] "Dutch Disbelief at American 'Defeatism'" *On the Record ICC*, Vol. 1, Issue 4, June 18, 1998. However, France also sent mixed signals with regard to its position on the trigger mechanism. In a meeting with NGO representatives, a French foreign minister implied that they might support the Singapore proposal, "if it feels satisfied with other aspects of the emerging draft."



C. Çakmak, *A Brief History of International Criminal Law and International Criminal Court*,
DOI 10.1057/978-1-137-56736-9_10

of the conference, Russia too reiterated its insistence that any court "act only on the recommendation of the UN Security Council or the request of the state involved."[3]

Conversely, civil society actors clearly stated that they favored a fairly independent court with no requirement to obtain state consent to proceed with investigations and prosecutions. In its statement to the Plenary Session, the European Law Students' Association declared that the court should be able to try the crimes under its jurisdiction "without being conditioned by the approval of any political body." The statement further provided that "No state consent should be required when a case can be prepared by an independent prosecutor."[4]

Over time, the rigid proposals for a limited jurisdictional regime that would have to rely on state consent were replaced with more moderate suggestions. The Dutch delegation proposed a regime under which the court would have to be authorized by a pretrial chamber before initiating an investigation. However, Britain strongly opposed this proposal and insisted that the territorial states be required to authorize the court before it could proceed with investigations or prosecutions.[5] At the same time, Spain proposed that the UN Security Council be allowed to prevent the court from initiating a prosecution for 24 months. However, this proposal alarmed the governments that favored an independent court and, naturally, the NGOs.[6]

One week after the inauguration of the Rome Conference, the initial four options were still on the table, with considerable support for each of them. For instance, Jordan, Ukraine, Italy, and Belgium agreed with the German proposal, which called for inherent jurisdiction, but Columbia, Tanzania, and Egypt expressed support for the British proposal, which

[3] "Russia Offers Few Surprises," *Terra Viva,* Issue 5, June 19, 1998, p. 2.

[4] "A Fair and Effective Court Should Be the first Building Block a Just World Order," Statement to the Plenary Session by the European Law Students' Association, *The International Criminal Court Monitor,* Special Issue 6, June 22, 1998, p. 4.

[5] "Dutch, UK Spar Over Whether States Should Veto Pre-Trial Investigations," *On the Record,* Vol. 1, Issue 9, June 29, 1998, available at: http://www.advocacynet.org/news_view/news_82.html.

[6] "Spain Muddies Water on Security Council Role," *On the Record,* Vol. 1, Issue 9, June 29, 1998.

provided a jurisdictional regime under which the territorial state's consent was required to initiate an investigation into the commission of crimes covered by the final statute.[7]

With the view that the proposals that envisioned a strong court were gaining considerable support, the United States decided to become more aggressive on its position regarding the jurisdictional regime of the future court. Specifically, David Scheffer, the US Ambassador for War Crimes and head of the US delegation, insisted, among other items, that states should have the discretion to address a situation or case before the International Criminal Court (ICC) took action. The United States also proposed that "states could also challenge the admissibility of a case in the event that the court finds a state unwilling or unable to prosecute."[8]

It appeared that the US opposition, albeit slightly, changed the course of the negotiations. Now there were two distinct and opposite possibilities, with no middle ground:

> Either the court will be granted substantial authority to prosecute criminals and deter atrocities—regardless of government opposition. Or this conference will place the court firmly under the control of governments and the UN Security Council.[9]

At that time, some governments openly expressed their defense of a strengthened role of states in the process of investigations and vs. They attempted to "ensure that the ICC prosecutor will be limited in his or her ability to conduct any pre-trial investigation without the consent and support of the government involved."[10]

---

[7] Ibid.

[8] "The Compromise Package: US Launches Long-awaited Preemptive Strike on ICC Statute," *On the Record ICC,* Vol. 1, Issue 15, July 8, 1998, available at: http://www.advocacynet.org/news_view/news_89.html.

[9] "Court in the Balance," *On the Record ICC,* Vol. 1, Issue 16, July 9, 1998, available at: http://www.advocacynet.org/news_view/news_88.html.

[10] "States Fight For Control Over Pre-Trial Investigations," *On the Record ICC,* Vol. 1, Issue 16, July 9, 1998.

## Negotiations Over the Authorities of the Prosecutor

Arguably, the most controversial issue at the Rome Conference was the role to be recognized by the court prosecutor. Should he be able to act independent of prior authorization and be free of external influence, or should the states and the UN Security Council hold the authority to allow him to go further in a particular case or situation? As noted earlier, from the beginning, certain states had advocated requiring prior authorization for prosecutorial discretion.[11]

The most commonly shared argument against an independent prosecutor that was voiced by the opponents was that a prosecutor with broad authorities could over time become a political figure and harm the interests of certain states. In addition to the already known, long-standing opposition of large powers such as the United States, China, and Russia, moderate powers that would normally have been expected to at least remain neutral with regard to the issue expressly stated concerns over a broadly authorized prosecutor. For instance, it was reported that the Cuban foreign minister in an interview speculated: "Who will guarantee that the Prosecutor will be free from interference, pressure, or even corruption?"[12] In an effort to counter the argument, the NGOs invited the Former Prosecutor of the ICTY, Richard Goldstone, to take the stage on the first day of the Rome Conference. Within this framework, Goldstone addressed the plenary session on behalf of the Coalition for International Justice and also briefed the NGOs at an informal meeting organized by a number of leading NGOs.

In his address at the Plenary Session, Goldstone dismissed the US' fears that "an independent prosecutor would run amok and launch

---

[11] Some states, for instance, the United States, also opposed the possibility that the court and the prosecutor would be able to receive information and evidence from NGOs with regard to particular situations or cases in question.

[12] Alejandro Kirk, "Cuba: Economic Blockades are Crimes against Humanity," *Terra Viva,* Issue 9, June 25, 1998, p. 2.

'politicized' prosecutions," and called those fears "shallow" and politically motivated.[13]

He further noted:

> If the ICC or its prosecutor are made subject to the control of political bodies, whether the Security Council or state parties, it will have no credibility and international justice will be seriously compromised. Amidst all the concerns being addressed at this conference—sovereignty, national interests—we risk forgetting about the victims. Without" an effective, independent court, it is the victims who will suffer the most. It is our responsibility not to let this happen.[14]

In an attempt to convince the delegates at Rome that an independent and broadly authorized prosecutor would not be politicized, in his briefing with the NGOs, Goldstone also asserted that no government would argue that he had acted politically during his term of office, and thus, there was no basis for the opposition to an independent prosecutor.[15]

However, the United States once more stated its opposition. David Scheffer noted that the United States would continue its objections and opposition against an independent prosecutor on the grounds that he would be "overburdened by requests from the NGO community and turn into a human rights ombudsman."[16] This statement marks a notable shift in the US position. Whereas the United States had been objecting to a court with a strong prosecutor on the grounds that it would pose a great challenge to state sovereignty, it now also based its objection on the alleged overburdening of the prosecutor. It now warned that "a prosecutor will have a difficult

---

[13] "Fears of "Politicized" ICC Prosecutors Ridiculed by a Former Hague Prosecutor," *On the Record ICC,* Vol. 1, Issue 3, June 17, 1998, available at: http://www.advocacynet.org/news_view/news_76.html.

[14] Remarks of Justice Richard Goldstone to the United Nations Diplomatic Conference on the Establishment of an International Criminal Court on behalf of the Coalition for International Justice, June 17, 1998.

[15] Fears of "Politicized" ICC Prosecutors Ridiculed by a Former Hague Prosecutor," *On the Record ICC,* Vol. 1, Issue 3, June 17, 1998.

[16] "The Role of the Prosecutory," *On the Record ICC,* Vol. 1, Issue 6, June 22, 1998, available at: http://www.advocacynet.org/news_view/news_117.html.

time in sorting through the mass of complaints that are likely to come in."[17] In the aforementioned statement, David Scheffer also noted that the United States would not ratify a final text that called for establishing a court with a broadly authorized prosecutor who would be empowered to launch ex officio investigations and prosecutions, simply because the United States could not "entrust such sensitive decisions to an individual."[18]

As the time for the conference was running out, there was little progress on the issue. Of course, there were position changes that increased the hopes and expectations of the NGOs with regard to adopting a statute that would have envisioned an independent prosecutor[19]; however, the overall situation was generally bleak. According to an NGO tally conducted in the first week of the conference, 39 governments expressed support for an independent prosecutor during the proceedings at the Committee of the Whole, and 24 stood against it. The same tally also reported that 58 delegations supported an independent prosecutor at the Plenary Session.[20]

However, despite the growing support, the opposition of China, the United States, and Russia to a court under which a prosecutor would have authority to launch investigations without prior consent or authorization by states or the UN Security Council was still effective. Moreover, just as with the supporting block, the group of states that opposed an independent prosecutor grew as well. Certain nonaligned states in particular, such as Syria, India, Pakistan, Uruguay, Nigeria, Algeria, and Turkey, joined the opposition camp.[21]

[17] *On the Record ICC,* Vol. 1, Issue 8, June 24, 1998.

[18] "The Role of the Prosecutory," *On the Record ICC,* Vol. 1, Issue 6, June 22, 1998, available at: http://www.advocacynet.org/news_view/news_117.html.

[19] For instance, the June 23 issue of *Terra Viva* asserts that "A growing number of nations is supportive of an 'ex officio' prosecutor who can begin proceedings on his or her initiative, according to delegates and NGOs following the negotiations for an International Criminal Court (ICC) this week." See "Momentum Builds for Powerful Prosecutor," *Terra Viva,* Issue 7, June 23, 1998, p. 1.

[20] "Support Growing for an Independent Prosecutor," *On the Record ICC,* Vol. 1, Issue 7, 23 June 1998, available at: http://www.advocacynet.org/news_view/news_80.html.

[21] Ibid.

Concerned that a statute that would create a court with a broadly authorized prosecutor would not be finalized during the conference, the CICC member organizations intensified their efforts in the following days. The New York-based Lawyers Committee for Human Rights prepared a detailed paper in which it strongly defended an independent prosecutor who would be authorized to launch investigations on his or her own. In an effort to justify the need for an independent prosecutor, the committee accused of the governments and the UN Security Council of not having taken action against the commission of large-scale atrocities so far:

> Political considerations have prevented states and the Security Council from reacting to mass atrocities in which hundreds of thousands, and in some cases millions, of people were killed over the last several decades. A proprio motu prosecutor is necessary to ensure that international crimes are investigated and prosecuted when states and the Security Council fail to respond for political reasons.[22]

In a similar endeavor, the NGOs sent a clear message to the conference delegates that they favored a strong court, not an alibi one. In the strongly worded "letter of solidarity," 250 NGO representatives called for establishing a strong ICC.[23] The undersigned representatives from those NGOs clearly stated that the statute to be finalized at the conference should provide for "an independent, impartial Prosecutor, empowered to initiate proceedings on her or his own initiative. The Prosecutor should be able to initiate proceedings based on information from any source, with appropriate safeguards."[24]

At nearly the same time, representatives from four leading CICC members—Amnesty International, Human Rights Watch, the International Commission of Jurists and the Lawyers Committee

---

[22] "Trigger Mechanisms: US, American Human Rights Groups Clash on Independent Prosecutor," *On the Record ICC*, Vol. 1, Issue 9, June 29, 1998.

[23] "Ottawa Review of 1992 Human Rights Conference Calls for Tough ICC," *On the Record ICC*, Vol. 1, Issue 10, June 30, 1998.

[24] "Letter of Solidarity on the International Criminal Court," From Representatives of Non-Governmental and Social Organizations Participating in the "International Forum, Vienna +5 Review."

for Human Rights—held meetings with the delegations from LMG countries and "expressed concern at the direction of negotiations." Subsequently, those NGOs also issued a joint appeal in which they made it clear that "a prosecutor with propio motu powers is nonnegotiable" and that they would not accept further restrictions on the prosecutor's ability to initiate prosecutions.[25]

During the same week in which the above joint appeal was issued, NGO alliances repeatedly made it clear that they would not compromise on their insistence on an independent and broadly authorized prosecutor. More than 40 NGOs from three continents issued a joint statement and declared that "the Statute and rules of the Court should ensure impartial investigation and prosecution by an independent Prosecutor" and that "the Court must be independent from any political interference."[26] At the same time, in an effort to express their particular concern over the opposition to certain African states' being able to block the prosecutor from initiating investigations on his own, African NGOs issued a separate statement. They noted that:

> In the face of political concessions by a certain number of African states, African NGO's are sounding the alarm and taking a firm stand in favour of a strong and independent prosecutor for the ICC. At a press conference held yesterday, several African based civil society organizations came out to voice their concern that the commitments made by their countries not be compromised away as a part of an apparent waning in some African states' support for a strong Court.[27]

---

[25] "An Appeal From Four Major Human Rights Organizations," *On the Record ICC,* Vol. 1, Issue 19, July 13, 1998. The appeal further concluded:

Above all, an effective court should not be sacrificed to unreasonable demands from the United States or certain other countries. About three-quarters of the countries here support almost every point made above, making clear that a court based on those points would enjoy broad enough support to succeed in promoting international justice and breaking the cycle of impunity. A court not based on those points would be a failure.

[26] "Joint Declaration of the Alliance of the Three Continents In an Unprecedented Show of Solidarity, a Joint Statement Was Approved by More than 40 NGOs From Asia, Africa and Latin America This Weekend," *The International Criminal Court Monitor,* Special Issue 17, July 7, 1998, p. 3.

[27] Robert Keller, "African NGOs Call for a Renewed Commitment to an Independent Prosecutor," *The International Criminal Court Monitor,* Special Issue 18, July 8, 1998, p. 1.

Meanwhile, it should be noted that there was substantial support for an independent prosecutor from the beginning of the conference. That is, although the issue was being debated, it had a certain base of support. The only ardently opposing countries from the very beginning were the United States, China, and Russia. In addition to the delegates from the LMG, many delegates from other blocks supported the idea of an independent prosecutor. However, the primary problem was that the supporting states simply did not have a clear vision and stance. In other words, they might have been ready to approve an independent prosecutor; but just *how* independent?[28]

[28] The official publication of the CICC during the Rome Conference, *On the Record,* raised corollary questions as the proceedings went forward: "How much authority and independence will be vested in the new court? The litmus test will be the function of its prosecutor. Will he or she be independent, and able to launch investigations proprio motu? Or will the prosecutor have to wait for the Security Council or states to refer a situation before investigating individual suspects?" *On the Record ICC,* Vol. 1, Issue 8, June 25, 1998.

# No Reservations, No Statute of Limitations in the Final Statute

One important and striking strength of the Rome Statute that established the International Criminal Court (ICC) is that it contained no provision referring to reservations, exceptions, or derogations. Many international treaties codified in the field of human rights recognize states' rights to derogate from certain provisions.[1] Even if there is no general clause of derogation or exception, nearly all international treaties and conventions include reservations that are annexed or attached to them by the signing or ratifying states. It is an essential tool for ensuring ratification by states by eliminating their respective concerns, if there are any. In other words, if a certain state, while agreeing with most provisions of a treaty, is not satisfied with a specific provision, the treaty in question makes room for reservations so that the state that opposed that

[1] For instance, one of the most authoritative and acclaimed documents in the field of human rights, the European Convention on Human Rights, formulates, in general terms, four types of restrictions: reservations, derogations, denunciations, and permissible restrictions. See Hugh Storey, "Human Rights and the New Europe: Experience and Experiment," *Political Studies,* Vol. 43, Special Issue, 1995, pp. 138–139.



C. Çakmak, *A Brief History of International Criminal Law and International Criminal Court*,
DOI 10.1057/978-1-137-56736-9_11

specific provision can ratify it by expressing its reservation. This ensures the highest possible number of ratifications, although too many reservations simply makes the treaty ineffective.

In a strong effort to prevent the adoption of a statute with reservations that would virtually make the court established therein ineffective, the Coalition for an International Criminal Court (CICC) members lobbied to exclude the option of reservations, exceptions, or derogations. The most commonly used tactic by the NGOs during the conference was to ensure the submission of package deals rather than proposals on specific issues.[2] Of course, this does not mean that they completely excluded such attempts. In fact, many NGOs made numerous statements, proposals, and submissions on various issues. However, in regard to negotiations, they generally preferred to submit whole packages to facilitate the adoption of a commonly accepted text. Otherwise, it would have been quite difficult to overcome more than 1,300 bracketed disagreements within such a very short time.

That the final statute does not allow reservations was an important achievement, given that at the beginning of the conference, at least some delegates were eager to adopt a document with reservations, which would have eliminated their particular concerns regarding the Court. The fact that the text transmitted to the conference contained so many contentious issues was the most visible factor behind this inclination. As soon as the conference opened, government delegates began forming their positions for including language that would allow reservations in the statute. Although most governments were in favor of including reservations, many NGOs feared "this would open a Pandora's box and turn the ICC into a 'Swiss cheese.'"[3]

As with reservations, the final statute also does not allow statutes of limitations, another outstanding achievement that was extensively contributed by the CICC members. From the very beginning, NGOs occasionally made it clear that they would not accept a court that

[2] The final package that was put forward by Philippe Kirsch is particularly worth mentioning. This proposal was so daring and challenging that it was referred to as a "take it or leave it!" package. See Alejandro Kirk, "Take it or Leave it," *Terra Viva*, Issue 22, July 14, 1998, pp. 1–2.

[3] "Too Many Ratifications Would Delay ICC'S Entry into Force, Say NGOs," *On the Record ICC*, Vol. 1, Issue 12, June 27, 1998.

allowed statutes of limitations, which they thought would be contrary to their insistence on the creation of a strong, fair, and effective court. For instance, the International Commission of Jurists recommended that the future court "not apply a statute of limitations, due to the seriousness of the crimes under the Court's jurisdiction and to the number of States that have national and international obligations preventing statutory limitations."[4]

## PrepComII Sessions in Brief

Even as early as the time when the pre-Rome negotiations were being held, there were various proposals referring to the need to adopt, at the Rome Conference, legal documents that would complement the future statute. For instance, the United States proposed drafting a text on Elements of Crimes, "which would set out the elements that must be proven by the Prosecutor for each individual crime."[5] Similarly, the Netherlands and Australia upheld that it would be better to adopt Rules of Procedure and Evidence during the conference. Philippe Kirsch and Valerie Oosterveld, who assumed leading roles during the Rome Conference and the PrepComII sessions in the aftermath, noted that while these and other similar proposals were "noted," most were "focused on gaining agreement on the drafting of the Statute."[6]

However, many contended that the time reserved for the negotiations in the Rome Conference would barely suffice to finalize a statute that would establish the court. Hence, the issue of adopting the additional documents was left to another international multilateral gathering, PrepComII. Most delegates were of the opinion that the Rome Statute should not refer to the multilateral gathering to be convened for the purpose of adopting the complementary documents. Instead, they

---

[4] International Commission of Jurists, "Definition of Crimes," ICJ Brief No. l, p. 5.

[5] Philippe Kirsch and Valerie Oosterveld, "Completing the Work of the Preparatory Commission: The Preparatory Commission for the International Criminal Court," *Fordham International Law Journal*, Vol. 25, Issue 3, 2002, p. 565.

[6] Ibid., p. 566.

agreed that PrepComII would be referred to as the Final Act of the Rome Diplomatic Conference.[7]

The Final Act[8] notes that a preparatory commission should be established to "take all possible measures to ensure the coming into operation of the International Criminal Court without undue delay and to make the necessary arrangements for the commencement of its functions."[9] Even though the priority to participate on the commission was given to the states that signed the treaty, the Final Act also allowed the non-signatory states to attend the sessions.[10] The commission was mandated to prepare the draft texts of Rules of Procedure and Evidence, Elements of Crimes, a relationship agreement between the court and the United Nations, basic principles governing a headquarters agreement to be negotiated between the Court and the host country, financial regulations and rules, an agreement on the privileges and immunities of the court, a budget for the first financial year, and the rules of procedure of the Assembly of States Parties.[11]

The Final Act further provided that among the drafts, the two most important ones, the Rules of Procedure and Evidence and those of the Elements of Crimes, were to be finalized by June 30, 2000.[12] The commission's mandate also included devising proposals on the thorny issue of aggression.[13] The Final Act required that the commission complete its entire work by the conclusion of the first session of the Assembly of States Parties.[14] In other words, the commission was

[7] Ibid., p. 566.

[8] Final Act of the United Nations Diplomatic Conference of Plenipotentiaries on the Establishment of an International Criminal Court, U.N. Doc. A/CONF.183/10, July 17, 1998, [Final Act], Resolution F.

[9] Ibid.

[10] Ibid., para. 2.

[11] Ibid., para. 5.

[12] Ibid., para 6.

[13] Ibid., para 7. The Final Act reads: "The Commission shall prepare proposals for a provision on aggression, including the definition and Elements of Crimes of aggression and the conditions under which the International Criminal Court shall exercise its jurisdiction with regard to this crime."

[14] Ibid., para. 8.

stipulated to set the infrastructure of the work until a date shortly after the Rome Statute's entrance into force.

The UN General Assembly, in its Resolution 53/105, requested that the Secretary-General convene PrepComII to "to discuss ways to enhance the effectiveness and acceptance of the Court."[15] The Resolution also noted that NGOs might participate in the plenary as well as open sessions, receive copies of the official documents, and distribute their documents to the delegates in attendance.[16] In similar Resolutions[17] adopted later, the UN General Assembly reiterated the same request upon the completion of the PrepComII sessions that were referred to in the respective resolution. In compliance with the aforementioned resolutions, the PrepComII convened ten sessions, three in 1999, three in 2000, two in 2001, and two in 2002.

The works of PrepComII have proven to be fruitful. As early as its second session, the commission was able to make substantial progress with regard to preparing the two most important documents, the Rules of Procedure and Evidence and the Elements of Crimes. It also devised a tentative procedural approach towards another thorny issue, the definition of the crime of aggression.[18] The third session was marked by the unanimous approval of both documents by the General Assembly. In reference to this accomplishment, the Commission Chair Ambassador, Philippe Kirsch from Canada, opined at the closing plenary, "Today, I am delighted to report that the PrepCom's performance record, on a scale of 1–10, has elevated to an almost

[15] "Establishment of an international criminal court," U.N. General Assembly Resolution No. 53/105, U.N. Doc. No. A/RES/53/105, 83rd Plenary Meeting, December 8, 1998, para. 4.

[16] Ibid., para. 7.

[17] "Establishment of an international criminal court," U.N. General Assembly Resolution No. 54/105, U.N. Doc. No. A/RES/54/105, 76th Plenary Meeting, December 9, 1999; "Establishment of an international criminal court," U.N. General Assembly Resolution No. 55/155, U.N. Doc. No. A/RES/55/155, 84th Plenary Meeting, December 12, 2000; "Establishment of an international criminal court," U.N. General Assembly Resolution No. 56/85, U.N. Doc. No. A/RES/56/85, 85th Plenary Meeting, December 12, 2001.

[18] Jennifer Schense, "Second Session of the Preparatory Commission," *The International Criminal Court Monitor,* Issue 11, 1999, p. 10.

perfect 10."[19] The Assembly's approval was followed by the commission's adoption of both documents at the end of its fifth session on June 30, 2000, as stipulated by the Final Act of the Rome Statute.[20]

At the same session, the PrepComII chair also appointed coordinators in advance to "facilitate work on the subjects remaining within the Preparatory Commission's mandate."[21] At the eighth session, seven working groups were active. The Working Groups on the Relationship Agreement, the Financial Regulations and Rules, the Agreement on the Privileges and Immunities of the Court, and the Rules of Procedure of the Assembly of States Parties completed their draft agreements, which were adopted for the inclusion in the Commission's final report. The working group on the basic principles governing the headquarters agreement and the working group on the 1st-year budget began their work at the same session.[22]

With a few exceptions, including the definition of the crime of aggression, PrepComII successfully completed its mandate and laid the groundwork for the ICC, and the number of states that were party to the statute was increasing. In the end, when the Rome Statute officially entered into force after the 60th ratification, the court's institutional and functional design was complete.

---

[19] David Donat-Cattin, "ICC Procedural Law: The Limited Mandate of the PrepCom on the Rules of Procedure and Evidence," *The International Criminal Court Monitor,* Issue 14, 2000, p. 8.

[20] Draft Report on the Eighth Session of the Preparatory Commission September 24, October 5, 2001 Coalition for an International Criminal Court October 7, 2001.

[21] Ibid., p. 3.

[22] Ibid., p. 3.

# Part III

## The International Criminal Court in World Politics

# Introduction

Human rights issues have not been paid much attention to at the international level until the end of World War II. One of the major obstacles before the realization of substantial improvements in the field of human rights was extensive concerns over national sovereignty. It should be noted that the concept of sovereignty is closely associated with the principle of "nonintervention," according to which sovereign states are strictly obligated not to intervene in matters falling into the domestic jurisdictions of other sovereign states.[1] As a consequence, "apart from [a] few examples, policymakers and intellectuals paid almost no attention to the concept of human rights before the Second World War."[2] After the end of World War II, "it became that human rights, formerly considered the *domain reserve* of States, were now a matter of concern for the whole international community" (emphasis in original).[3] Even though "the

[1] Jack Donnelly, *International Human Rights* (Boulder, CO: Westview Press, 1993), p. 5.

[2] Margaret E. Keck and Kathryn Sikkink, *Activists Beyond Borders: Advocacy Networks in International Politics* (Ithaca, NY: Cornell University Press, 1998), p. 43.

[3] Jastine Barret, "The Prohibition of Torture Under International Law: The Institutional Organization," *The International Journal of Human Rights,* Vol. 5, Issue 1, 2001, p. 2.



C. Çakmak, *A Brief History of International Criminal Law and International Criminal Court,*
DOI 10.1057/978-1-137-56736-9_12

doctrine of humanitarian intervention" formulated by the renowned Dutch scholar, Grotius, was legitimizing the intervention of states in the matters of state, which was believed to violate rights of its own citizens extensively, with a few exceptions, that doctrine was not exercised.

After the end of World War II, protection of human rights was placed on the agenda of international politics. The leading factor for the dramatic transformation toward the prevention of the abuses of fundamental rights and freedoms, which have long been overlooked by almost all global actors, including intergovernmental organizations, such as the League of Nations that was greatly concerned with nonintervention into domestic matters of sovereign states, and paid little attention to, and for the tendency toward the protection of rights of individuals is the Nazis' atrocities committed to the Jewish and other nations during World War II. The notorious Holocaust and genocide of Jews by the Nazis horrified all the humanity and accelerated the efforts and attempts to establish protection and promotion mechanisms of human rights worldwide.

The evolution of global human rights could be found in Buergenthal's analysis on this subject. He refers to four general stages in this evolution. The first stage is "the normative foundation," which "begins with the entry into force of the UN Charter and continues at least through the adoption in 1966 of the International Covenants on Human Rights."[4] The period saw the adoption of such principal human rights instruments as the Universal Declaration of Human Rights, Genocide Convention, and the Convention on the Elimination of All Forms of Racial Discrimination, such regional documents as the European Convention on Human Rights and the American Declaration on the Rights and Duties of Man, and such secondary documents as the Convention against Discrimination in Education and the Convention Concerning Discrimination in Respect of Employment and Occupation, promulgated by UNESCO and ILO, respectively.

The second stage is "institution building," which "begins in the late 1960s and continues for the next fifteen to twenty years."[5] The period

[4] Thomas Buergenthal, "The Normative and Institutional Evolution of International Human Rights", *Human Rights Quarterly,* Vol. 19, Issue 4, 1997, p. 704.

[5] Ibid., p. 708.

saw the emergence and consolidation of universal and regional treaty-based institutions for the protection of human rights. The UN Human Rights Committee, the Committee on the Elimination of Racial Discrimination, Inter-American Commission and Court of Human Rights, a special mechanism adopted by UNESCO for dealing with human rights violations that fall within its sphere of competence and several ILO institutions for dealing with human rights issues, consist only a partial list of institutions established in that period.

However, the institutions created in the period of "institution building" have not been effective until 1980s "when they could begin to focus on adopting effective measures to ensure state compliance with their international obligations."[6] This process is called "implementation." The leading factor that made implementation of treaties and conventions on human rights easy was the collapse of the Soviet Union and the dissolution of the Communist Bloc.

Buergenthal names the fourth stage as "Individual Criminal Responsibility, Minority Rights, and Collective Humanitarian Intervention."[7] Traditionally, the international community has shown a tendency to hold governments rather than individuals responsible for the violations of internationally guaranteed human rights. Although in the post World War II crimes trials, the Geneva Convention on Humanitarian Law, and some international human rights treaties, primarily Genocide Convention, individuals were held responsible for some of the most serious human rights abuses, such as genocide, crimes against humanity, and war crimes; international human rights law and efforts for its enforcement have for the most part focused on the obligations of governments.[8] Today, "the concept of international responsibility for massive violation of human rights is being expanded to include individuals and groups in addition to governments."[9] Therefore, while individuals have greater rights under international

[6] Ibid., p. 711.
[7] Ibid., p. 717.
[8] Ibid., p. 718.
[9] Ibid., p. 719.

human rights law, they are imposed corresponding duties not to violate those rights, and held responsible for their violation. We have also witnessed a growing interest by the international community in the establishment of international norms and institutions for the protection of members of national, racial, ethnic, linguistic, or religious minorities. Adoption of the Declaration on the Rights of Persons Belonging to National or Ethnic, Religious and Linguistic Minorities in 1992, the Framework Convention for the Protection of National Minorities in 1994, the establishment of the office of the OSCE High Commissioner for National Minorities are some of the attempts to focus international attention on the need for the international protection of minorities.[10] Collective humanitarian intervention is made possible by the UN Security Council, which is "increasingly taking action to deal with large-scale human rights violations by authorizing enforcement measures under the powers that Chapter VII of the UN Charter confers on it."[11]

Therefore, the final stage in the evolution of human rights is the recognition of private individuals as a new subject of international law. As the international legal system dates back to the 1600s, and since then, only states have been regarded as the main actors in global politics, the human rights regime has long been based on the enduring principle of state responsibility. For a long time, treaties, the primary instruments of international law, existed to regulate relations between states. However, the evolution in human rights politics brought individuals into the stage. Under the contemporary international legal system, individuals are recognized as the holders of rights.[12]

However, it is worth noting that they are not just holders of rights, a fact that implies that states are responsible to protect those rights; but they are, under international law, now assumed to be responsible for their acts as well. This state of responsibility, however, does not cover all

[10] Ibid., pp. 720–721.

[11] Ibid., p. 722.

[12] Chris Jochnick, "The Human Rights Challenge to Global Poverty," Retrieved on April 15, 2004, from http://www.cesr.org/text%20files/actors.PDF.

matters that fall into the scope of international law. Instead, the individuals are responsible for serious criminal acts only.

It is, therefore, the international criminal law that holds the individuals responsible for their acts. This seems to be unusual given that international law has regulated the inter-states relations. However, it should also be noted that the states have been given a wide discretion to deal with the criminal acts of the individuals. In other words, although the individuals have been held responsible in some particular cases, with a few exceptions, no international mechanism has been formed to address them.

The recently established permanent International Criminal Court is this international body to cover the issues pertinent to international criminal law. Until its establishment, nation-states have had the authority to try and punish the perpetrators of the most heinous crimes. However, it has been observed that this system has not worked very well, for that the world has witnessed several genocidal campaigns, much more massive killings of ethnic and national groups and numerous situations in which war crimes have been extensively committed.

In particular, the genocidal attempts in Former Yugoslavia and Rwanda are clear examples worth mentioning in this regard. Even though the international community has developed legal instruments to prevent those occurrences, it became evident that they did not succeed. The Genocide Convention of 1948[13] and the Geneva Conventions of 1949[14] hold the states responsible with regard to the rights they guarantee.[15] In addition, especially in case of the crime of genocide, it is generally

---

[13] *Convention on the Prevention and Punishment of the Crime of Genocide*, approved and opened for signature, ratification, and accession by the UN General Assembly Resolution 260 (III), December 9, 1948, and entered into force on January 12, 1951.

[14] These are: *Geneva Convention (I) for the Amelioration of the Condition of the Wounded, Sick and Shipwrecked Members of Armed Forces in the Field*, September 15, 1949, 75 U.N.T.S. 31; *Geneva Convention (II) for the Amelioration of the Condition of the Wounded, Sick and Shipwrecked Members of Armed Forces at Sea*, August 12, 1949, 75 U.N.T.S. 85; *Geneva Convention (III) Relative to the Treatment of Prisoners of War*, August 12, 1949, 75 U.N.T.S. 135; and *Geneva Convention (IV) Relative to the Protection of Civilian Persons in Time of War*, August 12, 1949, 75 U.N.T.S. 287.

[15] However, despite the breakthroughs the Genova Conventions have brought to fore, it is asserted that "they fell short of confirming rape and other sexual violence as grave breaches." Pam Spees, "Women's Advocacy in the Creation of the International Criminal Court: Changing the Landscapes of Justice and Power," *Signs: Journal of Women in Culture and Society*, Vol. 28, Issue 4, 2003, p. 1239.

accepted that it is an international customary rule that any state is responsible for its prevention and for its punishment in case it has been committed in its own territory, even if it is not bound by a treaty requiring doing so. However, notwithstanding these novel arrangements, there have been attempts to exterminate an ethnic group even as late as 1990s in Former Yugoslavia and Rwanda and since 2003 in Darfur, Sudan.

It is this observance that led the international community to create a permanent body to address the international criminal matters. The International Criminal Court is the outcome of the need to create such a body. This article explores the significance of this new actor in world politics. Although having an international legal personality, the Court is likely to affect the conduct of world politics. In this article, this effect is analyzed in three sections. First the impact of the Court on the perception and exercise of national sovereignty is discussed. Second, it is argued that the global civil society's impact was so great in the creation of the Court that it is now impossible to ignore it as a significant global actor. Finally, the US opposition to the Court and the subsequent developments suggest that the supremacy of the United States in world politics is likely to be questioned.

# Overview and Significance of the International Criminal Court (ICC)

Established as an intergovernmental organization, the International Criminal Court (the ICC or "the Court") is specifically designed to deal with the international crimes that are thought to be most severe and serious. It has generally been observed that the commissions of those crimes had gone unpunished, making the impunity of the perpetrators a usual and ordinary practice in international relations. Although the idea that a permanent international criminal court is strongly needed, and therefore, should be created, lingered for a very long time, the realization of that idea has become quite recently. Nation-states, the major and primary actors of the international system, have generally been lenient, if not reluctant, in addressing those kinds of acts. Particularly, concerns over sovereign rights of the states have made them reluctant to get together to discuss the issue up until 1998. Since sovereignty has been the underlying principle in the operation of the international system that is generally believed to be built by sovereign nation-states, states have long refrained from dealing with the issues pertinent to even the gravest crimes in order to show their tribute to the principle of nonintervention. As a consequence, apart from a few examples, human rights issues in



C. Çakmak, *A Brief History of International Criminal Law and International Criminal Court*,
DOI 10.1057/978-1-137-56736-9_13

general, and international crimes that are the most serious violations of human rights in particular, have not adequately been addressed by the state-based international system.

Therefore, the year of 1998 marked a historical moment, since there appeared for the first time a real possibility that the long-survived notorious practice of impunity would be unusual in the foreseeable future. In July 1998, the most important initial steps toward ensuring the globalization of justice and the end of impunity were taken at the Rome Diplomatic Conference to Establish an International Criminal Court,[1] and subsequently the Rome Statute[2] setting up such a Court was adopted and opened for signature, "half a century earlier than many predicted."[3] The Statute was authored by the representatives of the Participant States so as that the treaty would have entered into force after the number of 60 in ratifications is reached. That is to say, the Court was not automatically created at the conference. Although the vast majority of the participant states to the conference signed the treaty, showing their willingness and commitment to abide by the treaty content, the number of states that have signed the treaty but are not party to the ICC could be regarded as "significant." As of now, the number of the States Parties to the Rome Statute and to the ICC is 124, while the number of signatories is 139.[4]

On the other hand, it is worth noting that the threshold for the entrance into force of the treaty—which was 60—was impressively overcome in a very short time, "while many had predicted that this goal would not be realized for decades."[5] It is frequently stated that the fact that it took just four years for the Court to come into effect is unusual, given that the ratification of an international treaty is generally made by national assemblies, which are reasonably expected to be

[1] The United Nations Diplomatic Conference of Plenipotentiaries on the Establishment of an International Criminal Court), Rome, Italy, June 15–July 17, 1998.

[2] Rome Statute of the International Criminal Court, U.N. Doc. A/CONF.183/9. (hereinafter "the Rome Statute").

[3] William R. Pace, "A Victory for Peace," *The ICC Monitor,* Issue: 21, June 2002, p. 1.

[4] For the list of States Parties and signatories to the Rome Statute, see, the latest issue of *The ICC Monitor,* available at the NGO Coalition for an ICC website: http://www.iccnow.org.

[5] Pace, "A Victory for Peace," p. 1.

cautious toward such arrangements as the ICC, and therefore, to need much time for deliberating the treaty. After the required number of ratifications has been reached, the Rome Statute, along with the ICC, officially entered into force in July 2002.[6]

However, the Court did not become fully functional by the time it entered into force. In 2003, after a very complex and yet relatively democratic process ensuring a more and balanced gender, geographical and cultural representation, the judges and the independent prosecutors for the Court were elected and appointed. After then, the ICC began operating in its headquarters in The Hague, "the capital of international law."

Although it has not dealt with and thus not concluded any case for some time, first referrals by Uganda and Democratic Republic of Congo,[7] and the later ones by the UN Security Council and Central African Republic, have officially made it involved in the international criminal matters. It is commendable that the Court has received growing number of referrals either by state parties or the UN Security Council, an important sign for its effectiveness and credibility in dealing with the worst crimes and their perpetrators.

The Court is currently dealing with the gravest crimes, that is, the crime of genocide, crimes against humanity, war crimes, and the crime of aggression.[8] At the first sight, it might seem that the list is so narrow,

[6] Ten states concurrently deposited their accession instruments with the United Nations on April 11, 2002, increasing the number of ratifications of the Rome Statute of the ICC to 66. These ten countries are Bosnia and Herzegovina, Bulgaria, Cambodia, Democratic Republic of Congo, Ireland, Jordan, Mongolia, Niger, Romania and Slovakia.

[7] It appears that the DRC Government officials were *required* to refer the situation in the country to the Court. It is claimed that the referral is "the result of the Prosecutor's July 2003 announcement of his intention to follow closely the situation in the DRC." The Prosecutor previously informed the Assembly of States Parties that he had the intention to seek authorization from a Pre-Trial Chamber to start an investigation in accordance with his power under the Rome Statute. Jennifer Schense, "Prosecutor Receives DRC Referral," *The ICC Monitor,* Issue 27, June 2004, p. 3.

[8] Article 5(1) of the Rome Statute. However, the ICC will be unable to exercise its jurisdiction over the crime of aggression until a definition of that crime is adopted. Article 5(2) states, "The Court shall exercise jurisdiction over the crime of aggression once a provision is adopted in accordance with articles 121 and 123 defining the crime and setting out the conditions under which the Court shall exercise jurisdiction with respect to this crime."

suggesting that the Court is authorized to exercise its jurisdiction in too few cases. However, there are many "sub-crimes" that could perfectly be called as crimes against humanity, such as systematically committed rape, forced prostitution, and so on.[9] Furthermore, the inclusion of the crime of aggression as a crime to be dealt with by the Court on the list is an important step in preventing future conflicts. Although the jurisdiction of the ICC over the crime of aggression, defined in 2010, is yet to be exercised in comply with the provisions of the Rome Statute, there is an agreement that the definition and the exercise of jurisdiction would be consistent with the UN Charter.[10]

The Court's involvement with a criminal matter could be activated in three ways. First, the United Nations Security Council is given the authority to refer situations to the ICC. Second, as stated in the Statute, any State Party to the ICC is also authorized to refer a situation to the Court. And finally, the independent prosecutor has the power, although subject to some certain preconditions and limitations, to initiate an investigation for the events, in case the chief prosecutor believes that the reluctance, unwillingness, or the inability of the national authorities in adequately addressing them have been evident.

Since the end of World War II, the instruments of the international human rights law have steadily limited the state's absolute right to determine the treatment of its citizens.[11] That is to say, while the international human rights law has been evolving, the state's sovereignty has been eroded. In the evolution process of international human rights regimes, the nation-state's supremacy as the sole decision-maker in global affairs has been eroded. In this regard, the realization of the idea for establishing a permanent international criminal court is worth a close examination.

[9] For example, "the Rome Statute explicitly codifies for the first time many crimes of sexual and gender violence as war crimes and crimes against humanity." Spees, *supra,* "Women's Advocacy in the Creation of the International Criminal Court: Changing the Landscapes of Justice and Power," p. 1234.

[10] Article 5(2) of the Rome Statute.

[11] Marlies Glasius, "Expertise in the Cause of Justice: Global Civil Society Influence on the Statute for an International Court," in Marlies Glasius, Mary Kaldor and Helmut Anheier (eds.), *Global Civil Society 2002* (Oxford: Oxford University Press, 2002), p. 137

As one of the most recently established intergovernmental organizations, the ICC has the potential of influencing world politics deeply. However, at the same time, its creation triggered a major controversy between the EU and the United States,[12] which might affect its effectiveness and future roles and makes it a focus of political debates. The role recognized to the Prosecutor of the Court under the Rome Statute also raises a great political debate as to whether this position is likely to be politicized or a necessity for the realization of global justice. In short, in addition to its legal roles, it would be an important political actor as well.

First and foremost, the creation of the Court is a small revolution in international law and politics. Its establishment could be considered as one of the most important steps in the continuing transition from the state-centered world to a post-internationalist world order that is less based on the principle of state sovereignty, and more oriented and sensitive to the protection of individuals' fundamental rights and freedoms from the abuse of power-and-interest-based intergovernmental relations. Second, the contribution of global civil society and particularly of the coalition of large number of NGOs in the process which resulted in the adoption of the Rome Statute has been unprecedented in international treaty negotiations.[13]

Moreover, it is the first attempt to internationally hold individuals responsible for such crimes as genocide, crimes against humanity, and war crimes, and to punish them. Traditionally, international law has created responsibilities for states only. In other words, the main subject of international law has been "the nation-state." However, with the creation of the ICC, the individuals became responsible in international law. Although there has been individual criminal responsibility before the creation of the ICC, it was either temporary, or the individual concerned, while being responsible under the principles and rules of

[12] In this regard, it is commented that the ICC "has become a prominent feature of foreign policy in the world. The U.S. foreign policy on the ICC carries an array of disincentives designed to entice less powerful countries away from the Court, while European Union policy carries various incentives for ICC ratification." See, Spees, *supra,* "Women's Advocacy in the Creation of the International Criminal Court: Changing the Landscapes of Justice and Power," p. 1247.

[13] Ibid.

international law, was brought before justice by the state authorities. Even though such international treaties as the Genocide Convention of 1948[14] and the four Geneva Conventions of 1949 contain provisions that enable to hold individuals responsible for the violations of the respective rights they guarantee, the protection of those rights is almost entirely left to national authorities. However, none of them specifies an international authority to punish the individuals responsible for international crimes. That is to say, it is the national authorities that are anticipated to proceed against those who have committed the crimes covered by the above legal documents. However, there is no clearly and solidly defined sanction against the state that shows reluctance to effectively deal with the matter concerned.

Unlike the aforesaid Conventions, the Rome Statute that established the International Criminal Court provides precise procedures for the prosecution of the individuals responsible for the crimes concerned. In doing that, it has openly challenged the state's absolute sovereignty and dominance in the conduct of world politics, since it has, although in a limited way, replaced with the national courts. Traditionally, the enforcement of the treaty provisions and the implementation of an international treaty have been left to national authorities of States Parties to the treaty concerned. However, the Court is allowed to act independently of the states bound by the Rome Statute, and to request from the States Parties the handing over of the individuals accused of having committed the crimes it covers, and subsequently to try the accused. The States Parties have vested on the ICC the power of formally asking the handing over of a criminal suspect to the Court. Therefore, the Court is expected to act as if it is a national court, where the actual national court concerned has failed to handle the matter properly, or is impotent to conclude it.

It might be advanced that there are other international courts; thus, there is nothing new and original with the International Criminal Court. It is true that there are two permanent international courts: the European

[14] It is stated that the Genocide Convention has so far failed to effectively address the issue of genocide. For instance, see, Scott Straus, "Darfur and the Genocide Debate," *Foreign Affairs*, Vol. 84, Issue 1, 2005, p. 122.

Court of Human Rights and the Inter-American Court of Human Rights. However, they do not try individuals; rather, they receive complaints from individuals and make judgments against the State Party concerned. In this regard, the protection of the individuals' rights still remains at the State's disposal. In addition to those permanent Courts, a few ad hoc international tribunals have been established to try individuals for such crimes as genocide, crimes against humanity and war crimes. However, the Nuremberg and Tokyo Tribunals, the first of this kind, were established with the agreement of a relatively small number of states. Therefore, they were not genuinely international. The two recently established UN tribunals, the International Criminal Tribunal for Rwanda and the International Criminal Tribunal for the Former Yugoslavia, are also limited in time and in geographical scope.[15]

It is also worth noting that the ad hoc Tribunals established to deal with the crimes in Rwanda and Former Yugoslavia are temporary and responsible to the UN Security Council. The predecessors of this kind, the Nuremberg and Tokyo Tribunals, might be seen as the tools of the victorious powers after World War II. Moreover, all have and had limited power in terms of both time and scope. However, unlike these early examples, the ICC has a permanent seat, and a much more comprehensive authority. But most importantly, it is not controlled by the UN Security Council, where the major powers have the right to veto.[16] Although the Security Council is given prominent roles in the functioning of the ICC, it is the Assembly of States Parties that the ICC is held responsible to.

[15] Steven R. Ratner, "The International Criminal Court and the Limits of Global Judicialization," *Texas International Law Journal*, Vol. 38, Issue 3, 2003, p. 446.

[16] It has been commented that the Court's independence of the UN Security Council alone "has incurred the wrath of the defense and foreign policy establishment of the world's 'sole remaining superpower', the United States, which is a telling indicator of the potential of the new institution as an independent mechanism of accountability." Spees, *supra*, "Women's Advocacy in the Creation of the International Criminal Court: Changing the Landscapes of Justice and Power," p. 1233.

# The ICC Versus National Sovereignty: Analyzing ICC's Performance as a Legal and Political Institution

One of the most debated issues concerning the International Criminal Court (ICC) is that whether it constitutes a major threat to the international system that is based on the principle of national sovereignty. Relevant to this is also that whether the Court will be able to succeed to implement its mandate, given that states would strongly seek to retain their sovereign authority. Therefore, as one observer puts it clearly, "perhaps the central issue facing the ICC is its effect on sovereignty."[1] In this regard, he advances the question that must national sovereignty "be sacrificed to the international court?"[2] Especially, the role given to the Prosecutor under the Rome Statute, the way the Court is allowed to exercise its jurisdiction and its complementary role to the national judicial systems are worth noting for a clear analysis on whether the Court will undermine the sovereign right of the nation-state.

[1] David A. Nill, "National Sovereignty: Must It Be Sacrificed to the International Criminal Court?" *BYU Journal of Public Law,* Vol. 14, Issue 1, 1999, p. 127.
[2] Ibid., pp. 119–151.

 
C. Çakmak, *A Brief History of International Criminal Law and International Criminal Court,*
DOI 10.1057/978-1-137-56736-9_14

i. The role of the Prosecutor under the Rome Statute and its impact on and relevance to national sovereignty:

It is often stated that the Rome Statute recognizes a wide range of discretion to the Prosecutor in the proceedings against the alleged perpetrators of the crimes it covers. This role, it is argued, is so enormous that it poses a significant threat to national sovereignty. For instance, a Chinese representative that participated in the Rome Conference responds to the UN Chronicle's invitation for making a comment on the adoption of the Rome Statute of the ICC in the following fashion: "Granting the Prosecutor the right to initiate prosecutions placed State Sovereignty on the subjective decisions of an individual."[3] The discretion given to the Prosecutor has been criticized by academicians as well. Alfred P. Rubin of Tufts University states on the subject that "one key aspect is the authority of the prosecutor to initiate the process of the tribunal by charging particular individuals with violations of the law set out in the statute . . . the discretion given to the Prosecutor is enormous. Thus, the potential abuse of that discretion is also enormous."[4] Therefore, the underlying fear concerning the role of the Prosecutor is that this role is very likely to be politicized, even though the Office of the Prosecutor is one of the "judicial" organs of the Court described in Article 34 of the Statute.[5]

However, it seems that the role of the Prosecutor is unlikely to excessively affect the states' prerogatives in conducting global affairs. It is true that he has become a strong figure; but that does not necessarily mean that he would abuse or misuse his authority. The strength that role has is embedded in the Rome Statute. Under the Statute, the Court is authorized to exercise its jurisdiction if "The Prosecutor has initiated an investigation in respect of such a crime in accordance with article 15,"[6]

[3] "Permanent International Criminal Court Established," *United Nations Chronicle,* Vol. XXXV, Issue 3, 1998, p. 1.

[4] Alfred P. Rubin, "Challenging the Conventional Wisdom: Another View of the International Criminal Court," *Journal of International Affairs,* Vol. 52, Issue 2, 1999, p. 154.

[5] Under Article 34 of the Rome Statute, the other judicial organs of the Court are the Presidency, the Appeals, Trial and Pre-Trial Divisions; and the Registry.

[6] Article 13(c) of the Rome Statute.

which states that he "may initiate investigations proprio motu on the basis of information on crimes within the jurisdiction of the Court."[7] It should also be noted that under the Statute, the Prosecutor is the only figure that has the authority to "initiate" an investigation. In other words, while any state party to the Statute and the UN Security Council can "refer" a "situation" to the Court, the Prosecutor has the power to determine whether it is necessary to initiate an investigation based on the referrals made by the first two. This is severely criticized:

> The Prosecutor may decide not to proceed with an investigation if he or she believes there is a lack of sufficient evidence or because of some other reasons. On the one hand, the Statute places the Prosecutor above a State Party and the Security Council by entitling him or her the right to examine the decisions of a sovereign state and resolutions of the Security Council, at least to some extent. On the other, it puts the Prosecutor in a position to determine cases which might be related to the relationships between States or international politics so that he or she becomes a truly "world's Prosecutor."[8]

In this regard, it is also important to note that the Prosecutor does not solely depend on the information coming from such public authorities as national governments or intergovernmental organizations. Private entities such as NGOs are also legitimate sources of information for the Prosecutor. In addition, information coming about non-party states to the Statute is also taken into consideration. In effect, this is very important; since it has become evident that information on non-party states significantly contributed to the Prosecutor's information gathering. Between July 2002 and July 2003, the Office of the Prosecutor received about 500 communications from 66 countries. Twenty-three percent of this information was relevant to the states that are not parties to the Statute.[9] This is an important authority. However, it would have

---

[7] Article 15(1) of the Rome Statute.

[8] Lijun Yang, "Some Critical Remarks on the Rome Statute of the International Criminal Court," *Chinese Journal of International Law*, Vol. 2, Issue 1, 2003, p. 615.

[9] Annalisa Ciampi, "The International Criminal Court," *The Law and Practice of International Courts and Tribunals*, Vol. 3, Issue 3, 2004, p. 147.

been contrary to the nature of the prosecution act, if the Prosecutor were not given such a power.

While those kinds of criticisms refer to the role of the Prosecutor as a benign innovation for that it poses a major threat to national sovereignty, for some, it is in fact one of the most important accomplishments of the Statute of the ICC. For Steven R. Ratner of the University of Texas, the Statute's setting up an independent Prosecutor is one of the leading reasons for seeing the Court as a success.[10] Morten Bergsmo, Legal Adviser to the Office of the Prosecutor of the International Criminal Tribunals for Former Yugoslavia, points out that the authority the Prosecutor has under the Rome Statute is an effective measure for saving lives of potential victims: "A standing Prosecutor's Office can react quickly to emerging armed conflicts and other relevant situations, taking early steps to preserve evidence and spark the awareness of Governments of the importance of securing evidence when available. Such steps can have a deterrent effect among the parties to the conflict. Thus, *proprio motu* capacity of the ICC Prosecutor may contribute to saving some lives and evidence."[11]

It is also worth noting that the Prosecutor is not totally free in exercising his authority to initiate an investigation. That authority is granted to him for *initiation* an investigation. That is to say, it does not give him the authority to start it.[12] The Rome Statute lays down some certain limitations (or "safeguards," we might say) on the exercise of this power. Although the Prosecutor may receive information from non-state entities, i.e. non-governmental organizations, individuals, Article 15(2) stipulates that he would analyze the seriousness of that information.[13] After the analysis, he may proceed with an investigation if he concludes that there is a reasonable basis to do so; but he also has to submit to the Pre-Trial

[10] Ratner, *supra,* "The International Criminal Court and the Limits of Global Judicialization," p. 447.

[11] Morten Bergsmo, "The Jurisdictional Regime of the International Criminal Court (Part II, Articles 11–19)" *European Journal of Crime, Criminal Law and Criminal Justice,* Vol. 6, Issue 4, 1998, p. 41.

[12] Ibid., p. 38.

[13] Article 15(2) of the Rome Statute.

Chamber comprised of three judges "a request for authorization of an investigation, together with any supporting material collected."[14]

Article 15(4) further states;

> If the Pre-Trial Chamber, upon examination of the request and the supporting material, considers that there is a reasonable basis to proceed with an investigation, and that the case appears to fall within the jurisdiction of the Court, it shall authorize the commencement of the investigation, without prejudice to subsequent determinations by the Court with regard to the jurisdiction and admissibility of a case.[15]

What this implies is that in order to be able to proceed with the investigation, the Prosecutor has to be authorized by the Pre-Trial Chamber. However, for the critics of the ICC, it is not an effective safeguard; for that "with the approval of only the Prosecutor and two judges (a majority of a Pre-Trial Chamber), the ICC may hear a case, which might affect international relations and international politics."[16] Furthermore, "aside from such a limited judicial review, there seems to be no other formal check on the Prosecutor's authority in this regard."[17] This is surely a clear indication that the Prosecutor has a vast authority. But that does not necessarily mean that he would abuse this authority and be a political figure. The check applied by the Pre-Trial Chamber is based on "reasonableness," not "appropriateness." The Chamber is not expected to perform the role of the Security Council in empowering the Prosecutor of the ad hoc tribunals, which was in fact a political function. "The judicial nature of the Pre-Trial Chamber is thus protected, while at the same time there is control over the Prosecutor's commencements of investigations by a panel of professional judges."[18]

---

[14] Article 15(3) of the Rome Statute.

[15] Article 15(4) of the Rome Statute.

[16] Yang, *supra,* "Some Critical Remarks on the Rome Statute of the International Criminal Court," p. 616.

[17] Rubin, *supra,* "Challenging the Conventional Wisdom: Another View of the International Criminal Court," p. 158.

[18] Bergsmo, *supra,* "The Jurisdictional Regime of the International Criminal Court (Part II, Articles 11–19)," p. 39.

The denial of the Prosecutor's submission by the Pre-Trial Chamber does not necessarily prevent him from going further. Article 15(5) states that "The refusal of the Pre-Trial Chamber to authorize the investigation shall not preclude the presentation of a subsequent request by the Prosecutor based on new facts or evidence regarding the same situation."[19] This has also been a matter of controversy, for that it seems to be weakening the role of the Pre-Trial Chamber. However, the Statute is very clear that the new request by the Prosecutor will be based on new evidence acquired after the denial of the former request. It is quite probable that he would receive new information that would be sufficient to initiate an investigation about the situation.

The Statute further contains provisions securing the independence of the Prosecutor and preventing any external political exertion on him. Article 42(1) states that the Office of the Prosecutor will act as a separate organ and "A member of the Office shall not seek or act on instructions from any external source."[20] Under that article, the Prosecutor and the Deputy Prosecutors have to be of different nationalities.[21] It is also clearly stated that "The Prosecutor and the Deputy Prosecutors shall be persons of high moral character, be highly competent in and have extensive practical experience in the prosecution or trial of criminal cases."[22] More importantly, the impartiality of the Prosecutors is ensured in the process of their election. "The Prosecutor shall be elected by secret ballot by an absolute majority of the members of the Assembly of States Parties. The Deputy Prosecutors shall be elected in the same way from a list of candidates provided by the Prosecutor."[23] The election is made by the ASP, in which each member has a voice to be heard of. More safeguards against the politicization of the Prosecutor are provided in the same article. "Neither the Prosecutor nor a Deputy Prosecutor shall engage in any activity which is likely to interfere with his or her

[19] Article 15(5) of the Rome Statute.
[20] Article 42(1) of the Rome Statute.
[21] Article 42(2) of the Rome Statute.
[22] Article 42(3) of the Rome Statute.
[23] Article 42(4) of the Rome Statute.

prosecutorial functions or to affect confidence in his or her independence."[24] Under the Statute, "Neither the Prosecutor nor a Deputy Prosecutor shall participate in any matter in which their impartiality might reasonably be doubted on any ground."[25]

However, notwithstanding these checks, it is argued that the Prosecutor is still open to political pressure:

> For the purposes of our analysis is important to highlight the fact that the basic safeguards provided for in R.S. Art. 42, although an important step to isolate the Prosecutor from external political pressure, do not suffice to preserve her independence. As a result, the more political discretion is granted to the Prosecutor, the more political pressure will be put on her, and the less resistance she will be able to exercise to guarantee her independence. Hence, the introduction of a further safeguard consisting of the strict limitation of the amount of political discretion conferred upon the Prosecutor becomes of the greatest importance.[26]

It is possible to infer from the above that the Prosecutor of the ICC has a significant authority and role in international criminal matters. But this role is not designed to undermine national sovereignty; instead, it could be argued that states have willingly devolved some of the powers they had in international criminal matters to the Prosecutor of the ICC. Therefore, the assessment on the impact of the Prosecutor on national sovereignty will depend on how to see the arrangements on international criminal matters. On the one hand, it could be argued that states have partially withdrawn from the sphere of international criminal law; therefore, they are losing power. On the other hand, it could also be argued that the states themselves empowered the Prosecutor with such a vast authority in order to prevent future atrocities. In short, it could be said that the role of the Prosecutor will create a mild effect on national sovereignty. In fact, it would not be reasonable to expect that an

[24] Article 42(5) of the Rome Statute.

[25] Article 42(7) of the Rome Statute.

[26] Héctor Olásolo, "The Prosecutor of the ICC Before the Initiation of Investigations: A Quasi-judicial or a Political Body?" *International Criminal Law Review,* Vol. 3, Issue 2, 2003, p. 109

international organization like the ICC would have been designed to drastically change the nature of world politics.

ii. The ICC's exercising its jurisdiction and national sovereignty:

For the present time, the Court has automatic jurisdiction over the crime of genocide, crimes against humanity, and war crimes. It will have the power to exercise its jurisdiction over the crime of aggression as well, once a definition of that crime is adopted. However, in the Draft Statute prepared by the International Law Commission, only the crime of genocide was within the automatic jurisdiction of the Court. For other crimes covered in the Statute, the states themselves would have the authority to make the decision on whether they will refer them to the Court or not.[27]

However, under the Rome Statute, there are some preconditions for exercising this automatic jurisdiction. These preconditions are laid down in Article 12. In paragraph 1 of that Article, it is stated that "A State which becomes a Party to this Statute thereby accepts the jurisdiction of the Court with respect to the crimes referred to in article 5."[28] This demonstrates that once a state becomes party to the Statute, its acceptance of the jurisdiction of the Court too becomes compulsory. However, this provision also indicates that the jurisdiction of the Court is limited to the crimes referred to in Article 5. Another precondition for the jurisdiction of the Court is that either "The State on the territory of which the conduct in question occurred" (territorial state) or "The State of which the person accused of the crime is a national" (suspect state) should be "Parties to this Statute or have accepted the jurisdiction of the Court."[29] "In the case of States not party to the Statute on whose territory or by whose nationals core crimes have been committed, the competence of the Court may also be based on their acceptance of its jurisdiction on an *ad*

[27] Yang, *supra,* "Some Critical Remarks on the Rome Statute of the International Criminal Court," p. 600.

[28] Article 12(1) of the Rome Statute.

[29] Article 12(2) of the Rome Statute.

*hoc* basis."[30] By lodging a declaration with the Registrar, that state may "accept the exercise of jurisdiction by the Court with respect to the crime in question."[31]

In accordance with the above, the Court may exercise its jurisdiction if "A situation in which one or more of such crimes appears to have been committed is referred to the Prosecutor by a State Party,"[32] "A situation in which one or more of such crimes appears to have been committed is referred to the Prosecutor by the Security Council,"[33] or "The Prosecutor has initiated an investigation in respect of such a crime."[34]

The Prosecutor has the authority to initiate an investigation about a situation that occurs on the territory of a state party, or that involves a state party's national. Therefore, a non-party state's national may fall into his competence. The same applies to the cases where the state parties refer a situation to the Court. That is to say, a situation referred to by a state party to the Prosecutor may involve a non-party state's national. This was one of the major controversies during the Rome Conference. For instance, the United States strongly opposed the automatic jurisdiction of the Court and insisted that it would have optional jurisdiction with respect to war crimes and crimes against humanity.[35] In case of the referral by the Security Council to the Court, there are no jurisdictional conditions. In that case, the Court is authorized by the Council to investigate a situation which is related to even non-party states and nationals. Since a Security Council resolution is binding over both the UN members and non-members, once the Council adopts a resolution authorizing the Court to investigate the situation concerned, the Court is granted a universal jurisdiction over the crimes concerned.

[30] Hans-Peter Kaul, "Special Note: The Struggle for the International Criminal Court's Jurisdiction," *European Journal of Crime, Criminal Law and Criminal Justice,* Vol. 6, Issue 4, 1998, p. 49.

[31] Article 12(3) of the Rome Statute.

[32] Article 13(a) of the Rome Statute.

[33] Article 13(b) of the Rome Statute.

[34] Article 13(c) of the Rome Statute.

[35] Kaul, *supra,* "Special Note: The Struggle for the International Criminal Court's Jurisdiction," p. 55

The fact that the Court is authorized to exercise its jurisdiction over the situations involving nationals of non-party states to the Rome Statute is of greatest relevance to the debate on whether this poses a threat to the principle of national sovereignty. It seems that this authority is an important step toward establishing a right-based world order rather than the one based on national interests. Having the authority to investigate the situations involving even the nationals of non-party states, the Court is designed to focus on the crime committed and the prevention of further atrocities. In that sense, whether it is an intrusion on national sovereignty is not relevant. In other words, for the purposes of the creation of the ICC, the question should not be whether it undermines national sovereignty.

It is worth noting that while the Court has the authority described above in theory, it is hard to imagine that any state party to the Rome Statute would hand over any suspect of the gravest crimes who is not its own national to the Court, given that *reelpolitik* still plays a significant role in interstate relations. Therefore, this authority appears to be a great challenge to the long-standing principles of sovereignty and non-intervention on the paper, whether that it will ever be exercised remains unclear.

As for the authority given to the Security Council, on the one hand, it could be seen as an indication for the continuation of the former regime on international criminal justice where the Security Council had the authority to set up an ICC for particular cases. On the other hand, it could also be argued that the Security Council is given a complimentary role to the ICC, for the situations in which the Court would not be able to exercise its jurisdiction. In that sense, it could be said that while the Security Council was the sole authority in the former regime, the ICC is now the major player in the international criminal justice system and the Council is acting so as to ensure that the ICC's jurisdiction reaches everywhere.

But of course the role of the Security Council in the present system where the ICC seems to be the primary actor should not be underestimated. In fact, the Rome Statute itself recognizes that the Security Council has "primary responsibility for the maintenance of international peace and security under the Charter of the United Nations."[36] The

[36] Ciampi, *supra,* "The International Criminal Court," p. 149.

aforesaid authority of the Security Council under the Statute to refer situations to the Court reveals this recognition. More importantly, Article 16 of the Rome Statute authorizes the Security Council to defer the ICC's jurisdiction for a limited period. The article states that "No investigation or prosecution may be commenced or proceeded with under this Statute for a period of 12 months after the Security Council, in a resolution adopted under Chapter VII of the Charter of the United Nations, has requested the Court to that effect; that request may be renewed by the Council under the same conditions."[37]

Although this is a restrictive role over the Court's jurisdiction, the Draft Statute contained a more severe provision on this matter: "No prosecution may be commenced under the Statute arising from a situation which is being dealt with by the Security Council as a threat to or a breach of the peace or an act of aggression under Chapter VII of the Charter, unless the Security Council otherwise decides."[38] It means that if this provision were adopted, the Court would have to rely on the Council authorization in order to be able to proceed with the situation that is being dealt with by the Council. However, the present Statute dramatically changed the proposed article. "First, the mere placement of a situation on the agenda of the Security Council for an indefinite period of time will no longer be sufficient to deprive the ICC of its jurisdiction over individuals with respect to that situation. The role of the Security Council is preserved, but it would require a positive resolution directed specifically at the ICC under Article 16 of the Statute to prevent the ICC from proceeding."[39] In other words, the Security Council can block the ICC's jurisdiction, only if none of the permanent members in the Council would veto the resolution preventing the Court from exercising its jurisdiction. Moreover, for the passage of such a

[37] Article 16 of the Rome Statute.

[38] Olufemi Elias and Anneliese Quast, "The Relationship Between the Security Council and the International Criminal Court in the Light of Resolution 1422 (2002)" *Non-State Actors and International Law,* Vol. 3, Issue 2–3, 2003, p. 167

[39] Ibid., p. 168.

resolution, at least 9 out of 15 affirmative votes are required. Given that two permanent members, France and Great Britain, are parties to the Rome Statute, it is not conceivable that the Security Council would exercise this power in a broad sense. It is also stated that "the power of deferral by the Security Council will then be seldom used and the independence of the judicial activity by the Court will be effectively guaranteed."[40] The limited power given to the Security Council under the Rome Statute may not be directly relevant to the debate on whether the ICC is likely to undermine national sovereignty. However, at least from the perspectives of permanent members in the Council, it is obvious that their role in world affairs has been limited by the ICC.

iii. Complementarity principle under the Rome Statute and national sovereignty:

As noted earlier, the Court is designed to play a complementary role to national criminal jurisdictions. The Statue is clear on this matter. In its Preamble, it is emphasized that "the International Criminal Court established under this Statute shall be complementary to national criminal jurisdictions."[41] The same is reiterated in Article 1: the Court "shall be complementary to national criminal jurisdictions."[42] The fact that the Statute makes mention of the complementary role of the ICC twice is an indication that states parties to the Statute are concerned about their sovereign right and the probable impact of the ICC on it.

When compared to the formerly set up ad hoc international criminal courts, that is, the International Criminal Tribunals for Former Yugoslavia and Rwanda, it is observed that unlike these courts, "which have primacy over national courts should they choose to exercise it, the

[40] Ibid., p. 169 (quoted from L. Condorelli and p. Villalpando, "Referral and Deferral by the Security Council," in A. Cassese, P. Gaeta and J. Jones (eds.), *The Rome Statute of the International Criminal Court,* Vol. I, 2002, p. 745).

[41] Preamble of the Rome Statute.

[42] Article 1 of the Rome Statute.

ICC's jurisdiction is complementary."[43] Therefore, it is commented that "the ICC takes a far more timid approach to international criminal jurisdiction."[44]

Under the Statute, the national authorities have priority in investigating and prosecuting the crimes within the jurisdiction of the Court. Article 17 of the Statute clearly states this priority. A case will be determined as inadmissible by the Court, if "The case is being investigated or prosecuted by a State which has jurisdiction over it, unless the State is unwilling or unable genuinely to carry out the investigation or prosecution."[45] The same applies to the situations where the State which has jurisdiction over the crime has decided not to prosecute the person accused of that crime.[46] However, it should be noted that it is the Court who is authorized to decide whether the national authorities have carried out the proceedings against the accused, and dealt with the situation properly.[47] If "the proceedings were or are being undertaken or the national decision was made for the purpose of shielding the person concerned from criminal responsibility for crimes within the jurisdiction of the Court,"[48] "there has been an unjustified delay in the proceedings"[49] and "the proceedings were not or are not being conducted independently or impartially,"[50] the Court may decide that the state concerned is unwilling to proceed against the accused. Moreover, in determining the inability of the state in a particular case, "the Court shall consider whether, due to a total or substantial collapse or unavailability of its national judicial system, the State is

---

[43] Naomi Roht-Arriaza, "Institutions of International Justice," *Journal of International Affairs,* Vol. 52, Issue 2, 1999, p. 486.

[44] Bartram p. Brown, "U.S. Objections to the Statute of the International Criminal Court: A Brief Response," *International Law and Politics,* Vol. 31, Issue 4, 1999, p. 878.

[45] Article 17(1a) of the Rome Statute.

[46] Article 17(1b) of the Rome Statute.

[47] Olásolo, *supra,* "The Prosecutor of the ICC Before the Initiation of Investigations: A Quasi-judicial or a Political Body?," p. 97.

[48] Article 17(2a) of the Rome Statute.

[49] Article 17(2b) of the Rome Statute.

[50] Article 17(2c) of the Rome Statute.

unable to obtain the accused or the necessary evidence and testimony or otherwise unable to carry out its proceedings."[51]

There are further safeguards for the state parties in that matter. Before initiating an investigation, the Prosecutor is obligated to notify "all States Parties and those States which, taking into account the information available, would normally exercise jurisdiction over the crimes concerned."[52] Therefore, in addition to the fact that the state concerned has the priority in dealing with a situation involving elements falling into the Court's competence, that states would also have the opportunity to review and reconsider the situation even if the Prosecutor has decided that there is a reasonable basis to proceed with an investigation.

Therefore, it could be concluded that the Court is in fact designed to compel states to take preventive measures against the occurrence of the gravest crimes over which it has jurisdiction. Even when such crimes are committed, states would have the incentive to address those crimes in order to avoid the Court's jurisdiction. As a consequence, it is even asserted that given the stringency of the provisions that prioritize the states over the Court in the cases where the crimes falling under the ICC's jurisdiction have been committed, "the ICC is likely to see few cases from states even minimally functioning legal systems. States that hope to avoid prosecution of their own nationals by an institution over which they have only partial control can do so by investigating and, if warranted, prosecuting their national in their own courts."[53]

Apparently, the Court, despite its international legal standing, plays some major political roles as well. Its inevitable involvement in cases of civil war and internal conflicts add a political dimension to its mandate as a judicial institution. The political nature of its performance which has close relevance to the national sovereignty of the states attracts a great deal of criticisms. Obviously, the Court's political impact is not strong enough to change the course of international politics. Additionally, both the Court and its Prosecutor are at least partially susceptible to power politics.

[51] Article 17(3) of the Rome Statute.

[52] Article 18(1) of the Rome Statute.

[53] Roht-Arriaza, *supra,* "Institutions of International Justice," p. 487.

The ability and willingness of the Court and the Prosecutor to exercise its jurisdictional powers may sometimes depend upon the nature of the cases as well as the identities of the potential suspects and perpetrators. It is also likely that states showing little eagerness to honor principles of democratic accountability may tend to use the Court for their own political priorities and interests.

Specific cases can be cited to further elaborate on this argument. Even though it is not empowered to deal with interstate disputes, the Court may feel compelled not to take action in cases which will involve citizens of big and influential powers as perpetrators or suspects. In such delicate cases, the Prosecutor may refrain from exercising his/her powers. This does not necessarily mean that the Court surrenders to power politics and that it is extremely susceptible to political influence. However, it still draws some criticisms because of its alleged inaction to carry out its mandate in some cases where the relevant rules of international law has been clearly violated.

To this end, it should be recalled that the Court did not take action to prosecute possible international crimes committed during the US invasion in Iraq in 2003. Even though the Court's initial inaction was criticized, recent reports imply that there might be an attempt to prosecute alleged violations committed by British forces.[54] But this does not absolve the ICC from growing criticisms. African states, for instance, strongly condemn the Court for alleged selectivity in prosecution. The basis for this argument and criticism is the fact that the ICC has been in its initial years focused on cases in African continent alone. In fact, the criticism and condemnation did not remain as a discourse. Kenya has, in strong terms, accused the Court of acting hawkishly against Africa while remaining silent vis-à-vis big powers. Subsequently, Kenyan authorities declared that they may consider withdrawal from the Court. The Kenyan parliament joined the executive branch and supported the idea of withdrawal in a plenary session.[55] The government, confident after the backing by the parliament, continued to use withdrawal from the Court as a

[54] "ICC Prosecutor to Examine Alleged British Crimes in Iraq War," *Reuters*, May 13, 2014.
[55] "Kenya MPs Vote to Withdraw from ICC," *BBC News*, September 5, 2013.

trump card in its foreign relations.[56] African Union, the regional political organization in the African continent, endorsed the Kenyan attitude and further concurred with the accusation that the Court has acted selectively when deciding to take action.[57]

This is in fact a grounded criticism because the ICC's judicial performance since its entry into force in 2002 has been mostly relevant to dealing with violations in different parts of the African continent. Whether or not this unbalanced attention has been politically motivated requires further deliberation and verification. But even without such a verification, heavy involvement in situations in Africa at least justifies an attempt to question the impartiality of the Court. The principle of complementarity, specifically indicated in the Statute, can be cited as one reason because the Court has the authority to take action in cases where national judiciaries are unwilling or unable to perform their roles properly. In other words, the ICC may not be expected to become involved in judicial processes where the national authorities have effectively addressed the situation. This suggests that it will be more likely for the ICC to initiate an investigation in cases or situations where central authority lacks necessary resources or resolution to do so. Therefore, a failed state that does not have a strong central authority, and maintain broad and comprehensive legitimacy will more likely become a source of conflict that will then attract the attention of the ICC; such a state will also become susceptible to the Court's jurisdiction because of insufficient resources and mechanisms to prosecute international crimes to be committed during that conflict. And African continent, largely due to the repercussions of colonialization, is now home to the greatest number of failed states in the world.[58]

The Court currently handles 23 different cases in 10 situations. Some of these situations have been referred to by states parties whereas in some of them, the Court has been given authorization by the UN Security Council.

[56] "Kenya Issues Threat to Pull Out of ICC," *Daily Nation,* 22 November 2015.

[57] "African Union Members Back Kenyan Plan to Leave ICC," *The Guardian,* February 1, 2016.

[58] Ali Mazrui, "The Blood of Experience: The Failed State and Political Collapse in Africa," *World Policy Journal,* Vol. 12, Issue 1, 1995, pp. 28–34.

First referrals were made by Uganda and Democratic Republic of Congo (DRC). In December 2003, Ugandan government decided to refer the activities of Lord's Resistance Army (LRA) to the Court which officially admitted the referral on January 29, 2004.[59] Initial findings by the Court confirmed commission of international crimes in the conflict between LRA and the central government.[60] But the Court paid special attention to the use of children as soldiers and sex slaves in the Ugandan conflict. These violations were considered as crimes against humanity, mostly perpetrated by LRA forces. The Court issued arrest warrants for high-ranking commanders of the LRA in October 2005. Even though the government circles welcomed it, the decision raised concerns because it was considered potentially harmful due to the fragile situation in the country.[61]

There are several reasons for this concern. The prosecution at the Court, for instance, it was argued, may disrupt the peace talks between the conflicting parties. The government issued general amnesty in 2000 by which persons involved in the conflict since 1986 were granted immunity from criminal prosecution.[62] This raises a question as to what roles the Court should play in conflicts involving a huge number of potential suspects because its mandate calls for legal prosecutions whereas the situation on the ground may be something different for the sake of attaining social peace and harmony.

The situation in the DRC is also one of the initial referrals to the ICC. The widespread commission of international crimes was brought to the attention to the Prosecutor of the Court by the central administration in 2004. The Prosecutor, concluding that there is basis to proceed, decided to initiate an investigation into the longstanding conflict in 2006. Thomas Lubanga Dyilo, one of the prime suspects, was taken under custody on February 10, 2006. First hearing was held on January 26, 2009; and he

[59] 'President of Uganda refers situation concerning the Lord's Resistance Army to the ICC,' *International Criminal Court Press Release,* January 29, 2004.

[60] 'Rebels massacre 192 in Lira Camp,' *The Monitor,* February 23, 2004.

[61] Erin K. Baines, "The Haunting of Alice: Local Approaches to Justice and Reconciliation in Northern Uganda," *The International Journal of Transitional Justice,* Vol. 1, Issue 1, 2007, pp. 91–114.

[62] Ibid., p. 101.

was found guilty of recruiting child soldiers on March 14, 2012, and sentenced to 12 years in prison.[63] Other suspects Germain Katanga and Mathieu Ngudjolo Chui were brought to trial in absentia in July 2007 for the crimes they committed. The Court issued an arrest warrant referring to the different counts of crimes against humanity and war crimes including recruitment of child soldiers, targeting civilians, deliberate killings, sexual enslavement, and rape.[64] The Prosecutor further charged Bosco Ntaganda with almost identical counts.[65] Case against Callixte Mbarushimana was dropped on December 23, 2011.[66]

The situation in Central African Republic (CAR) was also referred to by the central government to the Court. Unlike the Ugandan case where only acts committed in certain parts of the country were brought to the attention of the Court, the referral covered the international crimes committed in the entire territory of CAR since July 1, 2002, when the ICC entered into force.[67] After "carefully" reviewing "information from a range of sources," the Office of Prosecutor concluded that there was reasonable basis to open an investigation because "grave crimes falling within the jurisdiction of the Court were committed" in the CAR.[68]

The decision was based on the belief that a huge number of people were murdered and raped, and stores were destroyed and looted during an armed conflict between the central government and the armed rebels. The Office described the situation as the first where "allegations of sexual crimes far outnumber alleged killings."[69] The government decided to take the situation to the ICC because the highest national judicial body concluded in an official note that it was unable to address the widespread violence.

[63] Democratic Republic of the Congo, ICC-01/04-01/06, The Prosecutor v. Thomas Lubanga Dyilo, http://www.icc-cpi.int.

[64] Ibid.

[65] Democratic Republic of the Congo, ICC-01/04-02/06, The Prosecutor v. Bosco Ntaganda, http://www.icc-cpi.int.

[66] Ibid.

[67] "Prosecutor receives referral concerning Central African Republic," ICC-OTP-20050107-86, January 7, 2005.

[68] "Prosecutor Opens Investigation in the Central African Republic," ICC-OTP-20070522-220, May 22, 2007.

[69] Ibid.

The Court issued, as part of the process, an arrest warrant for Jean-Pierre Bemba Gombo, alleged president and commander-in-chief of the Movement for the Liberation of Congo in 2008. Gombo was arrested by Belgian authorities in the same year and transferred to the Court premises. Gombo remains in detention and is being charged with two counts of crimes against humanity and three counts of war crime.[70] Additionally, Gombo and four other persons are being tried in connection with the Prosecutor v. Jean-Pierre Bemba Gombo case for offenses against "the administration of justice" through "corruptly influencing witnesses."[71]

Situation in Darfur, Sudan, is the first referred by the UN Security Council to the Court which did not have prior authorization because Sudan was not a state party. This referral[72] is also significant because the United States, despite its firm commitment that it would not be part of a process legitimizing the ICC's performance, had to give its tacit and indirect approval and consent. After three months of the referral, the Prosecutor decided to open an investigation into the situation. The review process was relatively short (particularly if compared to other situations handled by the Court) because there was already substantial evidence of commission of widespread international crimes previously verified by an UN-appointed Commission.[73]

The Darfur case is also important because, according to the Court, there have been violations that can be qualified as genocide committed during an armed conflict between the Sudanese forces and rebels. This indicates that the Court did not confine itself to the findings of the Commission which clearly stated that the violations did not amount to the level of genocide. The process of prosecution is, on the other hand, extremely crucial because it is the first time in the history of interstate relations that a head of state is being tried in an international court. Omar al-Bashir, currently serving as the President of the Sudan, stands

---

[70] "The Prosecutor v. Jean-Pierre Bemba Gombo," ICC-01/05-01/08.

[71] "The Prosecutor v. Jean-Pierre Bemba Gombo, Aimé Kilolo Musamba, Jean-Jacques Mangenda Kabongo, Fidèle Babala Wandu and Narcisse Arido," ICC-01/05-01/13.

[72] UN Security Council Resolution No. 1593 (2005), March 31, 2005.

[73] Report of the International Commission of Inquiry on Darfur to the United Nations Secretary-General, Geneva, January 25, 2005.

trial for five counts of crimes against humanity, two counts of war crimes, and three counts of genocide.[74]

The situation in the Republic of Kenya is the first for which an investigation has been sought by the Prosecutor in the absence of any referral by a state party or the UN Security Council. The Prosecutor, in relation to "the post-election violence of 2007–2008," the Prosecutor requested the Pre-Trial Chamber II to authorize "the commencement of an investigation into the situation."[75] The Chamber concluded that the relevant prerequisite criteria have been met and further authorized the Office of the Prosecutor for an investigation into the alleged commission of crimes against humanity covering the events that took place between June 1, 2005 (entry into force of the Statute for the Republic of Kenya) and November 26, 2009 (when the Prosecutor filed his request).[76]

The Court's decision sparked a great deal of reaction in Kenya which attempted to stop the process by appealing to the UN Security Council, as well as the ICC itself for the inadmissibility of the case. However, the Kenyan authorities still cooperated with the Court which started to proceed with opening three major cases in respect to the situation. In the Prosecutor v. William Samoei Ruto and Joshua Arap Sang, the Court holds Ruto, current deputy president, responsible as an indirect co-perpetrator for crimes against humanity. Similar charges are raised against Sang as well.[77] In The Prosecutor v. Walter Osapiri Barasa, the Court alleges that the suspect is "criminally responsible as direct perpetrator . . . of offences against the administration of justice . . . attempting to corruptly influencing three ICC witnesses."[78]

In a fairly controversial move, the Court, at the beginning of the process, pressed charges against Kenyan President Kenyatta for alleged crimes against humanity. In March 2011, the Pre-Trial Chamber II summoned Kenyatta to appear before the Court; despite appeals by Kenyan

[74] "The Prosecutor v. Omar Hassan Ahmad al Bashir," ICC-02/05-01/09.

[75] "Situation in the Republic of Kenya," Pre-Trial ChamberII, ICC-01/09, March 31, 2010, available at: https://www.icc-cpi.int/iccdocs/doc/doc854287.pdf.

[76] Ibid., pp. 50–52.

[77] "The Prosecutor v. William Samuoei Ruto and Joshua Arap Sang," ICC-01/09-01/11.

[78] "The Prosecutor v. Walter Osapiri Barasa," ICC-01/09-01/13.

governments, the Chamber further confirmed the charges in January 2012. However, on December 5, 2014, the Prosecution filed a notice stating that it "withdraws the charges against Mr. Kenyatta" because "the evidence remained insufficient to prove [his] alleged criminal responsibility beyond reasonable doubt."[79] Accordingly, the Court Chamber which reviewed the notice decided to terminate the proceedings.

Situation in Libya was referred to the ICC by the UN Security Council[80] which concluded that the bloody internal war that erupted during the Arab Spring process was a threat to international peace and security and that the Libyan government failed to honor its responsibility to protect (R2P) the Libyan people. It was Gaddafi who called for a military action in the first place when he vowed before entering Benghazi, a stronghold of the opponents, that he would show no mercy. There were reports of summary executions, indiscriminate shootings, and even rapes, indicating that inaction would have caused a massacre or a campaign of mass killings. Under the emergent international law, Libya, as well as its leader Gaddafi, was responsible to protect its people. The international political system still recognizes the primary role of the nation-state as the major actor, but redefines the concept of national sovereignty. Whereas the traditional understanding of the notion implied that the states as well as the heads were immune from criminal prosecution or condemnation in a tribute to the preservation of territorial integrity, the current interpretation gathers that the people cannot be left at the mercy of the national state.

Reference to the principle of R2P has relevance to intervention, as well as to justification for prosecution of the international crimes at the ICC. In other words, the Court has been involved in the process in the Libyan case as a potential actor to define the R2P and to determine its relevancy to the political arguments. Both the UN Human Rights Council and the UN Security Council underlined that violence in Libya might have amounted to the crimes against humanity and further

[79] "Decision on the withdrawal of charges against Mr Kenyatta," ICC Trial Chamber V(B), ICC-01/09-02/11, March 13, 2015.

[80] UN Security Council Resolution No. 1970 (2011), February 26, 2011.

pointed to the ICC prosecution as an effective remedy of post-conflict justice. The Prosecutor acted swiftly to decide as to whether there is reasonable ground to open an investigation. In pursuant to the resolution, he submitted a report to the UNSC, informing his decision of taking concrete action. The report notes that there are "reasonable grounds to believe that crimes against humanity have been committed and continue being committed in Libya." The prosecutable crimes include imprisonment or other severe deprivation of physical liberty, torture, persecution, rape, deportation, or forcible transfer, intentionally directing attacks against civilians not taking a direct part in hostilities and "intentionally directing attacks against buildings dedicated to religion, education, art, science or charitable purposes, historic monuments, hospitals and places where the sick and wounded are collected, provided they are not military objectives."

The Prosecutor further filed an application with Pre-Trial Chamber I requesting for the issuance of an arrest warrant for prominent figures who were considered liable for perpetration of grave crimes. Arrest warrants were issued for Muammar Gaddafi, Saif al-Islam Gaddafi and Abdullah al-Senussi on June 27, 2011. Case against Muammar Gaddafi was terminated on November 22, 2011, following his death during the conflict in Libya. On July 24, 2014, the Appeals Chamber confirmed the Pre-Trial Chamber I's decision declaring case against Senussi inadmissible, ending the legal proceedings at the ICC. Currently, Saif al-Islam Gaddafi is considered by the Court criminally responsible for two counts of crimes against humanity.[81]

The Court has become authorized to handle the situation in Ivory Coast through a declaration lodged by the government in pursuant to article 12(3) of the Rome Statute without joining the ICC. The Pre-Trial Chamber III has authorized the Prosecutor to investigate alleged crimes against humanity committed during post-election turmoil.[82] Initial findings by the prosecution indicate that both government and

[81] "The Prosecutor v. Saif al-Islam Gaddafi," ICC-01/11-01/11.

[82] "Decision Pursuant to Article 15 of the Rome Statute on the Authorisation of an Investigation into the Situation in the Republic of Cote d'Ivoire," ICC-02/11, October 3, 2011.

rebel forces are responsible for child recruitment, enforced displacements, and unlawful attacks.[83] Even though there is no individual case yet, the situation confirms the growing legitimacy of the Court to address international crimes that fall into its competence, given that it is viewed as the proper venue even by non-state parties like Ivory Coast.

On January 16, 2013, the Office of the Prosecutor opened an investigation into alleged crimes committed on the territory of Mali since January 2012 in response to decision of the Government of Mali to refer the situation on July 13, 2012. After a preliminary examination of the situation, including an assessment of admissibility of potential cases, the Prosecutor determined that there was a reasonable basis to proceed with an investigation.[84] According to the initial findings, the crimes committed in the territories of Mali include murder, mutilation, torture, pillaging, and rape.

On September 26, 2015, Ahmad Al Faqi Al Mahdi, an alleged member of an al Qaeda-linked terror organization, was transferred as a suspect of war crimes to the ICC on September 26, 2015, following an arrest warrant issued by the Court on September 18, 2015. Charges raised against him include war crimes of intentionally directing attacks against historic monuments and buildings dedicated to religion, including nine mausoleums and one mosque in Timbuktu, Mali. The initial appearance of Al Faqi Al Mahdi took place on September 30, 2015.[85]

Even though it is an international legal institution, most cases being reviewed by the Court have a political dimension as well. However, some of these cases are of more political in nature than others. Georgia is one of them. In legal appearance, the Court is investigating alleged crimes committed during Georgian-Russian War in August 2008. However, it also seems that the Court will be playing a political role because Russia,

---

[83] "Decision on the Prosecution's Provision of Further Information Regarding Potentially Relevant Crimes Committed Between 2002 and 2010," ICC-02/11, February 22, 2012.

[84] ICC Prosecutor opens investigation into war crimes in Mali: 'The legal requirements have been met. We will investigate,' Press Release, January 16, 2013.

[85] "The Prosecutor v. Ahmad al Faqi al Mahdi," ICC-01/12-01/15.

despite that it is not a state party, wants to use this institution to justify the invasion of South Ossetia, a breakaway region of Georgia.[86]

The Court's involvement in the situation on a registered vessel of the Union of Comoros further reflects its potential role for utilization as a political means and venue in a bilateral dispute. Interestingly, the Comoros has a very slight relevance, but is key to ensuring the Court's involvement in a major confrontation between Turkey and Israel. Israeli forces killed nine Turkish nationals onboard Mavi Marmara vessel carrying humanitarian cargo to Gaza in late May 2010. An Istanbul-based law firm, acting on behalf of the Union of Comoros, referred the situation to the ICC on May 14, 2013.[87] On November 6, 2014, the Prosecutor concluded that the legal requirements of the Rome Statute had not been met in the situation.[88] In response to an application filed by the legal representatives of the Union of Comoros who challenged this decision, the Appeals Chamber ruled for a reinvestigation of the situation by the Office of the Prosecutor.[89]

A review of the cases currently being handled by the Court as well as its potential involvement in other similar situations reveals that the ICC, as an international legal institution, plays a political role as well, and is affected by the political circumstances. Even though the advocates of the Court wants it to remain an institution of international justice, its works are inevitably influenced by the dynamics of power politics and global developments. But aside from its vulnerability to political games and intrigues, the Court has arguably performed fine so far.

---

[86] See Cenap Çakmak, "Rusya'nın Güney Osetya Politikası, Neo-Self Determinasyon ve UCM'nin Rolü" (Russia's South Ossetia Policy, Neo-Self Determination and ICC's Role), *Bilge Strateji,* Vol. 1, Issue 1, 2009, pp. 51–70.

[87] ICC Prosecutor receives referral by the authorities of the Union of the Comoros in relation to the events of May 2010 on the vessel 'MAVI MARMARA,' Statement, Office of the Prosecutor, May 14, 2013.

[88] Statement of the Prosecutor of the International Criminal Court, Fatou Bensouda, on concluding the preliminary examination of the situation referred by the Union of Comoros: "Rome Statute legal requirements have not been met," Statement, Office the Prosecutor, November 6, 2014.

[89] Charlotte Silver, "ICC Prosecutor Ordered to Investigate Israeli Attack on Mavi Marmara," *Electronic Intifada,* November 8, 2015, retrieved at https://electronicintifada.net/blogs/charlotte-silver/icc-prosecutor-ordered-investigate-israeli-attack-mavi-marmara. (April 12, 2016).

It is of course now good to know that the murderers and perpetrators of the most heinous crimes will not go unpunished anymore, claiming the shield provided for the heads of states. The classical custom suggesting that heads of state should not be responsible for their action is not applicable anymore under nascent international criminal law which upholds that the culprits of such egregious crimes as genocide, crimes against humanity, and war crimes should be prosecuted effectively regardless of their positions and status.

This implies that there is reason to be hopeful for the sake of future; however, success of the current international legal regime on the prosecution of international crimes very much depends on the cooperation between states and willingness of global actors to extend full support for the legal mechanisms set up to achieve global justice. Consideration of political priorities or intricate power relations would constitute the greatest barrier before delivery of justice and prevention of future atrocities.

Therefore, subscription to the works of the ICC towards achievement of justice needs to be promoted and encouraged worldwide; this is actually the obvious that must be done. But there are actually more complicated issues that need to be addressed properly. The ICC as well as global leaders should think about why the court is currently dealing with cases in regards to situations in African continent alone. This does not necessarily imply that the court is taking action against the weak, adopting a more lenient approach toward the stronger states. However, that the court handles only "African" cases in fact raises concerns as this points out to a structural problem.

Additionally, there are also reasons to believe that the Court will not be a panacea to problems of global injustice. Conventional methods of delivering justice will not help the warring factions achieve a lasting peace; in a unified nation with a sound legal system, measures and mechanisms for retributive justice may be sufficient; but such measures need to be backed and complemented by tools of restorative justice as well. In other words, justice is not fulfilled by focusing on the criminals alone; proper measures should also be taken to address the issues of the victims and attain internal peace that would satisfy all, including those who perpetrated crimes during the conflict.

For several cardinal reasons, involvement of the ICC in a situation where international crimes have been committed in a large scale by parties to a domestic armed conflict may not be of great help in achieving justice and lasting peace. Above all, a sense of revenge will most likely prevail; rebels or anti-government forces will believe that they have been repressed and persecuted by the central government, suffering from extensive brutality. Revenge is an innate feeling; but it does not help at all to achieve justice and a sound order.

Second, there will be no absolute winner in a civil war even if one party claims full power and control. In most cases of civil war, there is no strong nation or national identity; but instead there are different tribal, ethnic, or sectarian identities with certain goals and priorities. Therefore, it is likely that there will always be dissidents with the new political setting. Maintenance of full control by one of the warring parties will not end the disagreements and long-standing disputes between the different social groups and segments. It will be extremely difficult to come up with a wise solution or remedy for justice that would adequately address the concerns and priorities of all groups and tribes.

# Global Civil Society and the ICC

The codification of international treaties pertinent to such areas as human rights, environmental problems, poverty, and women's rights are quite appropriate for a better and larger involvement of civil activist groups. The contribution of NGOs, social movement organizations, religious groups, etc., might sometimes be substantial in the cases where the aforementioned issues are discussed, as those issues are very sensitive, and directly related to human beings; thus draw significant attention and a growing interest from the peoples of the world. Therefore, one should expect the direct involvement of a large number of civil activist groups in the process, when issues and problems relating to human rights are discussed.

Starting from the adoption of the UN Charter, when the NGOs ensured the inclusion of human rights language in the text, NGOs and other civil groups have actively been involved in the creation of international legal documents concerning human rights, and been represented in the international conferences, where human rights issues have been discussed. In doing so, they have proved that they are one of the major contributors to the making of international human rights



C. Çakmak, *A Brief History of International Criminal Law and International Criminal Court*,
DOI 10.1057/978-1-137-56736-9_15

documents and other relevant activities. They have used a different set of methods, ranging from lobbying to the dissemination of information they had gathered, in order to influence the states' stances toward the treaty under consideration.

After the adoption of the UN Charter, the national as well as international NGOs made substantial contributions to the creation of the Universal Declaration of Human Rights. However, because this was a declaration, and not a treaty, states did not become bound by this document. The civil groups have spent efforts to ensure the establishment binding rules. The two UN Covenants of 1966 were the results of these efforts. After the dissolution of the Soviet Bloc, and subsequently with the removal of the tension that has affected West-Soviet relations for several decades, the number of NGOs dealing with global human rights issues has proliferated, and their areas of activity have been broadened.

In this context, the world has witnessed more involvement of NGOs during the 1990s. The Vienna International Human Rights Conference in 1993 and the Beijing International Conference on Women's Rights in 1995 are worth noting in this regard. Both conferences were attended by a large number of NGOs and individual civil representatives. Many NGOs provided inputs to the final drafts of the conferences. The creation of the Rome Statute and the establishment of the International Criminal Court (ICC) are the most recent striking examples for the effectiveness and successes of civil activism in changing the direction and agenda of global politics.

The ICC case is worth examining, for that its creation was to a large extent ensured by the efforts and insistence of global civil society. While the contribution of civil society to the improvements in the field of human rights has been substantial for decades, until the Rome Conference, the civil groups have mostly worked individually. "Concerted efforts within the human rights community have been few and far between." Therefore, "prior to Rome, the contribution of civil society to the outcome of norm-creating international conferences for the promotion or protection of human rights has, for that reason, not been particularly spectacular."[1]

[1] Johan D. Van Der Vyver, "Civil Society and the International Criminal Court," *Journal of Human Rights,* Vol. 2. Issue 3, 2003, p. 426.

In this regard, it should be noted that human rights NGOs could not have made a great progress in convincing the concerned parties to create a permanent ICC until 1990s. The decision of the UN General Assembly in December 1994 not to take the International Law Commission (ILC)'s draft Statute to an international conference, where the Statute creating the Court would be adopted, shocked and disappointed several numbers of NGOs following the proceedings.

As a response to the resistance and reluctance of States, the activist groups developed new methods, considering the old ones did not work properly to obtain the optimum results. After the disappointing decision of the UN General Assembly, they sought new ways to change the States' attitudes. In this vein, they decided to form a Coalition that would be specifically designed to work on the establishment of a permanent ICC.

A few strong international human rights organizations took action in founding the coalition, but "they also carefully preserved their separate identities and influence."[2] On February 10, 1995, the NGO Coalition for an International Criminal Court (CICC) was founded as a "broad-based network of NGOs and international law experts." It was given a loose structure; it had no formal decision-making structure. In addition, at the beginning, the founders decided not to formulate a common position except "to advocate for the creation of an effective, just and independent International Criminal Court."

Such a decision was necessary, as any formulated common mandate-like text would cause serious clashes among the sub-groups. Moreover, this decision would make the Coalition focus on the main issue only. Otherwise, members of the Coalition would be distracted. Therefore, "the loose structure and lack of cumbersome procedures of the Coalition undoubtedly contributed to its flexibility and effectiveness."[3] Furthermore, given the high level of diversity among the members in the Coalition, it would be disruptive to build a strong and centralized organization.

---

[2] Fanny Benedetti and John L. Washburn, "Drafting the International Criminal Court Treaty: Two Years to Rome and an Afterword on the Rome Diplomatic Conference," *Global Governance,* Vol. 5, Issue 1, 1999, p. 19.

[3] Ibid., p. 147.

This new form of activism was welcomed by the civil groups with different backgrounds and mandates. While the Coalition was founded by a few NGOs, prior to the Rome Conference the number of participants in the CICC increased rapidly, and in the end, 134 NGOs were accredited by the Secretary-General's office to participate in the Conference.[4] The number of the NGOs in the Coalition has dramatically increased over the years. Today, over 2,000 NGOs are being represented in the CICC, and actively working on the effectiveness of the ICC.

During the conference, the Coalition members developed different strategies in order to achieve their goals. Various thematic sub-groups (teams) were formed and individual NGO representatives were allocated to those teams, "chaired in each instance by a designated coordinator and responsible for monitoring the debates and engaging in discussions and negotiations with government representatives in regard to a particular section of the proposed ICC Statute." Among these teams were the Definitions Team, the State Consent Team, the Trigger Mechanisms and Admissibility Team, the Investigation Team, the Trial, Appeal and Review Team, the Penalties Team, and the Enforcement Team. Furthermore, the Coalition members constituted different thematic and regional caucuses, such as the Women's Caucus and the Caucus on Children's Rights, and the ones for Africa and Latin America.[5] These caucuses were formed, "in order to ensure the perspectives of particular constituencies were incorporated into all aspects of the negotiations of the draft Statute for the ICC."[6]

Each of the caucuses played significant roles and made substantial contributions during the conference. The involvement of the caucuses in the conference proceedings remarkably affected its outcome. For instance, the Women's Caucus for Gender Justice was "responsible for the inclusion of the Rome Statute's clear definitions of crimes of sexual violence, such as the recognition of rape and other sexual violence as

---

[4] Vyver, *supra,* "Civil Society and the International Criminal Court," p. 428.

[5] Ibid.

[6] "Sectoral Caucuses Will Continue to Strengthen the ICC," *The ICC Monitor,* Issue 21, June 2002, p. 7.

both war crimes and crimes against humanity for the first time in international law. The Faith-Based Caucus made important contributions to the drafting Statute's preamble, which will be a reference in interpreting the spirit of law and thus in resolution of many cases before the ICC."[7]

After the Rome Conference, the caucuses did not simply dissolve themselves but began focusing on new goals. They have reshaped themselves and their goals and "continued to bring unique and important perspectives to the work of the Preparatory Commission, in particular to the negotiations of the draft Elements of Crimes and the Rules of Procedure and Evidence." They have also got involved in international ratification campaign, the efforts in the implementation of the Statute provisions into national legislations and the work of creating the Court itself. In addition to formerly established ones, a new Universal Jurisdiction Caucus was formed after the Court entered into force. Members of this caucus focus especially on "advocating for the inclusion of universal jurisdiction provisions as countries develop their implementing legislation."[8]

As members of the Coalition, the sub-groups mainly undertook such forms of action as lobbying state and intergovernmental representatives, writing expert documents and reports, convening seminars and conferences, disseminating the Court ideal to the masses, and street action. After the adoption of the Rome Statute, the Coalition began to engage in the ratification process, in order to bring the treaty into force. At that time, sub-groups intensified their actions in their own territories, in order to make the state concerned ratify the treaty. As a result, the threshold required for the treaty come into force was overcome in a very short time.

However, those groups did not simply end their activities even if the state they had been working on has acceded to the Rome Statute. National coalitions have also been formed with the purpose of affecting the domestic decision-making concerning the effectiveness of the ICC

[7] Ibid.

[8] Ibid.

since the ICC came into effect. For instance, it has been reported that national networks have been built in such countries as Belgium, Czech Republic, France, Germany, The Netherlands, Poland, Sweden, Switzerland, Turkey, Ukraine, United Kingdom, and Georgia.[9] More recently, a national NGO Platform on the ICC was founded in the Netherlands on January 28, 2004. It "consists of a fairly loose network of Dutch NGOs and academic institutions that are involved in activities relevant to the ICC. Some of the members may choose to work together on an ad hoc basis in order to influence policies and procedures of the Court."[10]

The Coalition members are still working for the effectiveness of the Court, and for increasing the number of States Parties to the treaty. They actively participated in the nomination and election process of the judges. It has been noted in this regard that "the NGO community participated in the development and monitoring of the nomination and election procedures for ICC judges in such an unprecedented manner."[11] The involvement of the Coalition in the process where the judges have been nominated and elected was seen as crucial, since the reputation and moral authority of the ICC for which global civil society has spent substantial efforts would suffer and the damage might have been irreparable in case the judges were not "well-qualified and representative." Therefore, "the CICC has engaged in a campaign to promote a transparent and consultative nomination process that will lead to a qualified and representative Court."[12] However, the principle that the Coalition will not take a position on individual candidates has been strictly observed in order to keep the Coalition's impartiality and credibility intact.

The Coalition, over the years, has become recognized all over the world for its outstanding efforts on making the ICC work properly and effectively. It is now inclusive of 95 percent of civil activist groups that are

---

[9] "Rome Statute Near 100 Ratifications," *The ICC Monitor,* Issue 26, February 2004, p. 9.

[10] "Dutch NGOs Combine Forces," *Insight on the ICC,* Issue 1, April 2004, p. 8.

[11] William Pace and Tanya Karanasios, "Expectations for the ICC Mount," *The ICC Monitor,* Issue 23, February 2003, p. 1.

[12] "Handling of Elections Will Affect the Future of the ICC," *The ICC Monitor,* Issue 21, June 2002, p. 3.

dedicated to promote the ICC and universal jurisdiction. In other words, it is the single, strong and legitimate voice of the masses that demand a fair and just world order. The Coalition's legitimacy and credibility is acknowledged by even "official" circles of international politics. For instance, William Pace, the convener of the Coalition, was invited to represent global civil society in the UN Secretary-General's office on the occasion of signing of the Relationship Agreement between the ICC and the UN[13] in pursuant of Article 2 of the ICC Statute.

The above implies that the world has witnessed a growing and organized influence of global civil society in world affairs. While the former attempts by the civil groups to create an impact on the outcome of international treaty negotiations pertinent to human rights have proven to be modestly successful, the strategies these groups developed before, during, and after the Rome Conference have by all means been unprecedented. These strategies worked very well, resulting in a people-oriented text and an effective Court that was designed to end notorious practice of impunity. Most importantly, these strategies, that is, building coalition with a loose and decentralized structure, focusing on the issue on the agenda only, creating thematic units, establishing partnerships with governments and international organizations, are now regarded as so promising that it is even argued that the Coalition set up a new type of diplomacy and that diplomacy will be adopted as a point of reference and model in the future activities of global civil society. Secretary-General of the UN Kofi Annan even labeled the Coalition's efforts as "the new functional diplomacy" and stated that a concerted partnership between civil society and the UN is of great necessity.[14] Given that necessity and the proven success of the Coalition, it is now hoped that the case of the CICC will remain the model for civil society in the future.

The involvement of the global civil society actors calls for evaluation of their interaction and cooperation with other actors of international politics during the creation of the ICC. This cooperation and interaction

[13] William Pace, "The ICC and UN at Crossroads of International Justice," *The ICC Monitor*, Issue 28, November 2004, p. 1.

[14] Vyver, "Civil Society and the International Criminal Court," p. 430.

represents a fine example of what is called new diplomacy involving the states, civil society actors and international institutions working together to attain a common goal. It should be noted that the topic of "new diplomacy" and its relevance to the activities of the Coalition has never been a commonly and frequently discussed subject even among the primary actors of the ICC process. Hence, it is only natural the issue did not attract substantial scholarly attention. However, occasionally the decision-makers of world politics as well as scholars of global civil society and transnational politics made mention of the impact of the Coalition's activities at Rome on the strengthening of the nascent "new diplomacy."

At the beginning of the Rome Conference, the UN Secretary-General put a special emphasis on the significance and workability of the "new diplomacy." Describing the harmony between the state delegations and civil society representatives and the excessive involvement of the NGO sector in the process as "new diplomacy," Annan said, "We at the U.N. travel the world encouraging participatory democracy; I think we should apply a bit of it to ourselves."[15] Again, soon before the gathering of the conference, Lloyd Axworthy, one of the most important individuals throughout the processes of the landmine ban treaty and the ICC,[16] discussed the relevance of "new diplomacy" to the ICC issue.[17]

Shortly after the completion of the conference, Kofi Annan once more recalled the significance and prominence of "the new diplomacy" in global arena. At the Hague Appeal for Peace Conference held on May 7, 1999, Annan noted:

> We have entered a new era of ever-greater partnership, and there are few limits to what civil society can achieve . . . it is clear that there is a new

[15] Charles Trueheart, "Clout Without a Country: The Power of International Lobbies," *The Washington Post*, June 18, 1998.

[16] It was asserted that "The striking achievement at Rome was the result of the efforts by Lloyd Axworthy and Boutros Ghali." Bernard E. Brown, "What Is the New Diplomacy?" *American Foreign Policy Interests*, Vol. 23, Issue 1, 2001, p. 7.

[17] Lloyd Axworthy, Minister of Foreign Affairs of Canada, "The New Diplomacy, the UN, the International Criminal Court and the Human Security Agenda," Conference on UN Reform, The Kennedy School of Harvard University, Cambridge, Massachusetts, April 25, 1998, available at: http://www.dfaitmaeci.gc.ca.

> diplomacy where NGOs, peoples from across nations, international organizations, the Red Cross, and governments can come together to pursue an objective... there is nothing we can take on that we cannot succeed it.[18]

William Pace, convener of the Coalition, in an interview after the Conference implied they furthered the pattern of "new diplomacy":

> We have much work before us. With the achievement of the ICC statute we have demonstrated another example of the extraordinary development of the "new diplomacy" characteristic of the post-Cold-War period which offers the hope of better global governance in the next century.[19]

Academic approaches towards the topic of new diplomacy could be roughly divided into two distinct lines. While one is more concerned about the likely impact of the new diplomacy on the US supremacy and its lead role in world politics, the other adopts a timid approach implying that the new diplomacy may not be so promising as the NGO community may anticipate.[20]

Recalling that "the new diplomacy is intended to be a rejection of and a replacement for traditional power politics, the triumph of political idealism over political realism," Bernard E. Brown suggests that the activities of the new diplomacy actors may negatively affect global policies of the United States. In a similar fashion, *American Foreign Policy Interests*, an academic journal dedicated to the promotion of US foreign policy, underlined that the United States has to learn how to live with the implications of the emerging new diplomacy.

---

[18] Address by Kofi Annan to Hague Appeal for Peace Conference: Greater Role for NGOs at the UN Welcomed, Hague Appeal for Peace Press Release, May 7, 1999, available at: http://www.globalpolicy.org/ngos/docs99/hap99.htm.

[19] Ethirajah Anbarasan, "A Decisive Victory," Interview with Bill Pace, The UNESCO Courier, available at: http://www.unesco.org/courier/1998_10_uk/dossier/txt23.htm.

[20] For instance see, Alistair Edgar, "Peace, Justice, and Politics: The International Criminal Court, 'New Diplomacy,' and the UN System," in Andrew F. Cooper, John English and Ramesh Thakur (eds.), *Enhancing Global Governance: Towards a New Diplomacy* (Tokyo, New York and Paris: United Nations University Press, 2002), pp. 133–152.

The journal especially drew attention to the growing role of NGOs and asserted that "The most difficult and novel challenge will be handling" civil society actors.[21]

Alistair D. Edgar questions the level of success secured through the so-called new diplomacy movement at the Rome Conference. He asserts that certain elements in the Court lead us to think that it is not so independent since the big powers will never be willing to "surrender their veto power."[22] Edgar also recalls that the creation of the Court did not drastically change the international system based on the mutual recognition of sovereign rights and prerogatives by the states; so it will be fair to conclude that the Court is a symbol of the continuation of the past.[23]

Likewise, Philip Ne, while acknowledging that the ICC process was a "normative innovation,"[24] implies that it will be hard to find anything as replacement for "sovereign impunity.[25] Nel contends that "the ICC process and statute have contributed to undermining the veto power of the great powers in at least some respects"; but he also notes that the restrictions "have no bearing on the role of the great powers in determining which 'situations' can be referred to the ICC and which cannot."[26] In conclusion, Nel expresses doubts on the effectiveness and influence of new diplomacy:

> It would be a mistake to assume that all attempts at breaking out of the strangle-hold of established great-power-dominated, top-down diplomacy are necessarily good simply by virtue of being counter-hegemonic . . . We

---

[21] "For the Record: The New Diplomacy and American National Interests," *American Foreign Policy Interests,* Vol. 23, Issue 1, 2001, p. 40.

[22] Edgar, "Peace, Justice, and Politics: The International Criminal Court, 'New Diplomacy,' and the UN System," pp. 140–141.

[23] Ibid., pp. 142–143.

[24] Philip Nel, "Between Counter-hegemony and Post-hegemony: The Rome Statute and Normative Innovation in World Politics," in Andrew F. Cooper, John English and Ramesh Thakur (eds.), *Enhancing Global Governance: Towards a New Diplomacy* (Tokyo, New York and Paris: United Nations University Press, 2002), p. 152.

[25] Ibid., p. 155.

[26] Ibid., p. 157.

should therefore make sure that our criteria of assessment of the new diplomacy have built into them a healthy dose of self-criticism.[27]

In its simplest form, the concept "new diplomacy" refers to the close collaboration between the UN, like-minded governments and progressive NGOs in a particular case. In practice, new diplomacy "creates coalitions of the willing to move difficult issues forward more quickly, while building international support."[28] It is asserted that the term "entails NGOs, progressive governments, and international organizations combining to take a treaty process forward even with major opposition from big powers."[29] The combination of forces essentially echoes "a common perception that the characteristics of global governance—the rules, norms, and institutions that govern public and private behavior across national boundaries—are changing in new and important ways."[30]

It appears that the most fundamental reason for this change is the—at least partial—shift of the world politics from a state-centered to a human-centered structure. In the new era, not the security of the states but the security of human beings is what matters most. The UN Secretary-General Kofi Annan succinctly expounds this fact putting a special emphasis on the key notion "human security":

> We know that we cannot be secure amidst starvation, that we cannot build peace without alleviating poverty, and that we cannot build freedom on foundations of injustice. These pillars of what we now understand as the

[27] Ibid., p. 159.

[28] Rob McRae, "Conclusion," in Rob McRae and Don Hubert (eds.), *Human Security and the New Diplomacy: Protecting People, Promoting Peace* (Montreal, Canada: McGill-Queen's University Press, 2001), p. 254.

[29] Amy Jeanne Bann, The Non-Governmental Organization Coalition for an International Criminal Court: A Case Study on NGO Networking, Unpublished Master's thesis, Virginia Polytechnic Institute and State University, 2001, p. 43.

[30] Michael Edwards, "Civil Society and Global Governance," Paper presented at the Conference "On the Threshold: The United Nations and Global Governance in the New Millennium," United Nations University, Tokyo, Japan, January 19–21, 2000, p. 2.

people-centered concept of "human security" are interrelated and mutually reinforcing. And perhaps most crucially, no country, however powerful, can achieve human security on its own, and none is exempt from risks and costs if it chooses to do without the multilateral cooperation that can help us reach this goal.[31]

Lloyd Axworthy, the leading figure who coined the term "new diplomacy," points to the paradigmatic shift:

> A key element of this new thinking is what has been called "human security." Essentially, this is the idea that security goals should be primarily formulated and achieved in terms of human, rather than state, needs . . . Soft power is particularly useful in addressing the many pressing problems that do not pit one state against another, but rather a group of states against some transnational threat to human security . . . we are increasingly able to draw on soft power to reinvigorate humanitarian law and develop new norms within it. My hope is that the international community will be able to use the same approach to resolve other pressing human security issues such as the proliferation of small arms and the use of child soldiers in armed conflicts.[32]

Hence, it would be fair and explanatory to assert that the growing interest in and the focus on the concept of "human security" pushes states to establish close ties with the civil society actors. Axworthy solidifies the point as follows:

> Advancing human security is also the reason for developing innovative global partnerships linking like-minded countries, institutions and NGOs. Such coalitions between governments and civil society are harbingers of the future, demonstrating the power of noble intent, good

[31] Kofi A. Annan, "Foreword," in Rob McRae and Don Hubert (eds.), *Human Security and the New Diplomacy: Protecting People, Promoting Peace* (Montreal, Canada: McGill-Queen's University Press, 2001), p. xix.

[32] Axworthy, address to "The New Diplomacy, the UN, the International Criminal Court and the Human Security Agenda."

> ideas, and pooled resources. Their energy, expertise, and ideas are indispensable in the pursuit of human security.[33]

The strength and effectiveness of such a coalition revealed itself during the Rome Conference. As one observer notes, the establishment of the ICC was "a powerful illustration of the ability and willingness of the international community to work collectively to address a pressing human security need."[34]

It should be noted that the shift is not only a normative tendency but also a necessary adaptation to the changing environment and priorities dictated by the new era, where "prestige is measured by human security, not military strength," and "single superpower hegemony is giving way to multilateralism and the rule of law."[35] This proposition implies that states are actually compelled to cooperate with the civil society actors in order to adapt to the new era and to resolve the global problems that concern all. The new diplomacy that requires active involvement of civil society actors and a working cooperation between those actors and like-minded states is the reflection of the new reality in global arena.

However, it should also be noted that not all states will be able to take part in new diplomacy endeavors no matter how eager they will be to do so.

> One requirement for the involvement of civil society in policy making is a plural society rich in knowledge and skills. In Russia, for instance, skills are not dispersed in the same way they are in Norway or in Canada. A second requirement for New Diplomacy to work is a good relationship among different segments/components of society and the state. Third, financial capacity must exist . . . A further prerequisite for New Diplomacy

---

[33] Lloyd Axworthy, "Introduction," in Rob McRae and Don Hubert (eds.), *Human Security and the New Diplomacy: Protecting People, Promoting Peace* (Montreal, Canada: McGill-Queen's University Press, 2001), p. 13.

[34] Darryl Robinson, "Case Study: The International Criminal Court," in Rob McRae and Don Hubert (eds.), *Human Security and the New Diplomacy: Protecting People, Promoting Peace* (Montreal, Canada: McGill-Queen's University Press, 2001), p. 170.

[35] Brown, "What Is the New Diplomacy?" p. 3.

> is a good relationship of Northern states with Southern states, usually established through development assistance.[36]

Perhaps, the most notable feature of new diplomacy is the visible role it recognizes to the nonstate actors. While the exacerbating global issues require closer attention by states, because it became evident they often do not have the necessary sources and sometimes willingness to address those problems, civil society actors feel they are obligated to take a lead role towards the rectification of global problems. Simply because "most existing international arrangements and organizations reflect processes that are largely intergovernmental and consensus-based," civil society actors are committed to create a human security agenda that "seeks to create a new international norm."[37]

But the most important feature of the nascent new diplomacy is its potential to change the commonly shared perceptions that the United States dominates the world politics. David Davenport recalls that

> The most powerful tool of the new diplomacy is replacing the leadership of the U.S. and other world powers with that of nongovernmental organizations and smaller states. The United States, for example, had been a key supporter of every international criminal tribunal created and had backed the processes that developed the International Law Commission draft. But when it became clear in Rome that the U.S. could not support some of the major shifts away from the ilc concepts of the court, the U.S. was left behind.[38]

The US opposition to this judicial institution which was essentially an almost-perfect design of the new diplomacy actors was mainly based on the infringement upon the long-survived national sovereignty caused by the tactics of the new diplomacy. Taking the probable devaluation of

---

[36] Iver Neumann, Paper presented at the Conference on New Diplomacy, cited at "Report from the Conference on New Diplomacy: The United Nations, Like-Minded Countries and Non-Governmental Organizations," Ontario, Canada, September 28–30, 1999.

[37] McRae, "Conclusion," p. 253.

[38] David Davenport, "New Diplomacy," *Policy Review,* Issue 116, 2002/2003, p. 25.

sovereignty by the new diplomacy, "several powerful nations, including the U.S., Russia, China, and India, have already signaled that this is not a tradeoff they are prepared to make."[39]

One last thing that should be recalled as the feature of the new diplomacy is its emotional characteristic. The language of the new diplomacy adds new words—mostly with a moral dimension—to the vocabulary of traditional pragmatic diplomatic approach. The terms "participation," "empowerment," "people-centered," and "consensus" are used to describe the emotional and moral character of the new diplomacy.[40] The unusually emotional celebration of the adoption of the Statute and the "extraordinary atmosphere of jubilation" at the end of the conference[41] was reflective of what was new with the "new diplomacy."

Interestingly, individuals and citizens have played remarkable roles during the cases of the new diplomacy. While most of the time they acted on their official capacities—that is, as heads of states, heads of delegations, or official representatives—in some occasions, their unofficial involvement in the negotiations have had visible impacts on the course of the deliberations. In addition to such prominent renowned figures as Lloyd Axworthy who coined the term of "new diplomacy" and Kofi Annan who contributed a great deal to the frequent use of the term, "citizen-diplomats" with little world-wide recognition have provided substantial inputs during the negotiations.[42]

Canadian diplomat Philippe Kirsch has also played remarkable roles during the negotiations in Rome. As a representative of Canada, a strong like-minded government that advocated a strong and independent Court, Kirsch was one of the best candidates for the civil society actors. NGO representatives and delegates from like-minded governments supported his election as the chair of "the pivotal negotiating body of the conference."[43] He established close ties with the NGO representatives

[39] Ibid., p. 25.

[40] Ibid., p. 25.

[41] Robinson, "Case Study: The International Criminal Court," p. 173.

[42] Axworthy, "Introduction," p. 5.

[43] Robinson, "Case Study: The International Criminal Court," p. 173.

and like-mined government delegates; they held frequent meetings to discuss the headway and devise new strategies to secure the adoption of a strong final text with no loopholes. Kirsch greatly contributed to the entire process; on some sensitive issues over which no "generally acceptable compromises" were not found, the bureau chaired by Kirsch drafted a final proposal which was "a carefully balanced package, reflecting the clear majority trends in the conference."[44]

The second group of actors that were influential during the process of new diplomacy was the one formed by like-minded governments. Even though it would not be correct to refer to a clear-cut group of states with certain boundaries and membership structure as like-minded group, certain states should be cited as the leading and dominant actors in this group of predominantly middle-power states. Countries with strong human rights record which placed human rights agenda into their foreign policy establishments and objectives, such as Canada, Norway, the Netherlands, and Germany, were the most prominent ones. In the case of the ICC, it was observed that the Nordic countries, Australia, New Zealand, and Canada were very influential and ambitious to finalize an effective text.[45] Particularly, Norway and Canada were the most active countries to ensure the establishment of a strong and independent Court.

Soon before the inauguration of the Rome Conference, these two countries furthered their commitment to the human security agenda and pledged themselves to promote its particular items. Through the Lysøen Declaration accorded between Norway and Canada on May 11, 1998,[46] a partnership was established to promote the establishment of the ICC. Later, "an additional group of nontraditional states" joined the core

---

[44] Ibid., p. 173.

[45] Andrew F. Cooper, "Like-minded Nations, NGOs, and the Changing Pattern of Diplomacy within the UN System: An Introductory Perspective," in Rob McRae and Don Hubert (eds.), *Human Security and the New Diplomacy: Protecting People, Promoting Peace* (Montreal, Canada: McGill-Queen's University Press, 2001), p. 11.

[46] For further details on the content of the declaration, see, Michael Small, "Case Study: The Human Security Network," in Rob McRae and Don Hubert (eds.), *Human Security and the New Diplomacy: Protecting People, Promoting Peace* (Montreal, Canada: McGill-Queen's University Press, 2001), p. 232.

group of a handful states. Cooper notes that especially South Africa stood out among this additional group.[47]

The partnership has over the time grown "to include thirteen countries which meet and communicate regularly on a variety of common interests and initiatives related to human security."[48] As narrated in the previous chapters, the like-minded group has expanded further to include more than 60 countries during Rome Conference. Furthermore, "the range of candidates for like-minded status has also expanded. From a narrow and well-established cohort of countries, the scope for possible coalition partners has become far more inclusive."[49]

However, it should be noted that the most important actors of the new diplomacy are civil society actors, since they have played a determinative role in the adoption of a progressive final text at the end of the conference. The reported remarks of a Western diplomat who participated in the deliberations at the Rome Conference are beyond explanatory: "Let me tell you, they are very, very, very, very important here."[50] And just as outlined by Brown, the new diplomacy marked by the achievements of the NGOs at the Rome Conference heralds a new global reality.[51] During the Rome Conference, NGOs "may have won themselves a greater ability to move politics and diplomacy in directions of their choosing."[52] This creates a new reality which suggests that "states are more prepared to overcome traditional sovereignty concerns in favor of indirect benefits of protecting individuals and human security," and that "civil society is having a more direct impact on international negotiations."[53]

---

[47] Cooper, "Like-minded Nations, NGOs, and the Changing Pattern of Diplomacy within the UN System: An Introductory Perspective," p. 11.

[48] Axworthy, "Introduction," p. 9.

[49] Cooper, "Like-minded Nations, NGOs, and the Changing Pattern of Diplomacy Within the UN System: An Introductory Perspective," p. 5.

[50] Charles Trueheart, "Clout Without a Country: The Power of International Lobbies," *The Washington Post*, June 18, 1998.

[51] Brown, "What Is the New Diplomacy?" p. 4.

[52] Edgar, "Peace, Justice, and Politics: The International Criminal Court, 'New Diplomacy,' and the UN System," p. 147.

[53] Robinson, "Case Study: The International Criminal Court," p. 175.

It should be recalled that the heavy and excessive involvement of NGOs in world politics has been criticized for their nondemocratic stance as observed during the Rome Conference where the "NGOs not fully supportive of the concepts of the court were essentially cut out of the process."[54] This move once more raised the issue with regard to the allegedly nondemocratic character of the NGOs, which were neither described as neither representative of nor accountable to citizens. The reported remarks by one observer during the deliberations at the Rome Conference asking, "Who elected these NGOs anyway?" are probably the best manifestation of the said criticism. To this connection, it was argued that "the new diplomacy rhetoric of 'soft power' and 'collaboration' masks major power plays and dramatic shifts in the process."[55]

In response to the criticism briefly outlined earlier, it is provided that the excessive involvement of the NGOs in foreign policy issues "helps form a base of a consensus-oriented society." In that case, the government will have the opportunity to rely "on the expertise and experience of the civil society it serves." Hence, the entire process will remain legitimate as long as transparency is ensured.

Another problem with the involvement of the NGOs in new diplomacy cases is the blurring line between the civil society actors and the states. The relationship between the two has mostly been ambiguous and temporary. Andrew F. Cooper notes on this matter that

> In a variety of other cases, there is a considerable element of flexibility built into the approach, with a great deal of short-term assessment about the value-added benefits of striking a constructive arrangement on an issue-by-issue basis. In overall terms this pattern of interaction remains fuzzy, fragmentary, and awkward, but nevertheless vital and important . . . Contacts and coalitions are built in an improvisational manner, but few in the way of coterminous roles are established.[56]

---

[54] Davenport, "New Diplomacy," p. 24.

[55] Ibid., p. 24.

[56] Cooper, "Like-minded Nations, NGOs, and the Changing Pattern of Diplomacy within the UN System: An Introductory Perspective," p. 7.

But it should be recalled that the case of the creation of the ICC could be considered an exception. In that case, the broader coalition established between the NGO Coalition and the group of like-minded governments has proven to be very effective and influential. Even though this cooperative coalition was occasionally improvisational, it became solidified in the long run.

NGOs should be given the credit for the effective collaboration. The tactics they have relied on throughout the entire process secured the preservation of the broad and diverse coalition intact and vibrant. The most important tactic was the special emphasis put on expedition. In an attempt to prevent "dissent and compromise," the NGOs present at Rome created "self-imposed deadlines," a special innovation "almost unheard of in the slow, deliberate world of customary international law."[57]

## US Opposition to the ICC

It is surely not sufficient to examine only the impact of the ICC's establishment on sovereignty and the revival of the global civil society for a complete analysis on the significance of the Court in world politics. One could easily cite many other issues that are perfectly relevant to the discussion. However, it is equally true that it is impossible to cover all relevant topics in a single study due to space limitations and other restrictions. Therefore, this article is intended to be an eclectic attempt to depict the probable influence and significance of the ICC as an international legal entity in world affairs with a special reference to its current and future impacts on state sovereignty and the opportunities its establishment created for a better involvement of global civil society in international political and legal affairs. The aforesaid limitations and the eclectic quality of this study notwithstanding, the US opposition to the Court[58] deserves a brief mention in this regard, since this opposition

[57] Davenport, "New Diplomacy," p. 23.

[58] That opposition has extensively been covered in the literature. Therefore, it should be noted that the following list is not exhaustive. For a general account on the US opposition to the ICC, see, Henry Kissinger, "The Pitfalls of Universal Jurisdiction," *Foreign Affairs,* Vol. 80, Issue 4,

signifies that the power politics that has been predominant throughout the twentieth century is becoming more and more irrelevant in international relations.

Although seriously and eagerly involved in the preparatory work for establishing an ICC, the United States showed hesitance to sign the Rome Statute at the Conference, being one of the seven participant but nonsignatory states. The United States at the conference insisted on the retaining the states' discretion over the criminal matters. In addition, it wanted the Court to be acting under the control and authority of the Security Council. However, other participants rejected some of the American proposals, while on some of them a compromise was reached. For example, it has been agreed that the Court would be "complementary" to the national authorities, and act only if it would be evident that the state party concerned is unable to deal with the matter.

During the Clinton Administration the United States signed the Rome Statute on December 31, 2000, the virtual deadline for signing, as, under the Statute, a state willing to accede to the ICC after that date would have to ratify it.[59]

However, the treaty was never introduced in the Senate for ratification. Indeed, the Bush Administration launched a campaign against the ICC.[60] First, sending a letter to the UN Secretary-General, the

2001, pp. 86–96; Robert W. Tucker, "The International Criminal Court Controversy," *World Policy Journal,* Vol. 18, Issue 2, 2001, pp. 71–81; David P. Forsythe, "The United States and International Criminal Justice," *Human Rights Quarterly,* Vol. 24, Issue 4, 2002, pp. 974–991; John R. Bolton, "The Risks and Weaknesses of the International Criminal Court from America's Perspective," *Law & Contemporary Problems,* Vol. 64, Issue 1, 2002, pp. 165–182; Jamie Mayerfeld, "Who Shall be Judge?: The United States, the International Criminal Court, and the Global Enforcement of Human Rights", *Human Rights Quarterly,* Vol. 25, Issue 1, 2003, pp. 93–129; Alfred P. Rubin, "Some Objections to the International Criminal Court," *Peace Review,* Vol. 12, Issue 1, 2000, pp. 45–50.

[59] Article 125(1) of the Rome Statute.

[60] It has generally been acknowledged that the US opposition to the Court is not well grounded. For instance, it is asserted that "it appears that US concerns about the dangers of the ICC for Americans are exaggerated. Either as a member or a non-member of the Court, the US would have no less jurisdiction over crimes involving Americans... than it already enjoys under the present extradite-or-prosecute regime. The complementarity provision would give the US clear jurisdiction over crimes committed either by Americans or on American soil." See, Giulio M. Gallarotti and Arik Y. Preis, "Toward Universal Human Rights and the Rule of Law: The Permanent International Criminal Court," *Australian Journal of International Affairs,* Vol. 53, Issue 1, 1999, p. 106.

United States formally denounced itself from its undertakings and commitments originated from its signature. This came to be known as "unsigning,"[61] a popular term, for which the debate that whether it is possible under international law is underway.

Then, the Congress adopted the American Service members' Protection Act (ASPA),[62] which gives the US President an extensive authority to deal with the ICC. Under the ASPA, the President is authorized to take "any" measure to free the American personnel from the ICC's jurisdiction. Although hypothetically, since ASPA contains the military intervention option, the Act came to be known as "The Hague Invasion Act," and caused serious tension and anger in Europe.

However, neither Clinton's ambivalence nor Bush's hostility to the Court could have prevented it from coming into existence. The Statute along with the ICC entered into force in a very short time despite the US efforts to undermine it. Unable to prevent its entrance into force, the United States started a struggle against the Court; however, it failed too. The United States also tried to wield its power in position within the UN Security Council to block the ICC jurisdiction. Pursuant to Article 16 of the Statute, the Security Council, obviously under the leadership and influence of the United States, has twice passed a resolution blocking the ICC's involvement in the situations relating to the US personnel.[63]

---

[61] For an analysis on whether the Bush Administration's denunciation itself of its obligations arising from the US signature to the Statute could be called "unsigning" and whether it is consistent with the international legal rules, see Konstantinos Magliveras and Dimitris Bourantonis, "Rescinding the Signature of an International Treaty: the United States and the Rome Statute Establishing the International Criminal Court," *Diplomacy &Statecraft,* Vol. 14, Issue 4, 2003, pp. 21–49.

[62] American Service-Members' Protection Act of 2002, Pub. L. No. 107–206, §§ 2001–2008 (2002).

[63] These are Security Council Resolutions 1422 (2002) and 1487 (2003). U.N. Security Council Resolution, UN. Doc. S/RES/1422 (2002), 4572nd meeting, July 12, 2002 (the text of the resolution could be reached at: http://www.un.org/Docs/scres/2002/sc2002.htm, accessed on May 31, 2005); U.N. Security Council Resolution, UN. Doc. S/RES/1487 (2003), 4772nd meeting, July 12, 2003 (the text of the resolution could be reached at: http://www.un.org/Docs/sc/unsc_resolutions03.html, accessed on May 31, 2005. In those resolutions, the Security Council requested that the ICC not commence or proceed with the investigation or prosecution of any case arising concerning acts or omissions relevant to an operation authorized by the UN involving current or former officials or personnel from a state contributing to that operation which is not a party to the ICC. It is worth noting that while Article 16 of the Rome Statute does not limit the Security Council authority to defer any case, these resolutions may apply to a few cases only.

However, it became evident that the members of the Security Council would resist a US proposal for the renewal of such a resolution once more, the United States pulled it back. Therefore, while the United States has succeeded to block the ICC with Security Council resolutions in 2002 and 2003, it could not have secured the passage of such resolution in 2004, due to the strong resistance to such an attempt.

In addition, the United States could not prevent the passage of the UN Security Council referring the situation in Darfur, Sudan, to the ICC.[64] While the US veto could have prevented this referral in this case, it did not wield this power and indirectly allowed the Court to get involved in investigating the incidents in Darfur. It is understandable that the United States cannot easily block the Court's jurisdiction under Article 16 of the Statute, given that none of the permanent members in the Council should cast a negative vote and at least nine members should cast affirmative votes for such a blocking. However, the US power in case the Court needs the authorization of the Security Council is highly significant as its veto would block the Council's referral to the ICC. Despite its power in the Council, the United States was required to abstain in the voting of the Security Council resolution authorizing the Court to investigate the situation in Darfur.[65] This is worth noting, since prior to the passage of this resolution, the United States declared that it would not take any action legitimizing the Court.[66] Like in the Sudan case, the United States had

[64] The UN Security Council referred the situation in Darfur to the ICC with its Resolution 1593(2005). U.N. Security Council, UN. Doc. S/RES/1593 (2005), 5158th meeting, March 31, 2005.

[65] US Representative to the UN Security Council Woods Patterson stated on the occasion of the passage of the Security Council Resolution authorizing the ICC to investigate the situation in Darfur that it is important that the international community has established a mechanism to try the perpetrators of the international crimes committed in Darfur. She continued saying that while the United States would be against the Court, the fact that the international community showed its willingness and its steadfastness with a single voice is important. For the text of this statement, see the following URL: www.un.org/News/Press/docs/2005/sc8351.doc.htm, accessed on May 18, 2005.

[66] US Ambassador Pierre-Richard Prosper stated that the United States would never be in a position legitimizing the Court. See, Judy Aita, "Darfur War Crimes Referred to International Criminal Court," http://usinfo.state.gov/dhr/Archive/2005/Apr/01-671037.html, accessed on May 19, 2005.

to acknowledge the role of the Court and its legitimacy tacitly in the case of Libya. Unlike its stance in the adoption of the UNSC Resolution 1593 on Darfur, the United States did not remain neutral in the voting and joined all other permanent members in the Council referring the situation in Libya to the ICC.[67]

[67] "In Swift, Decisive Action, Security Council Imposes Tough Measures on Libyan Regime, Adopting Resolution 1970 in Wake of Crackdown on Protestors," Security Council, 6491st Session, Department of Public Information: News and Media Division, February 26, 2011, http://www.un.org/News/Press/docs/2011/sc10187.doc.htm, accessed July 2, 2013.

# Conclusion

This study analyzes the significance of the International Criminal Court (ICC) as an institution of international law for a better understanding of the change in international politics. In this study where, in reference to the dynamic interplay between international law and international politics, it is implied that the Court serves as an important indicator and model for redefining international politics. This study is intended to be an eclectic attempt to depict the probable influence and significance of the ICC as an international legal entity in world affairs with a special reference to its current and future impacts on state sovereignty and the opportunities its establishment created for a better involvement of global civil society in international political and legal affairs. The aforesaid limitations and the eclectic quality of this study notwithstanding, the US opposition to the Court deserves a brief mention in this regard, since this opposition signifies that the power politics that has been predominant throughout the twentieth century is becoming more and more irrelevant in international relations.

Juxtaposing its impact on national sovereignty, the strong involvement of global civil society in its creation and the US failure in its



C. Çakmak, *A Brief History of International Criminal Law and International Criminal Court*,
DOI 10.1057/978-1-137-56736-9_16

'struggle' against it, one could conclude that the ICC is and will continue to be a significant actor in world politics. While it is true to say that power politics is still predominant, the ICC case shows that the possession of power does not always create positive results for its possessor. Masses organized in the form of loose but influential structure can affect the outcome of an initiative so as to meet the demands of ordinary people, even if major powers' interests are at stake.

However, the creation of the ICC is not to be seen as an abrupt and dramatic change in world politics. Instead, it could be regarded as the continuation of the tendency toward a more people-oriented world. It is by all means a significant breakthrough to create an institution like the ICC, but it would be realistic to assume that the Court will be unable to perform its roles unless states' consent for cooperation is obtained.

In this study, the current state of the international political system and the change observed in it is being discussed with particular reference to the ICC-nation-state and the ICC-international system relations. The political aspects of the Court, an international legal institution, have been generally ignored. This is particularly visible in the literature. There are only a few studies on the role of the civil society organizations in the creation of the ICC, the political meaning of the prosecutor, the potential impact of the Court's functioning upon the perception of the notion of sovereignty and the practical reflections. This study attempts to fill this void.

In essence, the ICC is both the result of the changes and modifications in the definition of the international system and the structure of the system itself and an important element contributing to this change. The ICC, a product of the states which are the main subjects of the international law, is also an outcome of a process where the nonstate actors joined the making of the international law. In this sense, the court refers to an important change in the way international politics operates. The individual, the real person, who has been recognized a broader sphere of action under the emerging international human rights law, has also become an important legal subject whose responsibilities have been clarified within the international criminal law where the ICC is one of the major players.

The change that occurred in the nature of the sovereignty of the state despite that it has remained one of the main determinants of the international system led to the idea that sovereignty yields to responsibility as well. The crises in Sudan and Libya attract attention as cases where the intervention in domestic affairs is justified in connection with this idea. In both cases, the ICC took action in cases where the state failed to observe its responsibility to protect the people in reference to sovereignty. The ICC plays an important role by virtue of its powers and in the practical implementation of the responsibility to protect principle to redefine the notion of sovereignty.

Some disputes have remained in place since the inception of the international relations discipline. One of the best examples of this is focused on the future of the state as well as sovereignty, its main component.[1] A corollary discussion and debate is about the nature of the international system.[2] Are there some major principles dominant in the international political and economic order? If there are some major features defining this system, do these features and characteristics change over the time? Or do these primary principles defining the nature of the international system repeat themselves?[3]

The establishment of the ICC is one of the global developments that may potentially affect the content of the analyses and approaches on the main dynamics defining the international political system as well as on the nation-state and its influence on the global stage.[4] The political impact of the Court suggests that its activities and performance may change the course of global politics. This does not of course necessary

---

[1] See Paul Hirst and Grahame Thompson, "Globalization and the future of the nation state," Economy and Society, Vol. 24, Issue 3, 1995, pp. 408–442; J. Samuel Barkin and Bruce Cronin, "The state and the nation: changing norms and the rules of sovereignty in international relations," International Organization, Vol. 48, Issue 1, 1994, pp. 107–130; Susan Strange, Retreat of the State: The Diffusion of Power in the World Economy, Cambridge, Cambridge University Press, 1996.

[2] See Barry Buzan, "From international system to international society: structural realism and regime theory meet the English school," *International Organization,* Vol. 47, Issue 03, 1993, p. 327–352.

[3] See James N. Rosenau, *Turbulence in World Politics: A Theory of Change and Continuity,* Princeton, NJ: Princeton University Press, 1990.

[4] For political analysis of the ICC, see Michael P. Scharf, "The Politics of Establishing an International Criminal Court," Duke Journal of Comparative and International Law, Vol. 6, Issue 1, 1995, pp. 167–173; Benjamin N. Schiff, *Building the International Criminal Court,* Cambridge: Cambridge University Press, 2008; Steven C. Roach, *Politicizing the International Criminal Court: The Convergence of Politics, Ethics and Law,* Lanham, MD: Rowman & Littlefield, 2006.

that the ICC will alone change the international system and redefine the role of the nation-state in international politics. However, the ICC should be seen as the symbol of a process of redefinition in world politics. To this end, the Court can be viewed as a product of the gradual change in the system.

A brief analysis of what the ICC means in terms of the change in the nature and conduct of the international politics is extremely important to better understand the characteristics of the globalized world where justice is becoming a pivotal notion. A review of the Court will mean that the idea suggesting that power is the main determinant in world politics should be at least questioned. Of course that does not necessarily mean that a fair and just order is being constructed in the world via the activities and performance of the ICC. But the influence of the ICC in the international system shows that international politics is far more complicated than many would think.

Perhaps the greatest contribution of the ICC to redefinition of the global politics is its emphasis on the individual as a person under international law. It is generally contended that the international political system that emerged out of the Treaty of Westphalia places emphasis upon the sovereign nation-state with its defined territories.[5] International law, playing a role of creating order in a community of states, was inevitably designed to be applicable to the state alone at the beginning. This remained the case until the end of World War II; in other words, nation-state stayed as the only subject of the international politics and law in this period.[6] International organizations were recognized as legal persons under international law after World War II; as subject of international law and politics, international organizations started to exercise some powers.[7] More recently, the individual was

---

[5] See Hendrik Spruyt, "The End of Empire and the Extension of the Westphalian System: The Normative Basis of the Modern State Order," International Studies Review, Vol. 2, Issue 2, 2000, pp. 65–92.

[6] See Malcolm N. Shaw, *International Law*, Cambridge: Cambridge University Press, 2008, p. 195–264.

[7] See Dan Sarooshi, *International Organizations and Their Exercise of Sovereign Powers*, Oxford: Oxford University Press, 2005.

added to the list of legally recognized persons under international law.[8] The two main mechanisms making the individual a person of international law are international human rights law and international criminal law. Under international human rights law, individual serves as beneficiary, whereas under international criminal law, the individual appears with its responsibilities.[9]

By institutionalizing the personality of the individual under international law, the ICC amended the design and definition of the international political system. As noted, under international criminal law, individual is a person and subject of international law. However, its personality is recognizable only when the universal jurisdiction doctrine is invoked in a national legal system.[10] In other words, the states theoretically have the power to prosecute international crimes, whether or not this power would be exercised is a decision an individual state would make.

In making the individual a person of international law under the doctrine of universal jurisdiction, the state plays the main role. The state is authorized to exercise this jurisdiction and prosecute suspects of international crimes under this doctrine. The ad hoc tribunals created in the aftermath of World War II performed trials as international institutions; however, it is not possible to view these prosecutions as part of universal jurisdiction. Above all, these tribunals were authorized to address the crimes referred to in their statutes and their jurisdiction were restricted by territoriality. In addition, they automatically disappear and are dissolved when they expiry.

From this perspective, it is possible to argue that the ICC confirmed the personality of individual under international law in three respects. First, the ICC makes the prosecution of an individual possible even when his state does not consent. It is also interesting to note that this

---

[8] See Thomas R. Van Dervort, *International Law and Organization: An Introduction,* Londra: Sage, 1998, pp. 95–317.

[9] See for instance, Philip Alston and Ryan Goodman, *International Human Rights,* Oxford: Oxford University Press, 2013, pp. 1047–1244. For individual responsibility under international criminal law, see, Edoardo Greppi, "The Evolution of Individual Criminal Responsibility Under International Law," *International Review of the Red Cross,* Vol. 81, Issue 835, 1999, pp. 531–553.

[10] For universal jurisdiction, see Luc Reydams, *Universal Jurisdiction,* Oxford: Oxford University Press, 2004.

state of responsibility is permanent. In other words, theoretically speaking, any individual in the world can be prosecuted by the ICC. This of course does not mean that the Court will be able to prosecute anybody it would indict given that it suffers from some systemic and structural flaws.[11] Yet the ICC still has the power to prosecute and try perpetrators of a crime that falls into its jurisdiction regardless of their positions and status. And because this power remains, individual becomes a person of international law via the Court.

Second, the exercise of universal jurisdiction doctrine in the national stage may be susceptible to the political concerns and considerations whereas the ICC is able to act more independently of these flaws and deficiencies. Of course, it is likely that both the Court and the Prosecutor may become politicized. The possibility that the Court may be selective in the cases it would review points to one of the realities of realpolitik.[12] However, given that the job description of the prosecutor and the Court is clarified, the prosecutor will have to act more responsibly. In addition, the risk of being politicized is further reduced because the Court is responsible to the Assembly of States Party which serves as some sort of parliament.[13]

Third, the Court is able to exercise its jurisdiction independently of the decisions and stances of the national judicial institutions. In other words, the decisions and actions of a national judicial body in a certain matter do not preclude the Court from being engaged in the same case. Even though its function is based on the principle of complementarity, the Court still holds the discretion to determine as to whether or not the decisions of a national judicial body in a certain case are legally well grounded. This suggests that when the perpetrators of a crime also

---

[11] Jack Goldsmith, "The Self-Defeating International Criminal Court," *The University of Chicago Law Review,* Vol. 70, Issue 1, 2003, pp. 89–104.

[12] For an analysis of how to address the politicization of the ICC Prosecutor, see Allison Marston Danner, "Enhancing the Legitimacy and Accountability of Prosecutorial Discretion at the International Criminal Court," *The American Journal of International Law,* Vol. 97, Issue 3, 2003, pp. 510–552.

[13] See Daryl A. Mundis, "The Assembly of States Parties and the Institutional Framework of the International Criminal Court," *The American Journal of International Law,* Vol. 97, Issue 1, 2003, pp. s.132–147.

prosecutable by the Court are tried by a national judicial body, the ICC has the power to determine whether or not the prosecution process is adequate or flawed.[14]

The ICC does not enjoy universal jurisdiction; however, the Court does not need prior authorization to exercise its powers. In other words, the ICC Prosecutor has the discretion to initiate an investigation without requiring a prior authorization into a criminal matter that falls into the competence of the Court. Where the ICC is unable to exercise automatic jurisdiction, the UN Security Council refers a situation to the Court for investigation.[15] Cases in Sudan and Libya confirm that the Security Council views the ICC as the only body that is able to deal with the prosecution of international crimes.

How does the creation and activities of the ICC contribute to the redefinition of the international system? It is generally argued that the international political system based on the supremacy of the nation-state as the primary actor has been subjected to radical transformations. During these processes of change and transformation, the interaction between international law and politics has become dynamic; and these two domains have become interlinked.[16] However, despite these changes, some major characteristics of the system have remained the same; both international politics and international law are built upon the principle of equality between states, the recognition of sovereignty and of the state as main subject.[17] This main principle is further backed the principle of nonintervention.[18]

[14] For instance, the ICC requested the extradition of Sayful Islam Gaddafi because it concluded that the trial process by a Libyan court was not legally satisfactory. Faith Karimi, "ICC to Libya: Hand over Gadhafi's son," *CNN,* June 3, 2013.

[15] See Corrina Heyder, "The U.N. Security Council's Referral of the Crimes in Darfur to the International Criminal Court in Light of U.S. Opposition to the Court: Implications for the International Criminal Court's Functions and Status," *Berkeley Journal of International Law,* Vol. 24, Issue 2, 2005, pp. 539–561.

[16] See Stepan Wood, Ann-Marie Slaughter and Andrew S. Tulumello, "International Law and International Relations Theory: A New Generation of Interdisciplinary Scholarship," American Journal of International Law, Vol. 92, Issue 3, 1998, pp. 367–397.

[17] Robert Rosenstock, "The Declaration of Principles of International Law Concerning Friendly Relations: A Survey," *American Journal of International Law,* Vol. 65, Issue 5, 1971, pp. 713–735.

[18] See Malcolm N. Shaw, *International Law*, Cambridge: Cambridge University Press, 2003, pp. 647–649.

Those two principles still constitute the basis of international politics as a construct. However, they simply refer to the rights and powers of the state as main unit of construction of the international law and politics. In addition to rights and powers, responsibilities of the subjects should also be defined within a community to create a working order. International law is the main mechanism prescribing those responsibilities.[19] In fact, international law is a logical product of a community because the presence of a community requires pursuit of order. The strongest norm suggesting that responsibilities should be observed in that system is *pacta sund servanda*. In other words, the principles of sovereignty and nonintervention refer to the rights of the states whereas *pacta sund servanda* prescribes their responsibilities.

As constructed, the system created by the nation-states which create the norms and make the international law and are obligated to comply with these norms at the same time is anarchical. However, anarchy does not necessarily mean lack of order and of community. "Anarchical society"[20] successfully defines how the international politics and system is defined and constructed. While main characteristics remained the same, international system has been redefined. In these periods of redefinition, the sovereignty of the state has been restricted by international law. For instance, war was prohibited in the aftermath of World War I.[21]And the use of force was monopolized to the UN Security Council after World War II.

The ICC is both the outcome of the changes in the way international politics is defined and in the system itself, and a significant element contributing to this chance. The ICC which can be seen a product of states as main subjects of the international law is also a major outcome of a process where nonstate actors join the making of the international law. In this sense, the Court refers to a significant change in the way international politics is defined and performed. Over the time, the

[19] For state responsibility, see Ibid., pp. 778–849.

[20] Hedley Bull, *The Anarchical Society: A Study of Order in International Politics,* New York: Columbia University Press, 2002.

[21] Leo Gross, "The Criminality of Aggressive War," *The American Political Science Review,* Vol. 41, Issue 2, 1947, pp. 205–225.

individual who was recognized rights under international human rights law has become a subject under international criminal law which prescribes responsibilities. In this process, new norms were developed and these norms partially changed the dynamics of international politics.[22]

In brief, the ICC is a product of the dynamic relation and interaction between international law and international politics. The change and transformation caused by the historical priorities and necessities in the definition of the international political system and community is being represented by the ICC. Even though it is hard to say that the Court is a very influential actor in itself, what really matters is the change this institution points to. In other words, the ICC is a good and illustrative indicator for proper reading and understanding of the change in international politics and in the way it is being constructed. The "After Hegemony"[23] period, the voids are filled by a diverse set of norm carriers and producers. The actors paying attention to their normative priorities serve as the carriers of this type of change in this process. But of course, the corollary question is whether or not this change will be permanent.

---

[22] For studies explaining norm entrepreneurship and norm diffusion, see Lesley Wexler, "The International Deployment of Shame, Second-best Responses, and Norm Enterpreneurship: The Campaign to Ban Landmines and the Landmine Ban Treaty," *Arizone Journal of International and Comparative Law,* Vol. 20, Issue 3, 2003, pp. 561–603; Kamil Zwolski and Christian Kaunert, "The EU and Climate Security: A Case of Successful Norm Enterpreneurship?," *European Security,* Vol. 20, Issue 1, 2011, pp. 21–43; Amitav Acharya, "How Ideas Spread: Whose Norms Matter? Norm Localization and Institutional Change in Asian Regionalism," *International Organization,* Vol. 58, Issue 2, 2004, pp. 239–275; Susan Park, "Theorizing Norm Diffusion Within International Organizations," *International Politics,* Vol. 43, Issue 3, 2006, pp. 346–361.

[23] Robert O. Keohane, *After Hegemony: Cooperation and Discord in the World Political Economy,* Princeton, NJ: Princeton University Press, 1984.

# Bibliography

Acharya, Amitav, "How Ideas Spread: Whose Norms Matter? Norm Localization and Institutional Change in Asian Regionalism," *International Organization*, Vol. 58, Issue 2, 2004.

Address by Kofi Annan to Hague Appeal for Peace Conference: Greater Role for NGOs at the UN Welcomed, Hague Appeal for Peace Press Release, May 7, 1999, available at: http://www.globalpolicy.org/ngos/docs99/hap99.htm.

Akhavan, Payam, "The International Criminal Tribunal for Rwanda: The Politics and Pragmatics of Punishment," *American Journal of International Law*, Vol. 90, Issue 3, 1996.

Alston, Philip and Ryan Goodman, *International Human Rights* (Oxford: Oxford University Press, 2013).

Andreasen, Scott W., "The International Criminal Court: Does the Constitution Preclude Its Ratification by the United States?" *Iowa Law Review*, Vol. 85, Issue 2, 2000.

Annan, Kofi A., "Foreword," in Rob McRae and Don Hubert (eds.), *Human Security and the New Diplomacy: Protecting People, Promoting Peace* (Montreal, Canada: McGill-Queen's University Press, 2001).



C. Çakmak, *A Brief History of International Criminal Law and International Criminal Court*,
DOI 10.1057/978-1-137-56736-9

Arnaut, Damir, "When in Rome? The International Criminal Court and Avenues for U.S. Participation," *Virginia Journal of International Law*, Vol. 43, Issue 2, 2003.

Axworthy, Lloyd, "Introduction," in Rob McRae and Don Hubert (eds.), *Human Security and the New Diplomacy: Protecting People, Promoting Peace* (Montreal, Canada: McGill-Queen's University Press, 2001).

Axworthy, Lloyd, Minister of Foreign Affairs of Canada, "The New Diplomacy, the UN, the International Criminal Court and the Human Security Agenda," Conference on UN Reform, The Kennedy School of Harvard University, Cambridge, MA, April 25, 1998, available at:, http://www.dfaitmaeci.gc.ca.

Bann, Amy Jeanne, The Non- Governmental Organization Coalition for an International Criminal Court: A Case Study on NGO Networking, Unpublished Master's thesis, Virginia Polytechnic Institute and State University, 2001.

Barret, Jastine, "The Prohibition of Torture Under International Law: The Institutional Organization," *The International Journal of Human Rights*, Vol. 5, Issue 1, 2001.

Barkin, J. Samuel and Bruce Cronin, "The State and the Nation: Changing Norms and the Rules of Sovereignty in International Relations," *International Organization*, Vol. 48, Issue 1, 1994.

Bassiouni, M. Cherif, *Crimes Against Humanity in International Criminal Law*, 2nd rev. ed. (Cambridge, MA: Kluwer Law International, 1999).

Bassiouni, M. Cherif, "Establishing an International Criminal Court: Historical Survey," *Military Law Review*, Issue 149, 1995.

Bassiouni, M. Cherif, "From Versailles to Rwanda in Seventy-Five Years: The Need to Establish a Permanent International Criminal Court," *Harvard Human Rights Journal*, Vol. 10, Issue 10, 1997.

Bassiouni, M. Cherif, "Negotiating the Treaty of Rome on the Establishment of an International Criminal Court," *Cornell International Law Journal*, Vol. 43, Issue 2, 1999.

Bassiouni, M. Cherif, "The Time has Come for an International Criminal Court," *Indiana International and Comparative Law Review*, Vol. 1, Issue 1, 1991.

Bassiouni, M. Cherif and Derby, Daniel H., "Final Report on the Establishment of and International Criminal Court for the Implementation of the Apartheid Convention and Other Relevant International Instruments," *Hofstra Law Review*, Vol. 9, Issue 1, 1981.

Beigbeder, Yves, *Judging War Criminals: The Politics of International Justice* (New York: St. Martin's, 1999).

Benedetti, Fanny and Washburn, John L., "Drafting the International Criminal Court Treaty: Two Years to Rome and an Afterword on the Rome Diplomatic Conference," *Global Governance*, Vol. 5, Issue 1, 1999.

Benison, Audrey I., "War Crimes: A Human Rights Approach to a Humanitarian Law Problem at the International Criminal Court," *Georgetown Law Journal*, Vol. 88, Issue 1, 1999.

Berg, Bradley E., "The 1994 I.L.C. Draft Statute for an International Criminal Court: A Principled Appraisal of Jurisdictional Structure," *Case Western Reserve Journal of International Law*, Vol. 28, Issue 2, 1996.

Bergsmo, Morten, "The Jurisdictional Regime of the International Criminal Court (Part II, Articles 11-19)," *European Journal of Crime, Criminal Law and Criminal Justice*, Vol. 6, Issue 4, 1998.

Best, Geoffrey, "Peace Conferences and the Century of Total War: The 1899 Hague Conference and What Came After," *International Affairs*, Vol. 75, Issue 3, 1999.

Bezlova, Anioaneta, "China Keeps Wary Eye on Interference by Tribunal," *Terra Viva*, Vol. 2, June 16, 1998.

Bos, Adriaan, "The International Criminal Court: A Perspective," in Lee, Roy S. (ed.), *The International Criminal Court: The Making of the Rome Statue: Issues, Negotiations, Results* (The Hague: Kluwer Law International, 1999).

Bowers, Paul, *The International Criminal Court Bill (HL), Bill 70 of 2000–2001*, Research Paper 01/39, Through House of Commons Library, United Kingdom, accessed via: 28 March 2002, available at: http://www.parliament.uk/commons/lib/research/rp2001/rp01-039.pdf.

Bolton, John R., "The Risks and Weaknesses of the International Criminal Court from America's Perspective", *Law & Contemporary Problems*, Vol. 64, Issue 1, 2002.

Brown, Bartram S., "U.S. Objections to the Statute of the International Criminal Court: A Brief Response," *International Law and Politics*, Vol. 31, Issue 4, 1999.

Brown, Bernard E., "What Is the New Diplomacy?" *American Foreign Policy Interests*, Vol. 23, Issue 1, 2001.

Buergenthal, Thomas, "The Normative and Institutional Evolution of International Human Rights", *Human Rights Quarterly*, Vol. 19, Issue 4, 1997.

Bull, Hedley, *The Anarchical Society: A Study of Order in International Politics* (New York: Columbia University Press, 2002).

Buzan, Barry, "From International System to International Society: Structural Realism and Regime Theory Meet the English School," *International Organization*, Vol. 47, Issue 3, 1993.

Cassese, A., Gaeta, P. and Jones, J. (eds.), *The Rome Statute of the International Criminal Court*, Vol. I, 2002.

Ciampi, Annalisa, "The International Criminal Court," *The Law and Practice of International Courts and Tribunals*, Vol. 3, Issue 3, 2004.

Clark, R. Floyd, "A Permanent Tribunal of International Arbitration: Its Necessity and Value," *American Journal of International Law*, Vol. 1, Issue 2, 1907.

Cooper, Andrew F., "Like-Minded Nations, NGOs, and the Changing Pattern of Diplomacy Within the UN System: An Introductory Perspective," in Rob McRae and Don Hubert (eds.), *Human Security and the New Diplomacy: Protecting People, Promoting Peace* (Montreal, Canada: McGill-Queen's University Press, 2001).

Crawford, James, "The ILC Adopts A Statute for an International Criminal Court," *American Journal of International Law*, Vol. 89, Issue 2, 1995.

Danner, Allison Marston, "Enhancing the Legitimacy and Accountability of Prosecutorial Discretion at the International Criminal Court," *The American Journal of International Law*, Vol. 97, Issue 3, 2003.

Davenport, David, "The New Diplomacy," *Policy Review*, Vol. 116, 2002–2003.

Davis, George B., "Doctor Francis Lieber's Instructions for the Government Armies in the Field," *American Journal of International Law*, Vol. 1, Issue 1, 1907.

Deschênes, Jules, "Toward International Criminal Justice," in Clark, Roger S. and San, Madeleine (eds.), *The Prosecution of International Crimes* (New Brunswick, NJ: Transaction Publishers, 1996).

Donat-Cattin, David, "ICC Procedural Law: The Limited Mandate of the PrepCom on the Rules of Procedure and Evidence," *The International Criminal Court Monitor*, Vol. 14, 2000.

Donnelly, Jack, *International Human Rights* (Boulder, CO: Westview Press, 1993).

"Dutch NGOs Combine Forces," *Insight on the ICC*, Issue 1, April 2004.

Edgar, Alistair, "Peace, Justice, and Politics: The International Criminal Court, 'New Diplomacy,' and the UN System," in Andrew F. Cooper, John English and Ramesh Thakur (eds.), *Enhancing Global Governance: Towards a New Diplomacy* (Tokyo, New York and Paris: United Nations University Press, 2002), pp. 133–152.

Edwards, Michael, "Civil Society and Global Governance," Paper presented at the Conference 'On the Threshold: The United Nations and Global Governance in the New Millennium,' United Nations University, Tokyo, Japan, January 19–21, 2000.

Ethirajah Anbarasan, "A Decisive Victory," Interview with Bill Pace, The UNESCO Courier, available at: http://www.unesco.org/courier/1998_10_uk/dossier/txt23.htm.

Farbstein, Susan Hannah, "The Effectiveness of the Exercise of Jurisdiction by the International Criminal Court: The Issue of Complementarity," *European Centre for Minority Issues*, Working Paper No. 12, 2001.

Finch, George A., "Draft Statute for an International Criminal Court," *American Journal of International Law*, Vol. 46, Issue 1, 1952.

Forsythe, David, "1949 and 1999: Making the Geneva Conventions relevant after the Cold War," *International Review of the Red Cross*, Vol. 834, 1999.

"For the Record: The New Diplomacy and American National Interests," *American Foreign Policy Interests*, Vol. 23, Issue 1, 2001.

Forsythe, David P., "The United States and International Criminal Justice", *Human Rights Quarterly*, Vol. 24, Issue 4, 2002.

Gallarotti, Giulio M. and Preis, Arik Y., "Toward Universal Human Rights and the Rule of Law: The Permanent International Criminal Court," *Australian Journal of International Affairs*, Vol. 53, Issue 1, 1999.

Glasius, Marlies, "How Activist Shaped the Court," Crimes of War Project, The International Criminal Court: An End to Impunity? *The Magazine* Section, December 2003, accessed via: http://www.crimesofwar.org/print/icc/icc-glasius-print.html.

Glasius, Marlies, *The International Criminal Court: A Global Civil Society Achievement* (London and New York: Routledge, 2006).

Glasius, Marlies, Kaldor, Mary and Anheier, Helmut (eds.), *Global Civil Society 2002* (Oxford: Oxford University Press, 2002).

Goldsmith, Jack, "The Self-Defeating International Criminal Court," *The University of Chicago Law Review*, Vol. 70, Issue 1, 2003.

Greppi, Edoardo, "The Evolution of Individual Criminal Responsibility Under International Law," *International Review of the Red Cross*, Vol. 81, Issue 835, 1999.

Gross, Leo, "The Criminality of Aggressive War," *The American Political Science Review*, Vol. 41, Issue 2, 1947.

Hall, Christopher K., "The First Proposal for a Permanent International Criminal Court," *International Review of the Red Cross*, Vol. 322, 1998a.

Hall, Christopher K., "The Third and Fourth Sessions of the UN Preparatory Committee on the Establishment of an International Criminal Court," *The American Journal of International Law*, Vol. 92, 1998b.

"Handling of Elections Will Affect the Future of the ICC," *The ICC Monitor*, Vol. 21, June 2002.

Haq, Farhan, "Bracket-Busting Time Begins," *Terra Viva*, Vol. 1, June 15, 1998.

Heyder, Corrina, "The U.N. Security Council's Referral of the Crimes in Darfur to the International Criminal Court in Light of U.S. Opposition to the Court: Implications for the International Criminal Court's Functions and Status," *Berkeley Journal of International Law*, Vol. 24, Issue 2, 2005.

Hirst, Paul and Grahame Thompson, "Globalization and the Future of the Nation State," *Economy and Society*, Vol. 24, Issue 3, 1995.

Hwang, Phyllis, "Defining Crimes Against Humanity in the Rome Statute of the International Criminal Court," *Fordham International Law Journal*, Vol. 22, Issue 2, 1998.

Jackson, William Eldred, "Putting the Nuremberg Law to Work," *Foreign Affairs*, Vol. 25, Issue 4, 1947.

Jamison, Sandra L., "A Permanent International Criminal Court: A Proposal that Overcomes Past Objections," *Denver Journal of International Law & Policy*, Vol. 23, Issue 2, 1995.

Jaura, Ramesh, "Legal Experts on ICC Compromise Yes, Clout No," *Terra Viva*, Vol. 1, June 15, 1998.

Jochnick, Chris, "The Human Rights Challenge to Global Poverty," Retrieved on 15.04.2004, from http://www.cesr.org/text%20files/actors.PDF.

Karimi, Faith, "ICC to Libya: Hand Over Gadhafi's son," *CNN*, 3 June 2013.

Kaul, Hans-Peter, "Special Note: The Struggle for the International Criminal Court's Jurisdiction," *European Journal of Crime, Criminal Law and Criminal Justice*, Vol. 6, Issue 4, 1998.

Keck, Margaret E. and Sikkink, Kathryn, *Activists Beyond Borders: Advocacy Networks in International Politics* (Ithaca, NY: Cornell University Press, 1998).

Keller, Robert, "African NGOs Call for a Renewed Commitment to an Independent Prosecutor," *The International Criminal Court Monitor*, Special Issue 18, July 8, 1998.

Kennan, George F. and Franck, Thomas M., *The Other Balkan Wars: A 1913 Carnegie Endowment Inquiry in Retrospect* (Washington, DC: Carnegie Endowment for International Peace, 1993).

Keohane, Robert O., *After Hegemony: Cooperation and Discord in the World Political Economy* (Princeton: Princeton University Press, 1984).

Kirk, Alejandro, "Cuba: Economic Blockades are Crimes against Humanity," *Terra Viva*, Vol. 9, June 25, 1998a.

Kirk, Alejandro "High Noon," *Terra Viva*, Vol. 23, July 15, 1998b.

Kirk, Alejandro "Take it or Leave it," *Terra Viva*, Vol. 22, July 14, 1998c.

Kirsch, Philippe and Holmes, John T., "The Rome Conference on an International Criminal Court: The Negotiating Process," *American Journal of International Law*, Vol. 93, Issue 1, 1999.

Kirsch, Philippe and Oosterveld, Valerie, "Completing the Work of the Preparatory Commission: The Preparatory Commission for the International Criminal Court," *Fordham International Law Journal*, Vol. 25, Issue 3, 2002.

Kissinger, Henry, "The Pitfalls of Universal Jurisdiction," *Foreign Affairs*, Vol. 80, Issue 4, 2001.

Latore, Roseann M., "Escape Out the Back Door or Charge in the Front Door: U.S. Reactions to the International Criminal Court," *Boston Collage International & Comparative Law Review*, Vol. 25, Issue 1, 2002.

Lemkin, Raphael, "Genocide," *American Scholar*, Vol. 15, Issue 2, April 1946, 227–230.

Lippman, Matthew, "Towards an International Criminal Court," *San Diego Justice Journal*, Vol. 3, Issue 1, 1995.

MacPherson, Bryan F., "Building an International Criminal Court for the 21st Century," *Connecticut Journal of International Law*, Vol. 13, Issue 1, 1998.

Maogoto, Jackson Nyamuya, *State Sovereignty and International Criminal Law: Versailles to Rome* (Ardsley, NY: Transnational Publishers, 2003).

Maxwell, John A. and Friedberg, James J. (eds.), *Human Rights in Western Civilization: 1600–Present*, 2nd ed. (Dubuque, IO: Kendall/Hunt Publishing, 1994).

Mayerfeld, Jamie, "Who Shall Be Judge?: The United States, the International Criminal Court, and the Global Enforcement of Human Rights", *Human Rights Quarterly*, Vol. 25, Issue 1, 2003.

McRae, Rob, "Conclusion," in Rob McRae and Don Hubert (eds.), *Human Security and the New Diplomacy: Protecting People, Promoting Peace* (Montreal, Canada: McGill-Queen's University Press, 2001).

McCormack, Timothy L.H., "Selective Reaction to Atrocity: War Crimes and the Development of International Criminal Law," *Albany Law Review*, Vol. 60, Issue 1, 1997.

Meray, Seha L., *Devletler Hukukuna Giriş*, 3rd ed., 2 vol. (Ankara: Ankara University Press, 1965).

Miller, Alexandra A., "From the International Criminal Tribunal for Rwanda to the International Criminal Court: Expanding the Definition of Genocide To Include Rape," *Pennsylvania State Law Review*, Vol. 108, Issue 1, 2003.

Morris, Madeline H., "The Trials of Concurrent Jurisdiction: The Case of Rwanda," *Duke Journal of Comparative and International Law*, Vol. 7, Issue 2, 1997.

Moshan, Brook Sari, "Woman, War and Words: The Gender Component in The Permanent International Criminal Court's Definition of Crimes Against Humanity," *Fordham International Law Journal*, Vol. 22, Issue 1, 1998.

Mullins, Christopher W., Kauzlarich, David and Rothe, Dawn, "The International Criminal Court and the Control of State Crime: Prospects and Problems," *Critical Criminology*, Vol. 12, Issue 3, 2004.

Mundis, Daryl A., "The Assembly of States Parties and the Institutional Framework of the International Criminal Court," *The American Journal of International Law*, Vol. 97, Issue 1, 2003.

Nel, Philip, "Between Counter-hegemony and Post-hegemony: The Rome Statute and Normative Innovation in World Politics," in Andrew F. Cooper, John English and Ramesh Thakur (eds.), *Enhancing Global Governance: Towards a New Diplomacy* (Tokyo, New York and Paris: United Nations University Press, 2002).

Neumann, Iver, Paper presented at the Conference on New Diplomacy, cited at "Report from the Conference on New Diplomacy: The United Nations, Like-Minded Countries and Non-Governmental Organizations," Ontario, Canada, September 28–30, 1999.

Nill, David A., "National Sovereignty: Must It Be Sacrificed to the International Criminal Court?" *BYU Journal of Public Law*, Vol. 14, Issue 1, 1999.

O'Connor, Gerard E., "The Pursuit of Justice and Accountability: Why The United States Should Support the Establishment of an International Criminal Court," *Hofstra Law Review*, Vol. 27, Issue 4, 1999.

Olásolo, Héctor, "The Prosecutor of the ICC Before the Initiation of Investigations: A Quasi-judicial or a Political Body?," *International Criminal Law Review*, Vol. 3, Issue 2, 2003.

Pace, William R., "A Victory for Peace," *The ICC Monitor*, Issue 21, June 2002.

Pace, William, "Awful and Awesome Responsibility Stands in Front of Us. We Cannot Fail," Statement at the Official Opening Plenary Session, *The International Criminal Court Monitor*, Vol. 2, Special June 16, 1998.

Pace, William, "The ICC and UN at Crossroads of International Justice," *The ICC Monitor*, Issue 28, November 2004.

Pace, William and Karanasios, Tanya, "Expectations for the ICC Mount," *The ICC Monitor*, Issue 23, February 2003.

Park, Susan, "Theorizing Norm Diffusion Within International Organizations," *International Politics*, Vol. 43, Issue 3, 2006.

Penfield, William L., "International Arbitration," *American Journal of International Law*, Vol. 1, Issue 2, 1907.

Pictet, Jean S., "The New Geneva Conventions for the Protection of War Victims," *American Journal of International Law*, Vol. 45, Issue 3, 1951.

Pritchard, R. John, "The Gift of Clemency Following British War Crimes Trials in the Far East, 1946–1947," *Criminal Law Forum*, Vol. 7, 1996.

Ratner, Steven R., "The International Criminal Court and the Limits of Global Judicialization," *Texas International Law Journal*, Vol. 38, Issue 3, 2003.

Reydams, Luc, *Universal Jurisdiction* (Oxford: Oxford University Press, 2004).

Roach, Steven C., *Politicizing the International Criminal Court: The Convergence of Politics, Ethics and Law* (Lanham, MD: Rowman & Littlefield, 2006).

Robinson, Darryl, "Case Study: The International Criminal Court," in Rob McRae and Don Hubert (eds.), *Human Security and the New Diplomacy: Protecting People, Promoting Peace* (Montreal, Canada: McGill-Queen's University Press, 2001).

Roht-Arriaza, Naomi, "Institutions of International Justice," *Journal of International Affairs*, Vol. 52, Issue 2, 1999.

"Rome Statute Near 100 Ratifications," *The ICC Monitor*, Issue 26, February 2004.

Root, Elihu, "The Outlook For International Law," *Proceedings of American Society of International Law*, Vol. 9, 1915.

Rosenau, James N., *Turbulence in World Politics: A Theory of Change and Continuity*, (Princeton, NJ: Princeton University Press, 1990).

Rosenstock, Robert, "The Declaration of Principles of International Law Concerning Friendly Relations: A Survey," *American Journal of International Law*, Vol. 65, Issue 5, 1971.

Rubin, Alfred P., "Challenging the Conventional Wisdom: Another View of the International Criminal Court," *Journal of International Affairs*, Vol. 52, Issue 2, 1999.

Rubin, Alfred P., "Some Objections to the International Criminal Court," *Peace Review*, Vol. 12, Issue 1, 2000.

Sadat, Leila Nadya, "The Establishment of the International Criminal Court: From The Hague to Rome and Back Again," *Michigan State University-DCL Journal of International Law*, Vol. 8, Issue 1, 1999.

Sarooshi, Dan, *International Organizations and Their Exercise of Sovereign Powers* (Oxford: Oxford University Press, 2005).

Schabas, William A., *An Introduction to the International Criminal Court* (Cambridge, UK and New York: Cambridge University Press, 2001).

Scharf, Michael P., "The Politics of Establishing an International Criminal Court," *Duke Journal of Comparative and International Law*, Vol. 6, Issue 1, 1995.

Schense, Jennifer, "Prosecutor Receives DRC Referral," *The ICC Monitor*, Issue 27, June 2004.

Schense, Jennifer, "Second Session of the Preparatory Commission," *The International Criminal Court Monitor*, Issue 11, 1999.

Schiff, Benjamin N., *Building the International Criminal Court* (Cambridge: Cambridge University Press, 2008).

"Sectoral Caucuses Will Continue to Strengthen the ICC," *The ICC Monitor*, Issue 21, June 2002.

Shaw, Malcolm N., *International Law* (Cambridge: Cambridge University Press, 2003).

Small, Michael, "Case Study: The Human Security Network," in Rob McRae and Don Hubert (eds.), *Human Security and the New Diplomacy: Protecting People, Promoting Peace* (Montreal, Canada: McGill-Queen's University Press, 2001).

Spees, Pam, "Women's Advocacy in the Creation of the International Criminal Court: Changing the Landscapes of Justice and Power," *Signs: Journal of Women in Culture and Society*, Vol. 28, Issue 4, 2003.

Spruyt, Hendrik, "The End of Empire and the Extension of the Westphalian System: The Normative Basis of the Modern State Order," *International Studies Review*, Vol. 2, Issue 2, 2000.

Steiner, Henry J. and Alston, Philip (eds.), *International Human Rights in Context: Law, Politics and Morals* (Oxford: Clarendon Press, 1996).

Stimson, Henry L., "The Nuremberg Trial: Landmark in Law," *Foreign Affairs*, Vol. 25, Issue 2, 1947.

Susan Strange, *Retreat of the State: The Diffusion of Power in the World Economy* (Cambridge: Cambridge University Press, 1996).

Storey, Hugh, "Human Rights and the New Europe: Experience and Experiment," *Political Studies*, Vol. 43, Special Issue, 1995.

Strapatsas, Nicolaos, "The European Union and Its Contribution to the Development of the International Criminal Court", *Revue de Droit Universite de Sherbrooke*, Vol. 33, Issue 2, 2002/2003.

Straus, Scott, "Darfur and the Genocide Debate," *Foreign Affairs*, Vol. 84, Issue 1, 2005.

Tomuschat, Christian, "A System of International Criminal Prosecution Is Taking Shape," *Review of the International Commission of Jurists*, Vol. 50, 1993.

Törnquiest-Chesnier, Marie, "NGOs and International Law," *Journal of Human Rights*, Vol. 3, Issue 2, 2004.

"Charles, Clout, "Without a Country: The Power of International Lobbies," *The Washington Post*, June 18, 1998.

Tucker, Robert W., "The International Criminal Court Controversy," *World Policy Journal*, Vol. 18, 2, 2001.

Van der Vyver, Johan D., "Civil Society and the International Criminal Court," *Journal of Human Rights*, Vol. 2, Issue 3, 2003.

Van Dervort, Thomas R., *International Law and Organization: An Introduction* (Londra: Sage, 1998).

Wexler, Lesley, "The International Deployment of Shame, Second-best Responses, and Norm Entrepreneurship: The Campaign to Ban Landmines and the Landmine Ban Treaty," *Arizona Journal of International and Comparative Law*, Vol. 20, Issue 3, 2003.

Williams, Sharon A., "The Rome Statute on the International Criminal Court: From 1947–2000 and Beyond," *Osgoode Hall Law Journal*, Vol. 38, Issue 2, 2000.

Willis, James F., *Prologue to Nuremberg: The Politics and Diplomacy of Punishing War Criminals of the First World War* (Westport, CT: Greenwood Press, 1982).

Wood, Stepan, Ann-Marie Slaughter and Andrew S. Tulumello, "International Law and International Relations Theory: A New Generation of Interdisciplinary Scholarship," *American Journal of International Law*, Vol. 92, Issue 3, 1998.

Yang, Lijun, "Some Critical Remarks on the Rome Statute of the International Criminal Court," *Chinese Journal of International Law*, Vol. 2, Issue 1, 2003.

Yingling, Raymund T. and Ginnane, Robert W., "The Geneva Conventions of 1949," *American Journal of International Law*, Vol. 46, Issue 3, 1952.

Zwolski, Kamil and Christian Kaunert, "The EU and Climate Security: A Case of Successful Norm Entrepreneurship?" *European Security*, Vol. 20, Issue 1, 2011.

# Official documents

*ABA Resolution* (Washington, DC: American Bar Association, 1998).

"A Decade of American Foreign Policy: Basic Documents, 1941–1949," (prepared by the Staff of the Committee and the Department of State) (Washington, DC: Government Printing Office, 1950).

Ad Hoc Committee on Genocide Report to the Economic and Social Council on the Meetings of the Committee, New York, 1948, U.N. ESCOR Supp. No. 6 at U.N. ESCOR Ad Hoc Committee, art. VII.

Affirmation of the Principles of International Law Recognized by the Charter of the Nuremberg Tribunal, G.A. Res. 95 (I), U.N. GAOR, U.N. Doc. A/236 (1946).

Alfaro, Ricardo J., International Law Commission, *Report on the Question of International Criminal Jurisdiction*, U.N. Doc. A/CN.4/15, reprinted in *The Yearbook of International Law Commission Volume II*, 1950.

Allied Control Council Law No. 10, Punishment of Persons Guilty of War Crimes, Crimes against Peace and against Humanity, 20 December 1945, Official Gazette of the Control Council for Germany, No. 3, Berlin, January 31, 1946; reprinted in Ferencz, Half A Century of Hope: An International Criminal Court: A Step Toward World Peace- A Documentary History and Analysis.

American Service-Members' Protection Act of 2002, Pub. L. No. 107-206, §§ 2001–2008 (2002).

Amnesty International, Establishing A Just, Fair and Effective International Criminal Court(Amnesty International: AI Index: IOR 40/05/94, 1994). A slightly revised and updated version of this report was later published in 1995: *Time for a Permanent International Criminal Court* (Amnesty International: AI Index: IOR 40/04/95, 1995).

Charter of the International Military Tribunal for the Far East, *Trial of Japanese War Criminals* (Washington, DC: United States Government Printing Office, 1946).

CONVENTION (I) FOR THE PACIFIC SETTLEMENT OF INTERNATIONAL DISPUTES (HAGUE I) (29 July 1899), entered into force September 4, 1900

CONVENTION WITH RESPECT TO THE LAWS AND CUSTOMS OF WAR ON LAND (HAGUE, II) (29 July 1899), entered into force September 4, 1900.

CONVENTION FOR THE ADAPTATION TO MARITIME WARFARE OF THE PRINCIPLES OF THE GENEVA CONVENTION OF AUGUST 22, 1864, adopted July 29, 1899, entered into force September 4, 1900.

Convention on the Non-Applicability of Statutory Limitations to War Crimes and Crimes Against Humanity, G.A. res. 2391 (XXIII), U.N. Doc. A/7218 (1968), entered into force November 11, 1970. Convention on the Non-Applicability of Statutory Limitations to War Crimes and Crimes Against Humanity, G.A. res. 2391 (XXIII), U.N. Doc. A/7218 (1968), entered into force November 11, 1970.

Convention on the Prevention and Punishment of the Crime of Genocide (Genocide Convention), December 9, 1948, 78 U.N.T.S. 1021, approved by UN General Assembly Resolution 260(III), 179th meeting, December 9, 1948.

Convention on the Prevention and Punishment of Crimes against Internationally Protected Persons, including Diplomatic Agents, GAOR 3166(XVIII), entered into force February 20, 1977.

Convention for the Suppression of Unlawful Acts against the Safety of Civil Aviation, 974 U.N.T.S. 178, entered into force January 26, 1973.

Declaration on Prohibiting Launching of Projectiles and Explosives from Balloons (Hague, IV);July 29, 1899, entered into force September 4, 1900.

"Draft Code of Crimes against the Peace and Security of Mankind," UN General Assembly Resolution 43/164, 43rd Session, 76th meeting, December 9, 1988.

Draft Code of Offences against the Peace and Security of Mankind. Reprinted in *Yearbook of* International Law Commission, Volume II, 1951.

Draft Convention on the Establishment of an International Penal Tribunal for the Suppression and Punishment of the Crime of Apartheid and other International Crimes, U.N. Doc. E/CN.4/AC/22CRP.19/Rev.1 December 10, 1980.

"Draft Convention for the Establishment of a United Nations War Crimes Court," UN War Crimes Commission, U.N. Doc.C.50(1), September 30, 1944.

"Draft Convention on Genocide," U.N. General Assembly180(II), 123rd meeting, November 21, 1947.

"Draft Code of Offences against the Peace and Security of Mankind," UN General Assembly Resolution 897(IX), 504th meeting, December 4, 1954.

"Draft Code of Offences against the Peace and Security of Mankind," Chapter III, Documents of the Sixth Session, including the Report of the Commission to the General Assembly, *Yearbook of the International Law Commission*, Volume II, 1954.

Draft Report on the Eighth Session of the Preparatory Commission September 24, October 5, 2001 Coalition for an International Criminal Court October 7, 2001.

"Draft Statute: International Criminal Tribunal," U.N. GAOR, 45th Sess., U. N. Doc. A/Conf. 144/NGO.7 (1990).

Draft Statute for an International Criminal Court, Report of the International Law Commission, U.N. GAOR, 49th Sess., U.N. Doc. A/49/10 Article 4 (1). (1994).

*Establishing an International Criminal Court: Major Unresolved Issues in the Draft Statute:* A *Position Paper* (New York: The Lawyers Committee for Human Rights, 1996).

*Establishment of an International Law Commission* GA Res. 174(II), UN GAOR, UN Doc. A/519 (1947).

Establishment of an International Criminal Court, The UN General Assembly Resolution No. 52/160, UN GAOR 52nd Session, U.N. Doc. A/RES/52/160, adopted December 15, 1997.

"Establishment of an International Criminal Court," U.N. General Assembly Resolution No. 53/105, U.N. Doc. No. A/RES/53/105, 83rd Plenary Meeting, December 8, 1998.

"Establishment of an International Criminal Court," U.N. General Assembly Resolution No. 54/105, U.N. Doc. No. A/RES/54/105, 76th Plenary Meeting, December 9, 1999.

"Establishment of an International Criminal Court," U.N. General Assembly Resolution No. 55/155, U.N. Doc. No. A/RES/55/155, 84th Plenary Meeting, December 12, 2000.

"Establishment of an International Criminal Court," U.N. General Assembly Resolution No. 56/85, U.N. Doc. No. A/RES/56/85, 85th Plenary Meeting, December 12, 2001.

Final Act of the United Nations Diplomatic Conference of Plenipotentiaries on the Establishment of an International Criminal Court, U.N. Doc. A/CONF.183/10, July 17, 1998.

Final Report of the Commission of Experts Established pursuant to Security Council Resolution 780 (1992), U.N. SCOR, 47th Sess., Annex, U.N. Doc. S/1994/674 (1994); Annexes to the Final Report, U.N. SCOR, 47th Sess., U.N. Doc. S/1994/674/Add.2 (1994).

Final Report of the Independent Commission of Experts Established in Accordance with Security Council Resolution 935 (1994), U.N. Doc. S/ 1994/1405(1994).

Formulation of the Principles Recognized in the Charter of the Nuremberg Trial and in the Judgment of the Tribunal General Assembly Resolution 177(II), U.N. Doc. A/519 (1948).

Geneva Convention for the Amelioration of the Condition of the Wounded and Sick in Armed Forces in the Field, 75 U.N.T.S. 31, entered into force October 21, 1950.

Geneva Convention for the Amelioration of the Condition of Wounded, Sick and Shipwrecked Members of Armed Forces at Sea, 75 U.N.T.S. 85, entered into force October 21, 1950.

Geneva Convention relative to the Protection of Civilian Persons in Time of War 75 U.N.T.S. 287, entered into force October 21, 1950.

Hall, Christopher Keith, Challenges Ahead for the United Nations Preparatory Committee Drafting a Statute for a Permanent International Criminal Court (AI Index: IOR 40/03/96, 1996).

"How much authority and independence will be vested in the new court? The litmus test will be the function of its prosecutor. Will he or she be independent, and able to launch investigations proprio motu? Or will the prosecutor have to wait for the Security Council or states to refer a situation before investigating individual suspects?" *On the Record ICC*, Vol. 1, Issue 8, June 25, 1998.

Human Rights Watch World Report. Special Issues and Campaigns: International Criminal Court, 1999, available at: http://www.hrw.org/worldreport99/special/icc.html.

"In Swift, Decisive Action, Security Council Imposes Tough Measures on Libyan Regime, Adopting Resolution 1970 in Wake of Crackdown on Protestors," Security Council, 6491st Session, Department of Public Information: News and Media Division, February 26, 2011, http://www.un.org/News/Press/docs/2011/sc10187.doc.htm (Accessed July 2, 2013).

Interim Report of the Commission of Experts Established pursuant to Security Council Resolution 780 (1992), U.N. SCOR, 48th Sess., Annex, at 20, U. N. Doc. S/25274 (1993).

International Commission of Jurists "Definition of Crimes," ICJ Brief No. l to the UN Diplomatic Conference of Plenipotentiaries on the Establishment of an International Criminal Court, Rome 15 June- 17 July 1998.

International Commission of Jurists, "The Third ICJ Position Paper on the International Criminal Court," August 1995.

International Convention against the Taking of Hostagesc, July 2, 2013 (XXXIV), U.N. Doc. A/34/46 (1979), entered into force June 3, 1983.

"International Criminal Responsibility of Individuals and Entities Engaged in Illicit Trafficking of Narcotic Drugs Across National Frontiers and Other Transnational Criminal Activities: Establishment of an International Criminal Court with Jurisdiction Over Such Crimes," UN General Assembly Resolution 44/39, 44th Session, 72nd meeting, December 4, 1989.

Instructions for the Government of Armies of the United States in the Field, prepared by Francis Lieber, LL.D., Originally Issued as General Orders No. 100, Adjutant General's Office, April 24, 1863, Washington, DC: Government Printing Office, 1898.

Judgment of the International Military Tribunal for the Trial of German Major War Criminals, Nuremberg, September 30th and October 1st, 1946.

*Laws of War: the Geneva Convention for Amelioration of the Condition of the Wounded on the Field of Battle* (also known as the Red Cross Convention); adopted at Geneva, August 22, 1864, entered into force June 22, 1865.

"Letter of Solidarity on the International Criminal Court," From Representatives of Non-Governmental and Social Organizations Participating in the "International Forum, Vienna +5 Review."

*Nuclear Weapons Advisory Opinion*, 1996 International Court of Justice, paragraphs 75, 79 (July 8).

*Official Records of the General Assembly, 12th Session, Supp. No. 16*, U.N. Doc. A/3574.

Pace, William R., "CICC NGO Papers," Workshop on International Criminal Accountability, Social Science Research Council, November 6–7, 2003, Washington, DC.

Pejic, Jelena, "Creating a Permanent International Criminal Court: The Obstacles to Independence and Effectiveness," *Columbia Human Rights Law Review*, Vol. 29, Issue 2, 1998.

Preliminary Report of the Independent Commission of Experts, U.N. Doc. S/1994/1125 (1994).

Principles of International Co-Operation in the Detection, Arrest, Extradition and Punishment of Persons Guilty of War Crimes and Crimes against Humanity, G.A. res. 3074 (XXVIII), U.N. Doc. A/9030/Add.1 (1973).

Progress Report of the Secretary-General on the United Nations Assistance Mission for Rwanda, U.N. Doc. S/1994/1133 (1994).

Project of an International Declaration Concerning the Laws and Customs of War, Adopted by the Conference of Brussels, August 27, 1874, reprinted in

*The American Journal of International Law*, Vol. 1, Issue 2, Supplement: Official Documents, 1907.

Proposal of Germany, A/AC.249/1998/DP.2, 1998.

Protocol additional to the Geneva Conventions of 12 August 1949, and relating to the Adoption of an Additional Distinctive Emblem (Protocol III).

Protocol Additional to the Geneva Conventions of 12 August 1949, and Relating to the Protection of Victims of International Armed Conflicts (Protocol I), 1125 U.N.T.S. 3, entered into force December 7, 1978.

"Question of Defining Aggression," UN General Assembly Resolution 688(VII), 408th meeting, December 20, 1952.

"Question of Defining Aggression," UN General Assembly Resolution 895(IX), 504th meeting, December 4, 1954.

"Question of Defining Aggression," UN General Assembly Resolution 1181(XII), 724th meeting, November 29, 1957.

Remarks of Justice Richard Goldstone to the United Nations Diplomatic Conference on the Establishment of an International Criminal Court on behalf of the Coalition for International Justice, June 17,1998.

Report of the Ad Hoc Committee on the Establishment of an International Criminal Court, adopted 6 Sept. 1995, U.N. GAOR, 50th Session, UN Doc. A/50/22 (1995).

Report of 1953 Committee on International Criminal Jurisdiction, GAOR Supp. (No. 12) U.N. Doc. A/2645 (1954).

Report of the Commission on the Responsibility of the Authors of the War and on Enforcement of Penalties, presented to the Preliminary Peace Conference, March 29, 1919, Official English text, reprinted from Pamphlet No. 32, Division of International Law, Carnegie Endowment for International Peace, Washington, DC, *American Journal of International Law*, Vol. 14, Issue 1, 1920.

Report of the International Law Commission, U.N. GAOR 46th Sess., U.N. Doc. A/46/10 (1991).

Report of the International Law Commission, U.N. GAOR 49th Session, U.N. Doc. A/49/10 (1994).

Report of the International Law Commission on the Work of its Forty-fourth Session, UN GAOR 47th Session, UN Doc. A/47/10 (1992).

Report of the International Law Commission on its Second Session, 5 June to 29 July 1950, Official Records of General Assembly, 5th Session, Supplement No. 12 (A/1316), reprinted in *The Yearbook of International Law Commission, Volume II*, 1950.

Report of the Preparatory Committee on the Establishment of an International Criminal Court adopted September13, 1996, UN GAOR, 51st Session, UN Doc. A/51/22, Vol. I (1996).

Report of the Preparatory Committee on the Establishment of an International Criminal Court, U.N. Doc. A/CONF.183/2 April 14, 1998.

*Report on the Proposed International Criminal Court* (New York: The Committee on International Law, and The Committee on International Human Rights of The Association of the Bar of the City of New York, 1996).

Report of the Secretary-General pursuant to paragraph 2 of Security Council Resolution 808 (1993), U.N. SCOR, 48th Sess., U.N. Doc. S/25704 (1993).

Respect for International Humanitarian Law, Handbook prepared by some of the members of the Inter-Parliamentary Union's Committee to Promote Respect for International Humanitarian Law, the International Committee of Red Cross Publication.

Report of the Secretary-General on the Situation in Rwanda, UN Doc. S/1994/640 (1994)

Report of the Working Group on the Question of an International Criminal Jurisdiction, in Report of the International Law Commission on the Work of its Forty-fifth Session, UN GAOR, 48th Session, UN Doc. A/48/10 (1993).

Rome Statute of the International Criminal Court, U.N. Doc. A/CONF.183/9

Sandstrom, Emil, International Law Commission, Report on the Question of International Criminal Jurisdiction, U.N. Doc. A/CN.4/20, reprinted in *The Yearbook of International Law Commission, Volume II*, 1950.

Statute of the International Criminal Tribunal for the Prosecution of Persons Responsible for Genocide and Other Serious Violations of International Humanitarian Law Committed in the Territory of Rwanda and Rwandan Citizens Responsible for Genocide and Other Such Violations Committed in the Territory of Neighbouring States between 1 January 1994 and 31 December 1994, annexed to S.C. Res. 955 (1994).

Statute of the International Tribunal for the Prosecution of Persons Responsible for Serious Violations of International Humanitarian Law Committed in the Territory of the Former Yugoslavia since 1991, U.N. Doc. S/25704, annex (1993) and S/25704/Add.1 (1993), adopted by Security Council on May 25, 1993, U.N. Doc. S/RES/827 (1993).

Study by the International Law Commission of the Question of an International Criminal Jurisdiction, UN General Assembly Resolution 260 B(III), U.N. Doc. A/810, December 9, 1948.

The Agreement for the Prosecution and Punishment of Major War Criminals of the European Axis, Aug. 8, 1945, 82 U.N.T.S. 279 (London Agreement).

The Agreement for the Prosecution and Punishment of the Major War Criminals of the European Axis, Aug. 8, 1945, Charter of the International Military Tribunal, 59 Stat. 1544, 1546, 82 U.N.T.S. 279, 284 (London Charter).

"The Crime of Genocide," UN General Assembly Resolution No. 96(I), 55th meeting, December 11, 1946.

The Convention for the Suppression of Unlawful Seizure of Aircraft, 860 U.N. T.S. 105, entered into force October 14, 1971.

The Draft Statute appears as Annex I to the Report of the Committee on International Criminal Jurisdiction, U.N. Doc. A/AC.48/4, September 5, 1951, reprinted as "United Nations: Committee on International Criminal Jurisdiction," American Journal of International Law, Vol. 46, Issue 1, Supplement: Official Documents, 1952.

The International Convention on the Suppression and Punishment of the Crime of Apartheid, G.A. Res. 3068 (XXVIII), U.N. Doc. A/9030 (1974).

The Proposal of the Republic of Korea, U.N. Doc. A/CONF.183/C.1/L.6, June 18, 1998.

The UN General Assembly Resolution, 898 (IX), "International Criminal Jurisdiction," Ninth Session, 512th meeting, U.N. Doc. A/2890, December 14, 1954.

The UN General Assembly Resolution, 1187(XII), International Criminal Jurisdiction, Twelfth Session, 727th meeting, U.N. Doc. A/3805, December 11, 1957.

The UN General Assembly Resolution No. 51/207, UN GAOR, 51st Session, UN Doc. A/51/49 (1996).

The United Kingdom Proposal, U.N. Doc. A/AC.249/WG.3/DP.1.

The United Nations Diplomatic Conference of Plenipotentiaries on the Establishment of an International Criminal Court), Rome, Italy, June 15–July 17, 1998.

The UN Security Council referred the situation in Darfur to the ICC with its Resolution 1593, 2005.

"Third Report Relating to a Draft Code of Offences against the Peace and Security of Mankind," U.N. Doc. No. A/CN.4/85.

Treaty of Peace Between the Allied and Associated Powers and Germany, concluded at Versailles, June 28, 1919 (Treaty of Versailles).

U.N. Doc. A/CONF.183/C.1/L.6.

U.N. ESCOR, art. VII, U.N. Doc. E/447 (1947) (Draft Convention on the Crime of Genocide).

UN GAOR 50/46, 50th Session, UN Doc. A/RES/50/46 (1995).

UN General Assembly Resolution, 489(V), 320th meeting, December 12, 1950.

UN General Assembly Resolution No. 47/33, UN GAOR, 47th Session, UN Doc. A/47/49 (1992).

UN General Assembly Resolution No. 48/31, UN GAOR, 48th Session, UN Doc. A/48/49 (1993).

UN General Assembly Resolution 687 (VII), Seventh Session, Resolutions adopted on reports of the Sixth Committee, "International Criminal Jurisdiction," 408th meeting, U.N. Doc. 2361, December 20, 1952.

UN General Assembly Resolution No. 5046 (L), 50th Session, Official Records, UN Doc. A/5249 (1997).

UN General Assembly Resolution on the Establishment of an International Criminal Court, UN Doc. A/51/627, December 17, 1996.

UN Security Council Resolution 918 (1994), UN Doc. S/RES/918, May 17, 1994.

UN Security Council Resolution, 925 (1994), UN Doc. S/RES/925 (1994).

UN Security Council Resolution. 935, U.N. SCOR, 49th Sess., U.N. Doc. S/RES/935 (1994).

U.N. Security Council Resolution, UN. Doc. S/RES/1422 (2002), 4572nd meeting, July 12, 2002.

U.N. Security Council Resolution, UN. Doc. S/RES/1487 (2003), 4772nd meeting, July 12, 2003.

U.N. Security Council, UN. Doc. S/RES/1593 (2005), 5158th meeting, March 31, 2005.

United Nations Security Council Resolution 771 (Concerning Information on Violations of International Humanitarian Law in the Territory of the Former Yugoslavia), S.C. res. 771, U.N. Doc. S/RES/771 (1992).

United Nations Security Council Resolution 780 (Establishing a Commission of Experts to Examine and Analyze Information Submitted Pursuant to Resolution 771), S.C. res. 780, U.N. Doc. S/RES/780 (1992).

## Articles

"A Fair and Effective Court Should Be the first Building Block a Just World Order," Statement to the Plenary Session by the European Law Students' Association, *The International Criminal Court Monitor*, Special Issue 6, June 22, 1998.

"Aggression Splits the Rome Conference," *On the Record ICC*, Vol. 1, Issue 5, available at http://www.advocacynet.org/news_view/news_78.html.

Aita, Judy, "Darfur War Crimes Referred to International Criminal Court," http://usinfo.state.gov/dhr/Archive/2005/Apr/01-671037.html, accessed on 19.05.2005.

"An Appeal From Four Major Human Rights Organizations," *On the Record ICC*, Vol. 1, 19, July 13, 1998.

"Attempt Begins to Water Down Crimes Against Humanity," *On the Record ICC*, Vol. 1, Issue 4available at http://www.advocacynet.org/news_view/news_77.html.

"Basic Principles for an Independent Effective and Fair International Criminal Court," *The International Criminal Court Monitor*, Special Issue 2, June 16, 1998.

"Britain Opposes Inclusion of Landmines as War Crime to Defend UK Nuclear Program," *On the Record ICC*, Vol. 1, Issue 16, July 9, 1998, available at: http://www.advocacynet.org/news_view/news_88.html.

"Campaigners Launch a Broadside," *On the Record ICC*, Vol. 1, Issue 2, June 16, 1998, available at: http://www.advocacynet.org/news_view/news_75.html.

"Court in the Balance," *On the Record ICC*, Vol. 1, Issue 16, July 9, 1998, available at: http://www.advocacynet.org/news_view/news_88.html.

"Definition of Crimes: Nuclear Cloud Over War Crimes Debate," *On the Record ICC*, Vol. 1, Issue 12, July 3, 1998, available at: http://www.advoca cynet.org/news_view/news_85.html.

"Dutch Disbelief at American 'Defeatism'" *On the Record ICC*, Vol. 1, Issue 4, June 18, 1998.

"Dutch NGOs Combine Forces," *Insight on the ICC*, Issue 1, April 2004.

"Dutch, UK Spar Over Whether States Should Veto Pre-Trial Investigations," *On the Record*, Vol. 1, Issue 9, June 29, 1998, available at: http://www.advocacynet.org/news_view/news_82.html.

"Editorial: It's All about Governance," *Terra Viva*, Issue 1, 15 June 1998.

"Fears of "Politicized" ICC Prosecutors Ridiculed by a Former Hague Prosecutor," *On the Record ICC*, 1998, Vol. 1, Issue 3, June 17, available at: http://www.advocacynet.org/news_view/news_76.html.

"Forget the Square Brackets, Go Back to Square One, Urges Trinidad and Tobago," *On the Record ICC*, 1998, Vol. 1, Issue 2, June 16, available at: http://www.advocacynet.org/news_view/news_75.html.

"Handling of Elections Will Affect the Future of the ICC," *The ICC Monitor*, Issue 21, June 2002.

"International Military Tribunal for the Far East," *International Organization*, Vol. 3, Issue 1, 1949.

"NGO Alliance Backs Widening List of Crimes," *Terra Viva*, Issue 17, July 7, 1998.

"Joint Declaration of the Alliance of the Three Continents In an Unprecedented Show of Solidarity, a Joint Statement Was Approved by More than 40 NGOs From Asia, Africa and Latin America This Weekend," *The International Criminal Court Monitor*, Special Issue 17, July 7, 1998.

"Momentum Builds for Powerful Prosecutor," *Terra Viva*, Issue 7, June 23, 1998.

"Non-Aligned Nations Target Nukes," *Terra Viva*, Issue 10, June 26, 1998.

"Ottawa Review of 1992 Human Rights Conference Calls for Tough ICC," *On the Record ICC*, Vol. 1, 10, 30 June, 1998.

"Permanent International Criminal Court Established," *United Nations Chronicle*, Vol. XXXV, Issue 3, 1998.

"Political and Legal Organizations," *International Organization*, Vol. 1, Issue 1, 1947.

"Rescinding the Signature of an International Treaty: the United States and the Rome Statute Establishing the International Criminal Court," *Diplomacy &Statecraft*, Vol. 14, Issue 4, 2003.

"Rome Statute Near 100 Ratifications," *The ICC Monitor*, Issue 26, February 2004.

"Russia Offers Few Surprises," *Terra Viva*, Issue 5, June 19, 1998.

"Sectoral Caucuses Will Continue to Strengthen the ICC," *The ICC Monitor*, Issue 21, June 2002.

"Spain Muddies Water on Security Council Role," *On the Record*, Vol. 1, 9, June 29, 1998.

"State Consent Could Weaken the Geneva Conventions Warns Red Cross Chief," *On the Record ICC*, Vol. 1, Issue 3, June 17, 1998, available at: http://www.advocacynet.org/news_view/news_76.html.

"States Fight For Control Over Pre-Trial Investigations," *On the Record ICC*, Vol. 1, Issue 16, July 9, 1998.

"Support Growing for an Independent Prosecutor," *On the Record ICC*, Vol. 1, Issue 7, June 23, 1998, available at: http://www.advocacynet.org/news_view/news_80.html.

"The Case for an International Criminal Court," *On the Record ICC*, Vol. 1, Issue 1, June 15, 1998, available at: http://www.advocacynet.org/news_view/news_59.html.

"The Compromise Package: US Launches Long-awaited Preemptive Strike on ICC Statute," *On the Record ICC*, Vol. 1, Issue 15, July 8, 1998, available at: http://www.advocacynet.org/news_view/news_89.html.

"The Relationship Between the Security Council and the International Criminal Court in the Light of Resolution 1422 (2002) " *Non-State Actors and International Law*, Vol. 3, Issue 2–3, 2003.

"The Role of the Prosecutory," *On the Record ICC*, Vol. 1, Issue 6, June 22, 1998, available at: http://www.advocacynet.org/news_view/news_117.html.

"The US in a Bind over Terrorism," *Terra Viva*, Issue 5, June 19, 1998.

"Too Many Ratifications Would Delay ICC'S Entry Into Force, Say NGOs," *On the Record ICC*, Vol. 1, Issue 12, June 27, 1998.

"Trigger Mechanisms: US, American Human Rights Groups Clash on Independent Prosecutor," *On the Record ICC*, Vol. 1, Issue 9, June 29, 1998.

# Index







C. Çakmak, *A Brief History of International Criminal Law and International Criminal Court*,
DOI 10.1057/978-1-137-56736-9

B



C